OECD Health Policy Studies

Strengthening Health Information Infrastructure for Health Care Quality Governance

GOOD PRACTICES, NEW OPPORTUNITIES
AND DATA PRIVACY PROTECTION CHALLENGES

This work is published on the responsibility of the Secretary-General of the OECD. The opinions expressed and arguments employed herein do not necessarily reflect the official views of the Organisation or of the governments of its member countries.

This document and any map included herein are without prejudice to the status of or sovereignty over any territory, to the delimitation of international frontiers and boundaries and to the name of any territory, city or area.

Please cite this publication as:
OECD (2013), *Strengthening Health Information Infrastructure for Health Care Quality Governance: Good Practices, New Opportunities and Data Privacy Protection Challenges*, OECD Health Policy Studies, OECD Publishing.
http://dx.doi.org/10.1787/9789264193505-en

ISBN 978-92-64-19348-2 (print)
ISBN 978-92-64-19350-5 (PDF)

Series: OECD Health Policy Studies
ISSN 2074-3181 (print)
ISSN 2074-319X (online)

The statistical data for Israel are supplied by and under the responsibility of the relevant Israeli authorities. The use of such data by the OECD is without prejudice to the status of the Golan Heights, East Jerusalem and Israeli settlements in the West Bank under the terms of international law.

Photo credits: Cover: © Alexander Lukin/Shutterstock.com; © vladis_studio/Shutterstock.com; © Zern Liew/Shutterstock.com; © George Paul/iStockphoto.com.

Corrigenda to OECD publications may be found on line at: *www.oecd.org/publishing/corrigenda*.
© OECD 2013

You can copy, download or print OECD content for your own use, and you can include excerpts from OECD publications, databases and multimedia products in your own documents, presentations, blogs, websites and teaching materials, provided that suitable acknowledgement of OECD as source and copyright owner is given. All requests for public or commercial use and translation rights should be submitted to *rights@oecd.org*. Requests for permission to photocopy portions of this material for public or commercial use shall be addressed directly to the Copyright Clearance Center (CCC) at *info@copyright.com* or the Centre français d'exploitation du droit de copie (CFC) at *contact@cfcopies.com*.

Foreword

All countries share common goals to improve the health of their populations and to improve quality in health care. Rising levels of chronic disease and multi-morbidity; concerns about the quality and safety of patient care; the need to measure and assure value for money for investments in health; and the need to allocate health system resources wisely are all too important to leave without good information for decision making.

What information infrastructure is needed to support decision making? To be useful for the assessment of progress in population health and the quality of care, health and health care data collections need to be organised in a systematic and efficient way, to be structured to support linkage across data sources, and to be accessible. At the same time, confidentiality of the data needs to be protected and privacy rights addressed.

This report is about the progress that has been made in OECD countries to develop national health information infrastructure. It focuses on two key dimensions: the development and linkage of health and health care data and the development and use of electronic health record systems. It signals important differences among countries in both the data that is available and its accessibility and use; and the opportunities that exist in all countries to continue to strengthen health information infrastructure in the future.

Acknowledgements

This OECD study was undertaken by the OECD HCQI (Health Care Quality Indicators) Expert Group as part of the 2011/12 programme of work of the OECD Health Committee. The authors would like to acknowledge the representatives from the countries who make up the HCQI Expert Group, all of whom gave generously of their time to provide input and guidance to this study. Additional thanks and recognition is extended to the experts from participating countries that provided responses to surveys and participated in case-study interviews.

The OECD would like to acknowledge the contributions of Jillian Oderkirk, Niek Klazinga and Elettra Ronchi who endeavoured to make this report possible. Sincere appreciation is extended to Mark Pearson for his review and comments and to Daniel Garley, Marlène Mohier and Nathalie Bienvenu for preparing the document for publication.

Table of contents

Acronyms and abbreviations 9

Glossary 11

Executive summary 13

Chapter 1. **Strengthening health information infrastructure matters** 17
    Issues examined in this report 20
    Study method 21
    Bibliography 23

Chapter 2. **Taking stock of the evidence – from data use to health system improvement**   25
    Multi-country projects 27
    Case studies 29
    Bibliography 45

Chapter 3. **National health information infrastructure** 49
    National databases 50
    National infrastructure for data linkage and analysis 51
    Sub-national infrastructure for data linkage projects 55
    Data linkages for public health research and health care quality monitoring 56

Chapter 4. **National electronic health record systems** 61
    Use of electronic medical and patient records in physician offices and hospitals . 63
    National plans and policies to implement electronic health records 63
    Implementation of a national electronic health record system 66
    Minimum data sets 68
    Structured data elements within electronic records 71
    Terminology standards in use 76
    Unique identifiers within EHR systems 77
    Smart cards 78
    Status and technical challenges of database creation from electronic health records today 79
    Analysis of data from electronic health records for statistical purposes and evaluations of data usability 83

Chapter 5. **Protection of privacy in the collection and use of personal health data** ... 87
    Variations in risk management lead to differences in OECD country practices ... 89
    Guiding principles and legislation 89
    Privacy principles in practice – country variation 92
    Multiple data custodianship and data sharing 96
    Data linkage activities and compliance with legislation 98

Electronic health record systems and compliance with legislation 101
Bibliography 102

Chapter 6. Governance of data collection, data linkages and access to data 103
De-identification of data 104
Secure facilities for access to data with a high re-identification risk 106
Project approval process for data linkages 107
The specific case of researchers requesting linkage of their own data cohort 110
Data security within public authorities 110
Data security when researchers receive data from public authorities 114
Multi-country projects 115
Bibliography 117

Chapter 7. Governance of national electronic health record systems data collection . 119
National bodies with responsibility for the development of National EHR infrastructure 120
Legal requirements to adopt electronic health records and adhere to standards . 124
Encouraging data quality within electronic health records 125
Data quality concerns and auditing 127
Engagement of third parties 129

Chapter 8. Progress and challenges in use of personal health data 131
Countries where it is becoming easier to use personal health data to monitor health and health care quality 132
Countries where it is neither easier nor harder today than five years ago to use personal health data to monitor health and health care quality 136
Countries where it is becoming harder to use personal health data to monitor health and health care quality 138
Outlook on the use of data from electronic health record systems 142
Countries that view monitoring within the next five years as very likely 142
Countries that view monitoring in the next five years as likely 144
Countries that are unsure monitoring will occur within the next five years 146
Countries that view monitoring within the next five years as unlikely 147
Countries that view monitoring within the next five years as very unlikely...... 147

Chapter 9. Strengthening health information infrastructure: Next steps 149
International action 152

Annex A. Questionnaire on secondary use of health data 153

Annex B. Telephone interviews on secondary use of health data 155

Annex C. Questionnaire on electronic health record systems and the secondary use of health data 156

Annex D. Supplementary tables 158

Annex E. Additional information on participating countries current use of electronic medical and electronic patient records by health care providers 179

Tables

2.1.	Belgium: Permanent sample of socially insured persons	29
2.2.	Canada: Pathways of care for stroke patients	30
2.3.	Canada, Ontario: Institute for Clinical and Evaluative Sciences	31
2.4.	Europe: Comparing diabetes outcomes across European countries	32
2.5.	Finland: Monitoring performance, effectiveness and costs of treatment episodes	33
2.6.	Germany: Effectiveness and safety of breast cancer screening	34
2.7.	Korea: Quality assessment of medical services	36
2.8.	Sweden: Quality and efficiency assessments of clinical guidelines	36
2.9.	Switzerland: Understanding the life expectancy of a nation	37
2.10.	United Kingdom, England: NHS Information Centre for Health and Social Care	38
2.11.	United Kingdom, England and Wales: Birth outcomes studies	39
2.12.	United Kingdom, England: Mapping pathways across health and social care – Torbay Care Trust	41
2.13.	United States: Understanding health care users and health outcomes	42
2.14.	United States: Kaiser Permanente Center for Health Research	43
	Summaries of further examples of policy-relevant data linkage projects	44
3.1.	Number of countries reporting linkable data and reporting data use	51
3.2.	National number that uniquely identifies patients and the main uses of this number	52
3.3.	Distribution of the regular occurrence of health-related record linkage projects by availability of databases with patient identifiers	57
8.1.	How likely is it that data from electronic health records will be used for national health care quality monitoring within the next five years?	143
A.1.	Countries that responded to the 2011-12 HCQI questionnaire on secondary use of health data	153
B.1.	Countries that responded to the 2011-12 HCQI telephone interview on secondary use of health data	155
C.1.	Countries that responded to the 2012 HCQI questionnaire on electronic health record systems and the secondary use of health data	156
D.1.	Data available at a national level	158
D.2.	National data used to regularly report on health care quality	159
D.3.	National data containing records for patients (persons)	160
D.4.	National data contains a unique patient identifying number that could be used for record linkage	161
D.5.	National data contains identifying variables such as name, sex, birth date, and address that could be used for record linkage	162
D.6.	Sub-national infrastructure for data linkage – regional or state-level record-linkage projects by type of data involved	163
D.7.	Sub-national infrastructure for data linkage – networks of health care organisations record linkage projects by type of data involved	164
D.8.	National data is used to undertake record linkage projects	165
D.9.	National data is used to undertake record linkage projects on a regular basis	166

D.10. National record linkage projects are used for regular health care quality monitoring. 167
D.11. Use of electronic medical and patient records by physicians and hospitals 168
D.12. National plan or policy and the inclusion of secondary data use. 169
D.13. Links to plans or policies to develop national EHR systems 170
D.14. Implementation of a national electronic health record system 172
D.15. Minimum data set defined as part of the National EHR system. 173
D.16. Data elements within electronic health records are structured. 174
D.17. Terminology standards for structured data elements 175
D.18. Encouraging quality of electronic health records 176
D.19. Building databases from EHR records for monitoring and analysis 177
D.20. Data usability evaluation and current secondary uses 178

Figures

3.1. Number of countries reporting national data used to conduct record-linkage projects on an occasional and on a regular basis 56
4.1. Number of countries reporting elements are structured using clinical terminology standards 72
5.1. Continuum of risk associated with the collection and use of personal health data 89
8.1. Over the past five years, has it become easier or harder to use personal healthdata to monitor health and health care quality? 135

This book has...

StatLinks

A service that delivers Excel® files from the printed page!

Look for the StatLinks at the bottom right-hand corner of the tables or graphs in this book. To download the matching Excel® spreadsheet, just type the link into your Internet browser, starting with the *http://dx.doi.org* prefix.
If you're reading the PDF e-book edition, and your PC is connected to the Internet, simply click on the link. You'll find StatLinks appearing in more OECD books.

Acronyms and abbreviations

AIHW	Australian Institute of Health and Welfare
AMI	Acute myocardial infarction
ASIP santé	Agency responsible for the electronic health record system, France
ATC	Anatomical Therapeutic Chemical Classification System
BIRO	Best Information for Regional Outcomes
CIHI	Canadian Institute for Health Information
CMS	Center for Medicare and Medicaid Services, United States
CMV	Controlled medical vocabulary
CNIL	Commission nationale de l'informatique et des libertés (data protection authority), France
CSIOZ	National Centre for Health Information Systems, Poland
CT	Computed tomography
DICOM	Digital Imaging and Communications in Medicine
DPA	Data protection authority
DRC	Dictionary of consultation results, France
EMR	Electronic medical record
EPR	Electronic patient record
EHR	Electronic health record
EU	European Union
EUBIROD	European Best Information through Regional Outcomes in Diabetes
EU epSOS	European eHealth Project
EuroCARE	European study of cancer survival
EuroHOPE	European Health Care Outcomes, Performance and Efficiency Project
Euro-PERISTAT	Perinatal health information in Europe
FSO	Federal Statistical Office, Switzerland
GP	General practitioner
HCPCS	Health Care Common Procedure Coding System, United States
HEAT	Health improvement, efficiency, access and treatment performance targets, United Kingdom
HES	Hospital Episode Statistics, United Kingdom
HIN	Health insurance number
HIRA	Health Insurance Review Agency, Korea
HL7	Health Level Seven international interoperability standards
HL7 CDA R2	Health Level Seven Clinical Document Architecture, Release 2
HMO	Health care maintenance organisation
ICD 9/10	International Classification of Diseases ninth revision/tenth revision
ICD 9 CM	International Classification of Diseases Ninth Revision Clinical Modification

ICD 10 PCS	International Classification of Diseases Tenth Revision Procedure Codes
ICES	Institute for Clinical and Evaluative Sciences, University of Toronto, Canada
ICF	International Classification of Functioning, Disability and Health
ICT	Information and communications technology
IMA-AIM	Intermutualist Agency, Belgium
INAMI-RIZIV	National Institute for Health and Disease Insurance, Belgium
IRB	Internal review board
IT	Information technology
KOSTOM	Korean Standard Terminology of Medicine
LOINC	Logical Observation Identifiers Names and Codes
MRI	Magnetic resonance imaging
NCHS	National Center for Health Statistics, United States
NCSP	Nordic Medico-Statistical Committee Classification of Surgical Procedures
NDI	National Death Index, United States
NHS	National Health Service, United Kingdom
NHS NSS	NHS National Services Scotland, United Kingdom
NIGB	National Information and Governance Board, United Kingdom
NWIS	NHS Wales Informatics Service, United Kingdom
OPCS-4	Office of Population Census and Surveys Classification of Interventions and Procedures, United Kingdom
PDF	Portable document format
PERFECT	Performance, Effectiveness and Cost of Treatment Episodes, Finland
READ	Medical diagnosis coding system used in general practice, United Kingdom
RDC	Research data centre, Canada and United States
REB	Research ethics board
SHIP	Scottish Health Informatics Programme
SHMI	Summary hospital-level mortality indicator
SNC	Swiss National Cohort
SNIR-AM	National Health Insurance Information System, France
SNOMED-CT	Systematised Nomenclature of Medicine – Clinical Terms
SSA	Social Security Administration, United States
SSN	Social security number
SURE	Secure data linkage environment, Australia
THL	National Institute for Health and Welfare, Finland
UMLS	Unified Medical Language System
UPI	Unique patient identifying number
WHO	World Health Organization

Glossary

Term	Definition
Clinical terminology standards	Standard sets of terms, names and codes to be used when entering data in electronic records. For example, SNOMED-CT (Systemised Nomenclature of Medicine – Clinical Terms) provides a broad set of standardised clinical terms for software applications.
Confidentiality	Confidentiality relates to disclosure or nondisclosure of information. Historically a duty to honour confidentiality has arisen with respect to information disclosed in the context of a confidential relationship, such as that between an individual and his or her physician, attorney, or priest. In such relationships, the confidante is under an obligation not to disclose the information learned in the course of the relationship. Now the law applies such duties to some holders of information who do not have a confidential relationship to a patient. The importance of confidentiality to the medical profession is reflected in the physician's "Oath of Hippocrates".
Controlled vocabulary	Controlled vocabulary requires data to be input using predefined, authorised terms that have been preselected by the designer of the vocabulary.
Data confidentiality	Data confidentiality is a property of data, usually resulting from legislative measures, which prevents it from unauthorised disclosure.
Data protection	Data protection refers to the set of privacy-motivated laws, policies and procedures that aim to minimise intrusion into respondents' privacy caused by the collection, storage and dissemination of personal data.
Database record	A database record is a row of data in a database table consisting of a single value from each column of data in the table. The data in the columns in a table are all of the same type of data, such as birth date or address, whereas the rows represent a given instance, such as a single patient or person or a group of patients or persons.
De-identified information	This is information which does not identify an individual directly, and which cannot reasonably be used to determine identity. De-identification, also referred to as anonymisation, requires the removal of name and exact address; and can also involve the removal of any other detail or combination of details that might support identification.
Deterministic record linkage	In this approach, often referred to as exact matching, a unique identifier or set of identifiers is used to merge two or more sources of data. In health linkages, the identifier used is often a unique patient identifying number or UPI.
Electronic health record	For this OECD study, an electronic health record (EHR) refers to the longitudinal electronic record of an individual patient that contains or virtually links records together from multiple Electronic Medical Records (EMRs) which can then be shared across health care settings (interoperable). It aims to contain a history of contact with the health care system for individual patients from multiple organisations that deliver care.
Electronic medical record/Electronic patient record	For this OECD study, an electronic medical record (EMR) or electronic patient record (EPR) is a computerised medical record created in an organisation that delivers care, such as a hospital or physician's office, for patients of that organisation. EMR/EPR is provider or organisation centric and allows storage, retrieval and modification of patient records.
Formal long-term care	Long-term care is the care for people needing support in many facets of living over a prolonged period of time. Formal long-term care can be provided in home, institutional or day-care settings, from public, not-for-profit and for-profit providers, with services varying from alarm systems to daily personal care.
Health data	Health data usually consists of individual, personal health and other related information. The European Group on Ethics in Science and New Technologies (EGE), in the Opinion No. 13 Ethical Issues of Health Care in Information Society[1] defines "health data" as including "a wide range of information about an individual, which all touch upon an individual's private life". A health biography could include not only basic medical data: a history of all medical diagnoses, diseases and medical interventions, medications prescribed, test results, including imaging, etc. but could also include more sensitive data: on mental health, relevant to family history, behavioural patterns, sexual life, social and economic factors, etc. and health care administrative data: admissions and discharge data routine operational data, insurance and financial transactional data, etc.

GLOSSARY

Term	Definition
Identifiable data	Data is identifiable if the information contains the name of an individual, or other identifying items such as birth date, address or geocoding. Data will be identifiable if the information contains a unique personal identifier and the holder of the information also has the master list linking the identifiers to individuals. Data may also be identifiable because of the number of different pieces of information known about a particular individual. It may also be possible to ascertain the identity of individuals from aggregated data where there are very few individuals in a particular category. Identifiability is dependent on the amount of information held and also on the skills and technology of the holder.
Interoperability	Interoperability is the ability of two or more systems to exchange information and to make use of exchanged information. It is an essential pre-condition to the development of electronic health records from the electronic medical records within multiple health care organisations.
Messaging standards	Messaging standards facilitate interoperability by defining how information will be communicated from one party to another. For example, Health Level 7 is a messaging standard for the exchange of clinical, financial and administrative data.
Network of health care organisations	A network of health care organisations provides a continuum of health care services. The network may provide integrated care under a parent holding company. Some networks have a Health Maintenance Organisation (HMO) component.
Population census	A population census is the total process of collecting, compiling, evaluating, analysing and publishing or otherwise disseminating demographic, economic and social data pertaining, at a specified time, to all persons in a country or in a well delimited part of a country.
Privacy	Privacy is not being observed or disturbed by others. Privacy is a concept that applies to data subjects, while confidentiality is a concept that applies to data.
Probabilistic record linkage	In this approach, a set of possible matches among the data sources to be linked are identified. For example, identifying information such as names, dates of birth, and postal codes, may be used to assess potential matches. Then statistics are calculated to assign weights describing the likelihood the records match. A combined score represents the probability that the records refer to the same entity. Often there is one threshold above which a pair is considered a match, and another threshold below which it is considered not to be a match. This technique is used when an exact match between records across databases is not possible, or when data capture errors have caused deterministic matches to fail.
Record linkage	Record linkage refers to a merging that brings together identifiable records from two or more sources of data with the object of consolidating facts concerning an individual or an event that are not available in any separate record.[2]
Structured data elements	Structured data elements are identifiable. The most common type of structured data is fields in a database. For example, when a field in a database contains dates where each date has the same structure, i.e. MM/DD/YY; a computer process can easily sort the data.
Unstructured data elements	Unstructured data elements have no identifiable structure. In health records, the most common example is free flowing text.

1. European Commission (2009), "European Group on Ethics in Science and New Technologies Option No. 13", *Ethical Issues of Healthcare in the Information Society*, www.ec.europa.eu/bepa/european-group-ethics/docs/avis13_en.pdf.
2. United Nations (1991), *Handbook of Vital Statistics Systems and Methods*, Vol. 1: Legal, Organizational and Technical Aspects, United Nations Studies in Methods, Glossary, Series F, No. 35, New York.

Executive summary

Health data constitutes a significant resource in most OECD countries and it makes economic and ethical sense to use this data as much as possible: to improve population health and to improve the effectiveness, safety and patient-centeredness of health care systems. Rising levels of chronic disease and multi-morbidity; concerns about the quality and safety of patient care; the need to measure and assure value for money for investments in health; and the need to allocate health system resources wisely are all too important to leave without good evidence for decision making. Understanding the progress of the health of populations and understanding the performance and quality of health care systems requires the ability to monitor the same individuals over time, as they experience health care events, receive treatments, experience improvements or deteriorations in their health and live or die.

On 7-8 October 2010, *Health Ministers* met in Paris to discuss how to improve value in health care. In their final communiqué, they underlined the importance of better health information systems and *called for more and effective use of health data that has already been collected*. Ministers also noted that expanded use of health information and communication technologies (ICTs), particularly electronic health records, can help to deliver better quality of care, reduce medical errors and streamline administration. They recognised the need to reconcile the legitimate concerns of citizens to protect their privacy with the use of health data to improve health sector performance and the quality of care.

This study indicates that national data infrastructure is improving across countries and the technical capacity to analyse and report from personal health information data assets is greater today than it was five years ago. Case studies included in this report demonstrate how many countries are linking and analysing personal health data to report on the quality and cost-effectiveness of treatments; to address underuse, overuse and misuse of therapies; to reduce variation in care practices; to assess and revise clinical care guidelines to ensure that the recommended practices are really the best practices; and to manage health expenditures.

In some countries, *there is potential to continue and to expand data linkage studies in the future* due to having reached a shared understanding with their data privacy officials of the requirements to respect principles of data privacy. This includes standardised processes for project approval, access to data and data security. *There is also potential for data from electronic health record systems to be used for health care quality monitoring* over the next five years. This is due to both the number of countries that plan to implement national electronic health record systems and the number of countries that consider it likely that the data from these systems will be used for some aspects of health care quality monitoring.

There are considerable and troubling differences across OECD countries, however, in the extent to which personal health data may be collected, linked and analysed and the extent to which such data are currently contributing to monitoring population health and the quality of health care. OECD privacy guidelines provide a unifying framework for the development of national data protection legislation. However, *cross-country differences in the application of privacy principles are significant and can be attributed to differences in risk management* in the balancing of individual rights to privacy and collective rights to safe and effective health care and to a high performing health system. Many countries report legislative barriers to the use of personal health data, including enabling data linkages and developing databases from electronic health records.

Some of the countries with weaker information infrastructure have decentralised the administration of health systems and have not reached a consensus within the country of how the levels of government could work together. *Data from decentralised systems needs to be brought together to support national information infrastructure* and capacity for data use at the level of the country. A principle challenge is the lack of clarity about the interpretation of legislations concerning the protection of data privacy at the national and sub-national levels. This includes the legality of data sharing among public authorities and providing access to data for research.

The resources required to comply with legislative requirements to enable data use is a secondary problem, as is the cost of developing the technical capacity to undertake the work. Countries have provided evidence of the considerable effort they put in to protect data security and to safeguard personal health data from loss or deliberately malicious acts. Efforts were clearly demonstrated in this study related to project approval processes; internal data security; and de-identification of data to protect privacy and security measures for external researchers. Efforts to balance protection of data privacy and access to data for research are also clearly evident. Resource limitations, and not meeting expectations of timeliness, are worries among bodies that approve project proposals and among bodies that conduct data linkages on behalf of others. New forms of whole-of-government approaches to project proposal review and data linkage services are very interesting developments. Not only do these help to standardise requirements and practices for both the government and external researchers, they have the potential to be more efficient.

A particular worry across countries today is that legislative reforms that are on the horizon, or that may be stimulated due to the implementation of electronic health record systems, may turn back the clock on the progress that has been made in enabling access to and use of personal health data for research. A second worry is that a transition to reliance on data from electronic health record systems has the potential to set back the quality of national databases, by creating holes in the health care pathway or lowering the quality of the data elements, such as the coding of diagnosis. A widely reported barrier to the use of data from electronic health record systems is concerns with the quality of the data, including both a lack of coded data and poorly coded data.

A role for the OECD in the coming years is to continue to support countries in reaching the goal of strengthening health information infrastructure so that privacy-respectful uses of data for health, health care quality and health system performance monitoring and research become widespread, regular activities. *On-going monitoring of the development of health information infrastructure* will help to promote shared learning about advancements and challenges in the development and use of health data; promote international comparability of data and data linkages; and uncover new opportunities for the development of internationally comparable indicators of the quality of care.

Another important step will be to *support countries in reducing unnecessary obstacles to data use* that can arise from differences in legislations regarding the protection of health information privacy and differences in the interpretation of what is necessary and helpful to assure that patients' privacy rights are respected in the conduct of health monitoring and research. A risk classification of data and data uses, to identify cases of higher risk to patient's information privacy and to associate recommended data privacy protection practices that will enable even very sensitive data to be used for research and monitoring, would support countries in developing privacy-respectful uses of data to improve health, health care quality and health system performance.

Chapter 1

Strengthening health information infrastructure matters

> *Health data constitutes a significant resource in most OECD countries that could be used to improve population health, the quality of health care and the performance of health systems. Well-intended policies to allay concerns about breaches of confidentiality and potential misuse of personal health data may be limiting data use. In 2010, Health Ministers called for OECD support to strengthen health information infrastructure.*
>
> *In 2011/12, 19 countries participated in an OECD study to better understand the extent to which countries develop and use personal health data and the reasons why data use may be problematic in some. In 2011/12, 25 countries participated in a related OECD study to describe the development and use of personal health data from electronic health record systems, including barriers and facilitators.*
>
> *This chapter describes why the privacy respectful use of personal health data is so important to strengthen information infrastructure for monitoring and research to improve health, health care quality and health system performance. It provides an overview of the issues to be examined in the next chapters of this report, as well as background information about how the studies were conducted.*

The statistical data for Israel are supplied by and under the responsibility of the relevant Israeli authorities. The use of such data by the OECD is without prejudice to the status of the Golan Heights, East Jerusalem and Israeli settlements in the West Bank under the terms of international law.

Health data constitutes a significant resource in most OECD countries and it makes economic and ethical sense to use this data as much as possible: to improve population health and to improve the effectiveness, safety and patient-centeredness of health care systems. Data to measure, monitor and compare performance are central to the assessment of both the health of populations and the quality and efficiency of health care services. Regional, national and international reports on health and health care are entirely dependent upon monitoring policies and investments in data infrastructure that either facilitate or restrict data and analysis (OECD, 2011). Rising levels of chronic disease and multi-morbidity; concerns about the quality and safety of patient care; the need to measure and assure value for money for investments in health; and the need to allocate health system resources wisely are all too important to leave without good evidence for decision making.

Understanding the progress of the health of populations and understanding the performance and quality of health care systems requires the ability to monitor the same individuals over time, as they experience health care events, receive treatments, experience improvements or deteriorations in their health and live or die. It also requires understanding the distribution of health and health outcomes across different groups in the population and understanding variations in care quality and health outcomes.

This work has a few very important prerequisites. First it depends on the collection and storage of data at the level of individual patients (for an entire population of patients or for a representative sample). The most common sources of health data are registries, administrative data, population surveys, patient surveys and clinical records. Second, it relies on the capacity to be able to follow individual patients across the care continuum and through different health events to measure change. Following patients through different health and health care events often requires the linkage of patient records across databases. This is because few databases have all of the needed information. This type of follow-up permits understanding of, for example, adverse drug reactions, medical errors, poor primary health care, deaths following treatments, and ineffective treatments. The capacity to construct accurate data to understand the pathways of patients through the health care system and to assess the health outcomes and costs that result is increasing rapidly. The health care sector is undergoing a significant transformation toward the adoption and use of information technologies. The computerisation of health care records and the development of capacity to exchange records to construct patient health care pathways is a promising new frontier for the advancement of measurement of the quality, efficiency and effectiveness of health care.

On 7-8 October 2010, Health Ministers met in Paris to discuss how to improve value in health care. In their final *communiqué*, they underlined the importance of better health information systems. They called for more and effective use of health data that has already been collected. Ministers also noted that expanded use of health information and communication technologies (ICTs), particularly electronic health records, can help deliver better quality of care, reduce medical errors and streamline administration. They recognised the need to reconcile the legitimate concerns of citizens to protect their privacy with the use of health data to improve health sector performance and the quality of care. In 2011 and 2012, the OECD undertook this in-depth study of the development and use of personal health data to understand patient pathways and outcomes via the linkage of personal health records across multiple datasets within countries and across multiple countries; and via the development and use of data from electronic health record systems.

The implementation of electronic health record systems amplifies concerns about the protection of confidentiality of data and privacy intrusion because EHR records can contain longitudinal patient histories and are meant to be transmitted across a computer network. Restrictions on content, storage and use of these records are necessary to mitigate risk of misuse. However, as EHR systems replace traditional health care databases, it is essential that secondary uses of data to monitor health care quality are given consideration. Otherwise, rather than improve monitoring of health care quality, stagnation and even deterioration in ability to monitor quality could occur over time.

While national implementation of EHR systems is still relatively new, the use of other forms of personal health data to report on patient health care pathways and outcomes is technically possible in most countries, due to advancements in detailed individual-level data and computer processing capacities. There is, however, evidence of significant cross-country variability in the extent to which these data resources are currently being used for health and health care monitoring and research.

Well-intended privacy and confidentiality decisions, which aim to allay concerns about breaches of confidentiality and reduce potential misuse of personal health information, may have made a contribution to this variation. In 2008, the Working Group on Data Protection of the EU NCA observed that diverging opinions on how to interpret the EU Directive on Data Protection (Directive 95/46/EC) and poor transposition into national data protection laws appeared to be a significant barrier for European public health monitoring and research. The Group recommended that best practice examples should be developed to provide guidance on the collection of high quality health data and that the privacy requirements be clarified and harmonised across countries (Verschuuren et al., 2008). Further, the group concluded that awareness of data protection issues among public health experts and researchers should also be promoted. Many other individuals and groups – especially medical researchers, public health officials, and health care delivery organisations – have countered that overzealous or misdirected privacy protections are thwarting efforts to use information to improve patient care and public health.

To be useful for the assessment of the quality of care, health and health care data collections need to be organised in a systematic and efficient way, to be structured to support linkage across data sources, and to be accessible. At the same time, confidentiality of the data needs to be protected and privacy rights addressed (OECD, 2010). In May 2011, the OECD Health Care Quality Expert Group proposed undertaking this in-depth study to better understand the challenges, the opportunities and the practices in the use of data to monitor and describe pathways of care and health care outcomes to enable health care quality and health system performance monitoring and research.

Issues examined in this report

This report focuses on country experiences in the development and use of data to understand patient pathways and outcomes via the linkage of personal health records across multiple datasets within countries and across multiple countries; and via the development and use of data from electronic health record systems. It explores the extent to which there are cross-country variations in data use and the reasons for them and proposes next steps for international action.

Chapter 2 presents case studies of policy-relevant uses of personal health data to improve health and health care quality and efficiency that were selected by countries as representing best practices in the protection of data confidentiality, respect for patient privacy and privacy legislations, excellent data security, using high quality data and having a sound research methodology.

Chapter 3 provides information on the status of health information infrastructure today including the availability of personal health databases at the national level, the sharing of data across national public authorities, national infrastructure for data linkages and analysis, regional and health care network infrastructure for data linkages, and regular uses of linked data for national health and health care monitoring and research.

The development and use of data from national electronic health record systems is presented in *Chapter 4*. This includes current uses of electronic records in physician offices and hospitals; national plans to implement electronic health record systems; a description of implemented national systems; the development of minimum datasets; the use of structure and terminology standards to code data; the status and technical challenges of database creation from electronic health records; and current uses of data from electronic health records including monitoring public health, patient safety and health system performance and conducting research.

Chapter 5 introduces issues regarding the protection of patient privacy in the collection and use of personal health data. It describes how cross-country variation in data use relates to differences in risk management in the balancing of individual rights to privacy and collective rights to patient safety and high performance health care. OECD guiding principles for the protection and transborder flow of personal data are presented and cross-country differences in the application of these principles are discussed, including the conduct of data linkage activities and the development of data from electronic health records.

Aspects of the governance of data linkages and the provision of access to data are discussed in *Chapter 6*. This include country experiences in the de-identification of data to protect the privacy of individuals; the development of secure facilities for access to data with high re-identification risk; project approval processes for data linkage projects; data security within public authorities holding data; data protection when public authorities provide data to external researchers; and governance of multi-country studies involving personal health data.

Chapter 7 provides country experiences in the governance of electronic health record systems and the use of data from these systems. This includes the development of national bodies to oversee national EHR implementations, the use of legal requirements to adopt EHRs or adhere to standards, the use of incentives and penalties to encourage quality in the use of EHRs, concerns with data quality and the use of data quality auditing, and the engagement of third parties to assist with building databases, de-identifying data and approving applications for data access.

Views of study participants regarding the strengths and weaknesses of their national information infrastructure and the potential for this infrastructure to support data use over the next five years are presented in *Chapter 8*, followed by conclusions and recommendations for international actions to support countries in their efforts to strengthen information infrastructure in *Chapter 9*.

Study method

A mail-back questionnaire sought information about the general environment in each country for the secondary use of personal health data as well as specific case studies. The questionnaire was sent to the members of the OECD Health Care Quality Indicators Expert Group in July 2011 and responses were received from 19 countries from September 2011 through to March 2012. Countries participating in the survey include Australia, Belgium, Canada, Denmark, Finland, France, Germany, Israel, Japan, Korea, Malta, Norway, Poland, Portugal, Singapore, Sweden, Switzerland, the United Kingdom and the United States (see Annex A).* Members of the Health Care Quality Indicators Expert Group represent the 34 member countries of the Organisation for Economic Co-operation and Development as well as a number of non-member countries who are participating actively in the HCQI project.

As part of this questionnaire, contact persons were identified who were knowledgeable about the general environment for secondary use of personal health data involving data linkages and multi-country studies. Experts with knowledge of national level studies, as well as regional, state and health care network specific studies were identified. Structured telephone interviews were conducted with 31 selected experts from September 2011 to March 2012 (see Annex B).

A second mail-back questionnaire sought information about progress in the development of electronic health record systems and the specific elements of the design that relate to the ability to extract high quality data from these records to monitor and report on health care quality. The questionnaire was sent to the members of the OECD Health Care Quality Indicators Expert Group in February 2012 and responses were received from 25 countries from March to August of 2012. Countries participating in the survey include Austria, Belgium, Canada, Denmark, Estonia, Finland, France, Germany, Iceland, Indonesia, Israel, Japan, Korea, Mexico, the Netherlands, Poland, Portugal, Singapore, Slovakia, Slovenia, Spain, Sweden, Switzerland, the United Kingdom and the United States (see Annex C).

* Italy participated in the telephone interview part of the study.

> ## Box 1.1. **Key concepts**
>
> **Secondary use of personal health data**
>
> Health data is often originally collected for administrative purposes or for direct patient care. Re-use of this data for purposes other than those for which it was originally collected is considered a secondary use. Some of the most common secondary uses of health data include:
>
> - identifying the causes of disease, the prevalence of risk factors and identifying populations at risk;
> - protecting public safety, especially with regard to infectious disease, but also in relation to prescription medicines, medical devices and environmental hazards;
> - needs assessment, monitoring and evaluation of services, with a view to providing an optimum performance of health care systems; and
> - improving the quality and safety of care in hospitals, practitioner's offices, clinics and other health care settings.
>
> Health data is personal when it is collected and stored at the level of individual patients or persons or can otherwise be related to an identified or an identifiable individual. Personal health data is needed to track events over time or across different health care settings and to investigate the potential role of risk factors in the development of disease or the effectiveness of treatments. Often such analysis requires the linkage of personal health data across two or more data sets. Linkage occurs when records from the same patient, or the same person, in two or more different databases are merged together, creating a more complete health biography. An example would be linking patient records in a hospital database to any death records for the same persons in a mortality database, in order to identify patients who died following treatment (see glossary).
>
> Public registries, administrative databases and clinical records, including electronic health records, are all important sources of personal health data where analysis and dissemination of results are a secondary use of the data. Other important sources of health data include population and patient surveys and population censuses or registries.
>
> **Electronic health records**
>
> There are varying interpretations of an appropriate definition of electronic health records. The OECD has been working toward the benchmarking internationally of information and communication technology (ICT) in the health sector. The benchmarking project aims to elaborate internationally agreed upon definitions of ICTs through a development process that began recently.
>
> For the purposes of this study, electronic health records (EHRs) were defined as the longitudinal electronic record of an individual patient that contains, or virtually links together, records from multiple electronic medical records (EMRs) which can then be shared (interoperable) across health care settings. It aims to contain a history of contact with the health care system for individual patients from multiple organisations that deliver care.
>
> For this study, an electronic medical record (EMR) is a computerised medical record created in an organisation that delivers care, such as a hospital or physician's office, for patients of that organisation. EMR are provider or organisation centric and allow storage, retrieval and modification of patient records. In some health care settings, the same type of record may be referred to as an electronic patient record or EPR.

Bibliography

Andrews, N. (2002), "The Value of Linked Data for Research into Surveillance and Adverse Events", *Symposium on Health Data Linkage Proceedings*, Australian Government Department of Health and Ageing, Sydney, pp. 36-39.

Black, N. (2008), "Maximizing Research Opportunities of New NHS Information Systems", *British Medical Journal*, Vol. 336, No. 7636, pp. 106-107.

Carinci F., C.T. Di Iorio, W. Ricciardi and N. Klazinga (2011), "Revision of the European Data Protection Directive: Opportunity or Threat for Public Health Monitoring?", *European Journal of Public Health*, Vol. 21, No. 6, pp. 684-685.

Challine, L.C., L.L.P. Pirard and P. Grosclaude (2003), "Epidemiological Surveillance of Cancer: Choosing a System for National Surveillance", *Environnement, Risques et Santé*, Vol. 2, No. 2, pp. 105-111.

Conway, P.H. and J.M. VanLare (2010), "Improving Access to Health Care Data: The Open Government Strategy", *Journal of the American Medical Association*, Vol. 304, No. 9, pp. 1007-1008.

Frank, L. (2001), "Epidemiology: When an Entire Country is a Cohort", *Science*, Vol. 287, No. 5462, pp. 2398-2399.

Gunter, T.D. and N.P. Terry (2005), "The Emergence of National Electronic Health Record Architectures in the United States and Australia: Models, Costs and Questions", *Journal of Medical Internet Research*, Vol. 7, No. 1.

Habib, J.L. (2010), "EHRs, Meaningful Use and a model EHR", *Drug Benefit Trends*, Vol. 22, No. 4, pp. 99-101.

Hakulinen, T. et al. (2011), "Harmonisation May Be Counterproductive – At Least for Parts of Europe Where Public Health Research Operates Effectively", *European Journal of Public Health*, Vol. 21, No. 6, pp. 686-687.

HM Treasury (2011), *The Plan for Growth*, London.

Holman, C.D.J., A.J. Bass, D.L. Rosman et al. (2008), "A Decade of Data Linkage in Western Australia: Strategic Design, Applications and Benefits of the WA Data Linkage System", *Australian Health Review*, Vol. 32, No. 4, pp. 766-777.

Jutte, D.P, N.L. Roos and M. Brownell (2011), "Administrative Record Linkage as a Tool for Public Health Research", *Annual Review of Public Health*, Vol. 21, No. 32, pp. 91-108.

Linder, J.A., J. Ma and D.W. Bates (2007), "Electronic Health Record Use and the Quality of Ambulatory Care in the United States", *Archives of Internal Medicine*, Vol. 167, No. 13, pp. 1400-1405.

Mladovsky, P., E. Mossialos and M. McKee (2008), "Improving Access to Research Data in Europe", *British Medical Journal*, Vol. 3, No. 36, pp. 287-288.

National Collaborative Research Infrastructure Strategy (2011), "Population Health Research Network", *www.ncris.innovation.gov.au/Capabilities/Pages/PopHealth.aspx*, accessed 23 August 2011.

OECD (2010), *Improving Value in Health Care: Measuring Quality*, OECD Health Policy Studies, OECD Publishing, Paris.

OECD (2011), "Meeting of the Health Committee at the Ministerial Level Final Communiqué", 7-8 October, *www.oecd.org/newsroom/46163626.pdf*, OECD, Paris, accessed 9 October 2012.

Peto, J., O. Fletcher and C. Gilham (2004), "Data Protection, Informed Consent and Research: Medical Research Suffers Because of Pointless Obstacles", *British Medical Journal*, Vol. 328, pp. 1029-1030.

Population Health Research Network (2011), *www.phrn.org.au*, accessed 23 August 2011.

Rahu, M. and M. McKee (2008), "Epidemiological Research Labelled as a Violation of Privacy: The Case of Estonia", *International Journal of Epidemiology*, Vol. 8, No. 37, pp. 678-682.

Roos, L.L., V. Menec and R.J. Currie (2004), "Policy Analysis in an Information-Rich Environment", *Social Science and Medicine*, Vol. 58, No. 11, pp. 2231-2241.

Safran, C., M. Bloomrosen, E. Hammond et al. (2007), "Toward a National Framework for the Secondary use of Health Data: An American Health Informatics White Paper", *Journal of the American Health Informatics Association*, Vol. 4, No. 1, pp. 1-9.

Tiik, M. (2010), "Rules and Access Rights of the Estonian Integrated e-Health System", *Studies in Health Technology and Informatics*, Vol. 156, pp. 245-256.

UKCRC R&D Advisory Group to Connecting for Health (2007), "Report of the Research Simulations", *www.ukcrc.org/publications/reports/*, accessed 15 April 2011.

Verschuuren, M., G. Badeyan, J. Carnicero et al. (2008), "The European Data Protection Legislation and Its Consequences for Public Health Monitoring: A Plea for Action", *European Journal of Public Health*, Vol. 18, No. 6, pp. 550-551.

Walsh, D., M. Smalls and J. Boyd (2001), "Electronic Health Summaries – Building on the Foundation of the Scottish Record Linkage System", *Studies in Health Technology and Informatics*, Vol. 84, Pt 2), pp. 1212-1218.

Wiktorowicz, M.E., J. Lexchin, K. Moscou et al. (2010), *Keeping an Eye on Prescription Drugs, Keeping Canadians Safe: Active Monitoring Systems for Drug Safety and Effectiveness in Canada and Internationally*, Health Council of Canada, Toronto.

Chapter 2

Taking stock of the evidence – from data use to health system improvement

> *Many countries are benefiting from the linkage and analysis of personal health data to provide the evidence needed for health policy decisions to improve the quality and efficiency of health care. Examples range from reporting on the cost-effectiveness and clinical appropriateness of care in Finland, Korea and Singapore; to assessments of the quality and efficiency of clinical guidelines in Sweden; to evaluating the safety of patient screening in Germany; to evaluating the quality of surgical outcomes in Israel and the United Kingdom; to examining care transitions in Australia and Canada.*
>
> *This chapter summarises 29 within-country projects and 10 multi-country projects deemed by country respondents to be policy relevant and to exemplify good practices in data protection. Among them, 14 study leaders were interviewed to provide additional information about their project and its relevance to health policy, as well as the steps taken to ensure privacy-respectful data use. For these 14 projects, a detailed case study summary is presented.*

The statistical data for Israel are supplied by and under the responsibility of the relevant Israeli authorities. The use of such data by the OECD is without prejudice to the status of the Golan Heights, East Jerusalem and Israeli settlements in the West Bank under the terms of international law.

There is a very large and growing body of evidence of the importance of the collection, analysis, linkage and reporting of results from personal health data assets for health care quality monitoring and improvement, population health policy, and health system performance measurement and evaluation. This OECD study asked respondents to identify up to three studies conducted in their country over the past five years that were relevant to policy makers and that demonstrated best practices in the protection of data confidentiality, respect for patient privacy and privacy legislations, excellent data security, high quality data, and a sound study methodology. Further, this study also asked respondents to identify a recent multi-country project involving the analysis of personal health data from health care administrative databases, disease registries or electronic medical record databases.

There were several very important examples provided by countries of the linkage of personal health data to follow the pathway of care and understand the health outcomes of care in order to evaluate the quality and effectiveness of health care treatments. The PERFECT study (Table 2.5) in Finland monitors the content, quality and cost-effectiveness of treatment episodes in specialised medical care and thus contributes to monitoring health system performance. The methodology developed for PERFECT is now having an impact on monitoring among other countries throughout Europe via the EUROhope study (see below). Korea's quality assessment of medical services includes assessment of the clinical appropriateness and cost effectiveness of health care by reporting on quality and inducing service providers to make improvements in response to the evidence (Table 2.7). It aims to identify underuse, overuse and misuse of therapies and to reduce variation in care practices through the regular reporting of quality indicators. There are also quality and efficiency assessments of clinical care guidelines in Sweden (Table 2.8). For areas of care subject to national guidelines, such as cardiac and stroke care, care for selected cancers, dental care, diabetes care and mental health care, data linkages are undertaken to develop indicators to evaluate the effectiveness of recommended therapies and the evidence contributes to revisions of the care guidelines. To monitor and study health care consumption and expenditures, Belgium has developed a permanent sample of socially insured persons via the linkage of health care reimbursement invoice data to create longitudinal histories of health care encounters (Table 2.1). Results inform policy decisions to manage health care expenditures.

In Germany there have been projects to evaluate the effectiveness and safety of breast cancer screening (Table 2.6). A project examined the quality of breast-cancer mammography as a diagnostic tool and involved a follow-up of women who had experienced breast pain or a suspicious lump through subsequent health care encounters and cancer outcomes. A second project involves an evaluation of early detection guidelines for mammography screening where patients who participated in a clinical trial and those who did not will be followed up for health outcomes. In so doing, the benefits and the potential adverse effects of exposure to mammography screening can be evaluated and the evidence used to develop policy.

Two data linkage projects are underway in the United Kingdom to improve understanding of infant health (Table 2.11). These involve overcoming gaps in existing information to provide a more comprehensive and consistent picture of maternity outcomes and to enable statistics of births and infant deaths by key characteristics, such as gestational age and ethnicity. To extend the information available about pathways of stroke care beyond the acute care setting, a pilot data linkage project is underway in Canada (Table 2.2).

In Switzerland, a linkage of population Census data and mortality data is enabling a better understanding of the socio-economic and socio-demographic characteristics of mortality and life expectancy and forms a base cohort from which additional data may be linked for specific, approved, studies (Table 2.9). In the United States, a platform has been developed to support health and health services studies, including a repository of surveys that have been readied to support linkage projects and two key linkages: the linkage of population health survey data to mortality data; and the linkage of population health survey data to data on health care encounters for Medicare and Medicaid insurance beneficiaries (Table 2.13). In the United Kingdom, there is an initiative to facilitate research involving personal health data that is in the public's interest. The service can both produce tabulations and conduct data linkages on behalf of clients with approved projects (Table 2.10).

A care trust in England has a new project to link records across health and social care databases to produce pathways of services and associated costs on an on-going basis (Table 2.12). A Canadian province has established a university-based research centre to conduct linkage of individual-level data to inform on health system performance, patient safety, population health, diagnostic services and primary care (Table 2.3). A health care maintenance organisation in the United States has accumulated 50 years of experience in research and monitoring involving personal health data and linkages to improve health care services and patient outcomes and is now analysing data from an electronic medical record system (Table 2.14).

Other examples of projects involving data linkages summarised in this chapter include health care quality monitoring through understanding care pathways and outcomes for chronic disease patients, for cancer patients, for patients suffering a heart attack, and for patients after key surgeries; studies of the health effects of radiation exposure; the development of disease registries; monitoring pregnancy outcomes; and monitoring health care use and expenditures.

Multi-country projects

The European Best Information through Regional Outcomes in Diabetes (EUBIROD) project (Table 2.4) is a public health project funded by the European Union that aims to implement a sustainable European diabetes register to monitor diabetes complications and the health of diabetes patients (EUBIROD, 2011). EUBIROD is amalgamating aggregate data from 18 diabetes registries across Europe and it was challenging for the participants to find common ground where the local requirements for data security and privacy would be respected. The solution was the Best Information for Regional Outcomes or BIRO system (Di Iorio et al., 2009). In BIRO, each disease registry provides aggregated data for their region with very little to no re-identification risk using an on-line data transfer system. In working with participating countries, the conclusion of the EUBIROD team is that the sharing of de-identified person-level data from diabetes registers would not be possible and still succeed in securing the participation of a large set of countries.

The Nelson trial is a randomised trial of the potential to use low-dose CT scans to screen at risk patients for lung cancer (van Klaveren et al., 2009). Data are from Belgium and the Netherlands. The trial began in 2004 and is continuing until 2015. The world is waiting for the trial results because this is the only study where patients were recruited from population registries where it could be certain that those in the no-screening group indeed had not been screened. Results will have worldwide implications for health system policy regarding the uptake of and guidelines for lung-cancer screening.

EuroHOPE, the European Health Care Outcomes, Performance and Efficiency project, is a new initiative funded by the European Union and co-ordinated by the National Institute for Health and Welfare in Finland to evaluate the performance of European health care systems in terms of outcomes, quality, use of resources and costs through data linkages. Participating countries all have the necessary health information infrastructure and legal framework to undertake the data linkages and include Norway, Sweden, Scotland, regions in Italy and the Netherlands. For EuroHOPE, each participating country will link health care administrative databases for in-patient hospitalisations, pharmaceutical data, and cancer registry and mortality data in order to begin to generate indicators of the quality of hospital-based treatments across the whole cycle of care that would be comparable across the participating countries. The five focus areas for the development of these health care quality indicators are acute myocardial infarction, stroke, hip fracture, breast cancer and low birth-weight infants.

EuroHOPE aims to develop indicators that could be recommended to the European Union for routine reporting, develop methods for international comparative health services research based on data linkages of person-level data; and inform about the policy-relevant drivers of health care quality, including treatment practices, use of medicines and new medical technologies, waiting times, financing, and the organisation of care. EUROHOPE is following the analytical model established by National Institute for Health and Welfare in Finland (Table 2.5).

EURO-PERISTAT is a European project to monitor and evaluate perinatal health in the European Union by establishing a sustainable system for reporting perinatal health indicators (EURO-PERISTAT, 2011). The Deepening our Understanding of Quality Improvement in Europe (DUQuE) project is funded by the European Union to study the effectiveness of quality improvement systems in European hospitals by assessing the relationship between hospitals quality improvement systems, management and culture and the quality of hospital care, such as clinical effectiveness, patient safety and patient involvement (DUQuE, 2011).

There are numerous multi-country projects exploring dimensions of cancer incidence, treatment and survival. The *Cancer Incidence in Five Continents* series, published by the World Health Organisation is a reference for international comparison of cancer incidence (IARC, 2011). EUROCARE is a study of cancer survival across Europe (EUROCARE, 2011). Australia, Canada, Denmark, Norway, Sweden, and the United Kingdom participated in an International Cancer Benchmarking Project to better understand both how and why cancer survival varies among countries (Coleman et al., 2011).

Denmark, Finland and Sweden collaborated in a study of mortality and life-expectancy trends from 1987 to 2006. This study required each country to link hospital discharge registers to cause of death registers to examine the excess mortality and life expectancy gaps for people hospitalised with severe mental health disorders. Results helped to inform about the quality of psychiatric services (Wahlbeck et al., 2011). Canada and the United States collaborated to conduct the Joint Canada-US Survey of Health (JCUSH) to compare access to and use of health care services and population health between the two countries (Gulley and Altman, 2008; Altman and Gulley, 2009).

Case studies

Table 2.1. **Belgium: Permanent sample of socially insured persons**

Study title	Permanent sample of socially insured persons
Lead organisation	National Institute for Health and Disease Insurance (INAMI-RIZIV), Belgium.
Project description	Belgium has developed a permanent sample of socially insured persons involving the collection and linkage of health care reimbursement invoice data from the seven Belgian health insurance organisations (Commission Technique d'Échantillon Permanent au Conseil Général de l'INAMI, 2011). Data are linked to create longitudinal histories of health care encounters to study health care consumption and expenditures. The seven health care insurance organisations entered into a partnership for this project and the data is collected and linked by a trusted third party operating on behalf of the insurers called the Intermutualist Agency or IMA-AIM. Other partners in the project are government departments including the Belgian Health Care Knowledge Centre (KCE), National Institute for Health and Disease Insurance (INAMI-RIZIV), and the cancer registry. The management committee of the project consists of the partners and representatives of the Belgian Privacy Protection Commission.
Project approval	The permanent sample is authorised by law. The law establishes the IMA-AIM as the party that would select from the universe of social security numbers in Belgium a representative sample of the population of one in 40 persons and one in 20 persons aged 65 and older. The law requires that the data only be used for statistical purposes related to management and research and forbids participating partners from undertaking operations that might directly or indirectly identify an individual. The management committee is authorised to approve studies using the permanent database. This includes the approval of any extension of the database involving linkages to other databases within the custody of the partners (Committee for Social Affairs). Extensions of the database involving linkages to databases outside of the participating partners, such as linkages to databases in the custody of the Committee for Public Health, are not part of the legal authorisation and would require all of the steps for approval of the Privacy Protection Commission of any new project and may require the legislation authorising the permanent sample to be amended.
Data and data linkage	Included in the permanent database are records from primary health care, a subset of hospital data and information on reimbursed medications. Data is composed of reimbursement codes by procedure, service, admission, and drug delivery that include dates, providers, institutions and costs. Virtually all health care encounters have an associated Social Security Number. Missing from the data would be a small number of cases of foreign persons receiving health care and infants born in hospital who have not yet received a Social Security Number. According to the law authorising the permanent database, Social Security Numbers within the micro data are re-coded by the seven health insurance mutualities before being sent to an intermediate party which also re-codes the social security number a second time and then transmits the micro data to the IMA-AIM. The insurers also further de-identify the data by removing other direct identifiers including names, exact birth dates and addresses. The IMA-AIM link the records using the coded Social Security Number to create a longitudinal view of each selected insured person in the sample. Partners are provided access to micro data that includes the coded Social Security Number, the year of birth and a city code. IMA-AIM provides partners with access to the permanent sample using a secure electronic data transfer. Data for the sampled insured persons is linked for a maximum of ten years before it is destroyed. Each year a new sample is drawn and thus the database itself is maintained permanently.
Protection of data privacy	There is no prior consent requested of insured persons to be selected for inclusion in the database. However, Belgian health interview surveys can only be approved to be linked to the permanent sample database if the survey respondents have consented to this linkage. Government partners receiving micro data are required by law to control access to the permanent database. Only a small number of individuals (4-5 persons) are permitted access to detailed micro data within each organisation. More aggregated data views where, for example, year of birth is grouped to five year intervals, may be accessible to a broader number of employees. Government partners are required to consult with experts in data security and privacy protection as well as a health care practitioner to ensure that internal practices conform to the intent of the law. Further, access to data and uses of data must be tracked and may be verified through an external audit by the Privacy Protection Commission. Academic partners can obtain access to aggregated results from the permanent database from IMA-AIM that have been screened to protect data confidentiality.

Table 2.1. **Belgium: Permanent sample of socially insured persons** (cont.)

Study title	Permanent sample of socially insured persons
Study results and future directions	The permanent database was developed to better inform policy decisions and it is directly used by policy makers, particularly in the area of managing health care expenditures. Work includes monitoring the costs of treating patients with chronic diseases, monitoring out-of-pocket payments for health insurance, monitoring the use of health technologies, and monitoring the recurrence of diagnostic exams and biological tests, such as blood tests. Also examined has been exposure of patients to radiation from medical imaging. Results influence the development of clinical guidelines. Overall the database helps the government to explore new ways of financing health care and to explore policy scenarios. The permanent database is focused on insurance transactions and therefore does not have information on the results of lab tests nor diagnosis. Diagnosis can, for some conditions, be inferred from prescription medicines. There are new proposals to link the permanent database to the hospital clinical minimum dataset to enable the study of readmission to hospital by the reason for the readmission. This request falls outside of the authorising legislation for the permanent database and will require the approval of the Privacy Protection Commission and a legal amendment is noted as required. A second proposed project is to understand the degree to which cancer patients may have a caregiver in their household. This will also require a linkage that is outside of the legislation and a separate approval process. There is a new research requirement to examine the histories of health care use of sampled persons for a period of up to 30 years. This change to the permanent database would require a legal amendment. Overall the governance of the permanent database with the establishment of the management committee has increased the ability of project partners to generate evidence for the management of the health system by reducing the heavy burden of documentation and the time lag required that would occur if each study were a separate application to the Privacy Protection Commission. Through the management committee all stakeholders are around the table and decisions to undertake projects can be made efficiently. In future, the permanent database can be used to develop health care quality indicators related to primary care and prescription medicines. The database could also be used to contribute new international quality indicators. While overall in Belgium it has become more difficult to undertake data linkage studies in health over the past five years, the development of the permanent sample has made it easier to analyse health insurance data than it would otherwise be. New concerns by the privacy commissioner of the risk of re-identification from small cells in aggregate tables will have to be addressed. A technical commission has been established to develop more documentation on managing disclosure risks from small cells.

Table 2.2. **Canada: Pathways of care for stroke patients**

Study title	Pathways of stroke care
Lead organisation	Canadian Institute for Health Information (CIHI).
Project description	This pilot project links data from in-patient hospitalisation data, emergency department visits and data on rehabilitative care in the Canadian province of Ontario in order to determine the additional information that could be gained on the outcomes of stroke care through data linkage (Canadian Institute for Health Information, 2012).
Project approval	The project was approved by CIHI senior management and the CIHI Committee on Privacy and Confidentiality, which includes the Chief Privacy Officer for CIHI. This committee grants approval for all projects involving the linkage of patient records across databases in the custody of CIHI. Elements of the application for approval include a description of the linkage project, the value of the project, restrictions to access to the linked data, the retention period for the linked data and protection of confidentiality of data in any published results. The approved retention period for the linked file prepared for this study was three years. The elapsed time between the submission of the application and the approval to conduct the study was three months.
Data and data linkage	Data for Ontario from several databases were linked at the level of the patient including inpatient hospitalisations, emergency department data, inpatient rehabilitation data, and complex continuing care data. Complex continuing care is a specialised programme providing continuing, medically complex and specialised services to patients over an extended period of time. It can be provided in either a free-standing facility or through designated beds within acute care hospitals for chronically ill patients. These patients require skilled, technology-based care that is not available through other long-term care facilities or home care programmes. All of the databases were in the custody of CIHI. There was no requirement for patient consent for the linkage of these administrative databases. Individual-level data is shared with CIHI from Canadian provinces to build national databases. All provinces have a health insurance number that is unique to the province and is used for health care encounters. Some jurisdictions encrypt the health insurance numbers on their databases before sending individual-level data to CIHI. These provinces apply the same encryption algorithm to each file and over time so that data linkage is possible. Other provinces provide CIHI with files with original health insurance numbers. For these provinces, one of the first data processing steps within CIHI is to encrypt the health insurance numbers. The standard encryption algorithm renders the original health insurance number unrecognizable. For this project the analytical team was provided with the data needed for the project and the team conducted a deterministic linkage using encrypted health care number, date of birth and sex. The quality of the linkage was high with over 90% of records successfully linked across the databases involved. Provincially issued HINS make it very difficult to trace patients who move province and introduce bias into record linkage studies. For the pathways of stroke care this bias was considered to be minimised because the period of follow-up was only four years.

Table 2.2. **Canada: Pathways of care for stroke patients** (cont.)

Study title	Pathways of stroke care
Protection of data privacy	Analytical teams never have access to data with original health insurance numbers. Access to this identifiable data is restricted to a data processing unit. Access to the analytical files necessary for the pathways of stroke care project was limited to a small number of named individuals approved to complete the work. The data is stored on a secured server. As the study has not yet been published, no external researchers have requested access to the linked database prepared for this project.
Study results and future directions	The publication of the results is expected to have implications for the care of stroke patients in Ontario and particularly for the organisation and co-ordination of their care. The analytical team would like to repeat the project in the future and to extend the linkage to other aspects of the care of stroke patients including long-term care data; home care data; pharmaceutical medicines data; and primary care data. Due to gaps in the coverage of these databases they were not included in the first pilot project. As the data holdings of CIHI expand and improve over time, greater insight into pathways of care would be possible.

Table 2.3. **Canada, Ontario: Institute for Clinical and Evaluative Sciences**

Study title	Institute for Clinical and Evaluative Sciences
Lead organisation	Institute for Clinical and Evaluative Sciences, University of Toronto.
Project description	The Institute for Clinical and Evaluative Sciences is a university-based research centre providing population-based health services research for Canada's largest province, Ontario (Institute for Clinical and Evaluative Sciences, 2011). ICES reports on many topics including health system performance; drug safety and effectiveness; population health; diagnostic services; and primary care. The research programme of ICES depends on the linkage of individual-level data from a variety of sources. ICES is sponsored by the Ontario Ministry of Health and Long-term Care and also receives academic grants for research projects.
Project approval	Under Ontario's Personal Health Information Protection Act, ICES is identified as a prescribed entity. This status enables ICES to receive and to use personal health information without patient consent for the purposes of analysis and statistics about Ontario's health care system. ICES must ensure that it can demonstrate that the collection and use of the information is in the public good and furthering medical research. Projects are approved by ICES science leaders. A form is then completed describing the project, the databases involved, the project team, and the benefit to the public of the project. This form is signed off by the lead investigator, the Chief Privacy Officer, the satellite site director if the study will take place at a satellite site and the ICES CEO. Many projects have benefited from scientific grants and have also fulfilled the requirements of the granting agencies involved.
Data and data linkage	ICES receives personal health data from the Ontario Ministry of Health and Long-term Care and also negotiates to receive data transfers from other Ontario prescribed entities, such as disease registries. Data sharing agreements are used to describe the terms of the data transfer including data privacy protection and data security. ICES data holdings of personal health data from the Health Ministry go back to 1988 and ICES is authorised to hold this data until such time as ICES is closed or the ministry ends its agreement with ICES. The legislation does not place limits on the retention of personal health data and the ministry understands that a long time series is necessary for epidemiological research. For data transfers to ICES from other Ontario data custodians, the data sharing agreement will specify a date of data destruction. The Ontario Health Insurance Number is used for all patient encounters for public health care services, including physician claims, drug benefits, and hospital encounters. The Ontario Registered Persons Database includes all HINS associated with individuals by name, address and birth date. ICES receives fully identifiable personal health data from various data custodians, including administrative health data from the Ontario Ministry of Health and Long-term Care. As a first use, ICES encrypts the health information numbers to create an ICES key number (IKN) and further de-identifies the data by removing other direct identifying variables. ICES uses the same encryption algorithm for all files and throughout time to enable data linkage. Files received from the Health Ministry do not contain the original Health Insurance Number, names or addresses. Data linkages at ICES depend on the ICES key number and tend to be undertaken using a deterministic method.

Table 2.3. **Canada, Ontario: Institute for Clinical and Evaluative Sciences** (cont.)

Study title	Institute for Clinical and Evaluative Sciences
Protection of data privacy	To fulfil the requirements of prescribed entity status within PHIPA, ICES policies and practices for data use and data security are reviewed by the Ontario Information and Privacy Commission on a tri-annual basis. ICES is required to have a data privacy and security framework complying with a manual prepared by the Privacy Commission. A threat and risk assessment of ICES information security takes place annually by an independent organisation hired to audit ICES data security and to try to penetrate it (ethical hacking). All data inflows and outflows to ICES use an encrypted transfer system. The retention period for linked databases is set on a project-by-project basis when a project is approved. ICES has a network of academic researchers working throughout the province of Ontario and only researchers affiliated with ICES or collaborating with an ICES researcher may be approved for access to ICES databases. Access is provided at the ICES headquarters or through a network of secure satellite centres providing access to ICES databases over a secure network. Researchers are always required to access data holdings within a secure facility. Approval is limited to the databases and the variables within the databases that the researcher needs to undertake a project. To make it easier for researchers to plan a project, ICES provides information about the databases and the variables within them on its Intranet site. There is a separation of duties at ICES where researchers analysing data can only see de-identified data and only specially designated individuals may encrypt health insurance numbers and de-identify data. There is no electronic link between computers used to process identifiable data and computers used for analysis. As a prescribed entity, ICES is able to process personal health data from administrative sources without consent. ICES informs the public about its research programme through its website. ICES also publishes an information brochure. When ICES is involved in primary data collection, such as a recent survey of homeless persons, participant consent to data linkage is sought. ICES has various documents to help staff inform staff about the protection of data confidentiality and privacy, including policies and a manual provided to new staff members. Staff are reminded of requirements and updated on new guidelines or policies through staff meetings, the Intranet site and an employee newsletter dedicated to data privacy and security. Employees are required to sign an agreement annually to protect data confidentiality.
Study results and future directions	ICES researchers have published thousands of research studies using data linkages at a population level. This research has informed about the effects of treatments in real-world settings which can differ from results of clinical trials. For example, a recent study of patients who had received an implantable cardio defibrillator determined that after six months there were important variations across care settings in the occurrence of inappropriate shocks and deaths (Krishnakumar et al., 2011). The evidence produced by ICES contributes to policy planning and evaluation within the Ontario Ministry of Health and Long-term Care. While access to databases of ICES have been restricted to staff, adjunct staff and sponsored collaborators, there has recently been an exception created by ICES and another entity, Cancer Care Ontario. Cancer Care Ontario requested a linkage of its cancer database to ICES databases for a project to be undertaken by researchers at Cancer Care Ontario. To provide data to these external researchers, ICES engaged in a more sophisticated process of data de-identification, including the removal of all direct identifying variables, the conversion of dates to indicators of elapsed time, and the inclusion of less-specific geographic identifiers. The de-identification process used was developed by Dr. Khaled El Emam and is called the Privacy Analytics Risk Assessment Tool (PARAT). The resulting de-identified data was provided to the external researcher on a CD. ICES is interested in exploring the option to use the PARAT process for other similar projects in the future. When researchers are interested in a project involving other Canadian provinces, the process has been to develop code for data processing together and then to have a researcher affiliated with each province responsible for the linkage of their own data and the analysis of that data. There is interest within ICES in further developing mechanisms to improve the ability to undertake analysis among Canadian provinces. There is also interest in further exploring linkages of health data to other areas, such as education or transportation.

Table 2.4. **Europe: Comparing diabetes outcomes across European countries**

Study title	European Best Information through Region Outcomes in Diabetes (EUBIROD)
Lead organisation	The Department of Internal Medicine at the University of Perugia (Italy) is coordinator of the project which involves 20 partners and two collaborating institutions from at least 20 countries, including EU member states and other countries.
Project description	The EUBIROD project is amalgamating aggregate data from 18 disease registries across Europe to create a sustainable European Diabetes Register to monitor diabetes indicators including complications and health outcomes. The three-year project has been sponsored by the European Union (EUBIROD, 2011).
Project approval	It is the responsibility of regions to obtain approval to participate.
Data and data linkage	Project participants use the BIRO system to submit aggregate data from their disease registry using an on-line data transfer system. Each disease registry receives a statistical programme and technical support from EUBIROD which helps to ensure consistency in the submitted indicators. The BIRO system produces pre-defined tables with pre-defined views. It is not possible to generate new table views.

Table 2.4. **Europe: Comparing diabetes outcomes across European countries** *(cont.)*

Study title	European Best Information through Region Outcomes in Diabetes (EUBIROD)
Protection of data privacy	Some diabetes registries have a strong infrastructure for data security and protection of data privacy while others have grown up from a local advocate and have achieved governmental support with a weaker infrastructure. It was important for the EUBIROD project to understand the the management of data privacy protection among the different registries within the countries participating, as different approaches could affect the completeness of the information within the registries and the comparability of results. To build this knowledge, EUBIROD developed an on-line tool for privacy performance assessment that enables participating registers to evaluate their level of respect for the privacy principles enshrined through the EU Data Protection Directive (Di Iorio et al., 2010). Key findings of the privacy performance assessment included that privacy principles have been implemented heterogeneously across Europe, with some interpretations restrictive to the point of limiting development and use of the registries that would be consistent with research in the public interest. The EUBIROD project has sought common ground where local requirements for data protection would be respected to ensure the greatest number of countries could particpate. The project did not attempt to amalgamate individual-level data. Instead, the data submitted to the project through BIRO are aggregate indicators that would not reveal the identity of a patient. Further, as it is not possible to generate new tables, the risk of revealing the identity of individuals from repeated generation of detailed tables is mitigated. In the first published report, anticipated for fall 2011, regions contributing to EURBIROD will be identified by a study number and not by country. This is because some countries have only one region participating and identification of the country could then reveal the identity of a particular diabetes care centre.
Study results and future directions	The first EUBIROD report will cover approximately 120 000 subjects and yield 72 indicators. Regions contributing to EUBIROD will be identified by study number. In the future, as more health care centres contribute data it may be possible to publish indicators by country. The European Commission is also interested in the possibility of using the BIRO system to populate indicators required by the European Union. This is not possible in the short run, but may become possible in the future as more care centres participate and data becomes more representative of countries.

Table 2.5. **Finland: Monitoring performance, effectiveness and costs of treatment episodes**

Study title	PERFECT – PERformance, Effectiveness and Cost of Treatment Episodes (Finland)
Lead organisation	THL National Institute for Health and Welfare, Finland.
Project description	PERFECT monitors the content, quality and cost-effectiveness of treatment episodes in specialised medical care and thus contributes to monitoring health system performance. Indicators and models were created to monitor selected disease groups and procedures (stroke, premature newborns, hip fracture, breast cancer, schizophrenia, acute myocardial infarction, and orthopaedic endoprosthesis including hip and knee replacement surgery, and invasive heart surgery). These disease groups and procedures were selected because of the number of patients treated and/or the level of treatment costs. Through the linkage of individual-level data, the project is able to go beyond reporting on single health care events to examining the whole cycle of care including patient outcomes, treatments and use of health system resources for well defined, and risk-adjusted, patient groups (Häkkinen, 2011). The performance measurement data generated from the PERFECT project enables benchmarking clinical practices against best-practice guidelines and assessment of the degree to which guidelines are being followed. The data can also be used to investigate the policy-sensitive factors explaining differences between hospitals and regions The project creates a database of about 200 indicators for hospitals and regions that are identified by name.
Project approval	The project was initiated by a consortium of researchers and clinical experts who received a scientific grant for health services research. On initiation, there was no requirement for research ethics approval of this project as it involved only registry data. Two years ago, however, legislative requirements changed and a research ethics board was created within THL (National Institute for Health and Welfare) to act as the approval body for data linkage projects involving registry data. If a project requires data from Statistics Finland, such as mortality and cancer statistics, an approval process takes place within that organisation as well. As necessary, Statistics Finland will also consult with the national privacy office. Because of the on-going development of PERFECT, the team presents an application for data linkage approval at nearly every monthly board meeting. The requirements for board approval places an administrative burden on the PERFECT team and project plans must take into account the additional time required to prepare and follow-up applications.
Data and data linkage	The project depends on high-quality and linkable individual-level data from within a set of databases including hospital in-patient records, out-patient records, birth records, disease-specific registers, prescribed medicines data, social care data, death records, and data on care reimbursement (Peltola et al., 2011). The data linkages required for the project take place at THL (National Institute for Health and Welfare). The main linkage key is the Personal Identity Number which is used in all data collections for public services including health care. Overall the quality of the data linkages is high for Finland, particularly when the research team compares linkage results to those of other countries attempting similar work.

Table 2.5. **Finland: Monitoring performance, effectiveness and costs of treatment episodes** (cont.)

Study title	PERFECT – PERformance, Effectiveness and Cost of Treatment Episodes (Finland)
Protection of data privacy	THL has a right to collect and use personal health data under law and patient consent is not required for the use of registry data and mortality data, including data linkages. If a survey is to be included in a PERFECT study, however, survey respondents need to have been asked for consent to link their survey responses to the registries for the linkage to be approved. An agreement was negotiated between Statistics Finland, the social insurance authority and THL for the data to be shared to undertake the PERFECT study. The agreement ensures that the requirements for data security and data privacy of each data supplying organisation will be respected. The PERFECT team ensures that the data custodians receive copies of published reports so that they can monitor how their data have been used. Only one individual within THL holds the code used to encrypt the Personal Identity Number (PIN) and the data with direct identifiers is stored in a locked room. The PIN is converted to an encrypted identifier using an algorithm that is consistently applied across all of the databases required for linkage. Any names on the files are converted to an encrypted code that cannot be reversed. The original names and PIN are then removed from the databases that are provided to THL staff that will perform the record linkage with the encrypted identifiers. The linked files will contain address information and dates which have some risk of re-identification of individuals, however, all of the data are stored within the secure THL facility and are only accessed by staff who have been approved for this access and who have signed an undertaking to protect the confidentiality of the data. Computers are password protected and other computer security protections are implemented. Data can be provided by the PERFECT team to researchers outside of the THL. In this case, however, the content of the file would be reduced to the minimum needed for the researcher to undertake their project. The external researchers would be required to sign an agreement with the THL which commits them to protect data confidentiality and security and which binds them to not share the data with third parties.
Study results and future directions	Across the disease groups and procedures examined, a wide range of patient outcome indicators have been published including mortality rates at different time intervals, such as at seven days, 30 days, 90 days or one year after an event; emergency room visits and rehospitalisation rates overall and for specific reasons such as infections and surgical complications; and days spent at home and/or in long-term care facilities after events (Peltola et al., 2011). The study found that centralisation of care of new-borns in the five university hospitals would reduce infant mortality rates. This lead to a change in the law requiring new-borns to be treated in university hospitals. Further, as one of the university hospitals had a higher infant mortality rate than the other four, it was subject to a quality audit. Results published include that, after risk-adjustment for differences in the characteristics of patients across regions, as much as 20-30% of the cost of treatment of AMI patients could be contained if all regions in Finland could match the costs of the best performing region (Häkkinen et al., 2011). Further, better outcomes could be obtained for AMI and stroke patients, including a reduction in deaths. Hospitals have used the PERFECT indicators to initiate quality improvement. Currently PERFECT is focussing on monitoring the quality of hospital care but there are plans to extend this work to examine primary care, elder care and social services. Municipalities have agreed to participate in the extension and Statistics Finland has presented the proposal to the privacy office for Finland for approval. The PERFECT project is also having an international impact through the launch of EuroHOPE, which involves a set of countries developing quality monitoring indicators for hospital care using the PERFECT methodology.

Table 2.6. **Germany: Effectiveness and safety of breast cancer screening**

Study title	Evaluation of early detection guidelines for mammography screening and examination of the quality of breast-cancer mammography as a diagnostic tool
Lead organisation	Institute of Clinical Epidemiology/Institute of Cancer Epidemiology, University of Luebeck, Germany.
Project description	Two key projects evaluate breast cancer screening effectiveness and safety. A project to evaluate early detection guidelines for mammography screening requires a large population cohort to compare with health outcomes of participants in a clinical trial. Mammography screening involving spectrum mammography was delivered to women who took part in a clinical trial in Germany. This screening process exposes women to radiation and thus it is important to evaluate the benefits and harms of population-level screening. Particularly, of interest are the rates of interval cancers, which are cancers that were not detected from screening and still occurred between screening intervals. This study will examine the health outcomes of screened women and compare them with outcomes of a representative cohort of women who did not participate in the trial. A second project to examine the quality of breast-cancer mammography as a diagnostic tool focussed on a cohort of women who had experienced breast pain or a suspicious lump, who had sought medical care, and where a physician had requested a mammography screen as a diagnostic tool (Obi et al., 2011).

Table 2.6. **Germany: Effectiveness and safety of breast cancer screening** *(cont.)*

Study title	Evaluation of early detection guidelines for mammography screening and examination of the quality of breast-cancer mammography as a diagnostic tool
Project approval	The early detection guideline is part of federal legislation for statutory health insurance. The legislation states that an evaluation of the guidelines would take place and that results would be shared with government. While the women who took part in the clinical trial provided informed consent, the comparison cohort of non-trial participants would be drawn from administrative data. The guideline authorised that the evaluation would require the use of administrative records from a large population cohort and therefore without patient consent. In Germany, legal data protection requirements are established partly on the Federal level and partly on the state (Land) level. Data protection supervision for federal public sector entities and social security administration is the remit of the (Federal) Data Protection Commissioner. Each of the 16 states in Germany has a Data Protection Commissioner with jurisdiction at the state level and their responsibilities include social security administration at the state level. Data linkages in Germany only take place at the state level and only when authorised by law. Because of the necessity to examine a population cohort for the country from administrative data without consent; the study must be incorporated into law within each of the 16 states. Thus far, a few states have implemented the changes in law required for the project. For the study of the quality of mammography as a diagnostic tool, the cohort to be studied was all women who had consented to participate. As a result, the study protocol was approved by the research ethics boards within the German states as it satisfied the requirements of existing legislation.
Data and data linkage	Both projects required data from clinical trials to be linked to records for the same patients within the cancer registries of the participating German states. There is no patient number in Germany to facilitate data linkages. Linkages take place using a set of identifiers including name, date of birth, location, and, if available, place of birth. Approved linkages take place within participating German states, and data files that have been anonymised are provided to the researcher. There is a national pseudonymisation algorithm used by all German states and this helps to limit the bias that could occur as a result of cross state mobility of patients. The algorithm is tolerant of small spelling errors in names. Name changes can occur, however, particularly for women. Where possible, the birth name of women is incorporated into the linkage framework. Linkages depend on probabilistic techniques and are resource intensive requiring skilled technicians and significant time. Other identifiers may remain on a linked file for analysis, such as date and place of birth, if they have been justified as necessary for the analytical project. Evaluations of the quality of the linkages indicate results are of reasonably high quality.
Protection of data privacy	The national data protection law and accompanying federal guidelines have strict provisions for data security. The Institute for Cancer Epidemiology in the state of Schlewig-Holstein has strong physical security including doors that cannot be opened from the outside without a key; and password-protected computers. Lap-top computers are encrypted to protect against risk in the event of a lost or stolen machine. Individuals are only authorised access to data they need for their work and only staff involved in data processing ever has access to patient identifiers. Staff involved in processing of data is under a clean desk policy where they must have all files locked away at the end of each day. Every staff member is issued a handbook on data protection. Cancer registry data may be held for 110 years after the birth of an individual, which enables long-term studies of cancer survival to take place. Data with encrypted identifiers (de-identified data) may be held indefinitely. The retention of linked data files is negotiated with the data protection authorities for each project and the scientific standard which is recommended is to retain the files for ten years. If the study has the informed consent of participants, the participants will be informed that the data will be linked for ten years.
Study results and future directions	The project to evaluate early detection guidelines for mammography screening is an example of the value to policy of research requiring data linkages, as the evaluation study was incorporated into legislation. The probabilistic linkages required for these studies are costly. It may be possible to make a case in the future to encrypt a health information number, as is the process currently in Germany for the pseudonymisation of names, but with the result being more successful and less resource intensive linkages. It remains unclear whether or not the changes that would be required to enable deterministic linkages in Germany would be supported by the population.

Table 2.7. **Korea: Quality assessment of medical services**

Study title	Quality Assessment of National Health Insurance Benefits, Korea
Lead organisation	Health Insurance Review and Assessment Service (HIRA).
Project description	This project aims to assess the clinical appropriateness and cost effectiveness of health care and to improve health care quality by reporting on quality and inducing service providers to make improvements to any services determined to be inadequate (Health Insurance Review and Assessment Service, 2011). It aims to identify underuse, overuse and misuse of therapies and to reduce variation in care practices through the regular reporting of quality indicators. Indicators from the linkage of hospital in-patient data to mortality data include 30-day case fatality for acute myocardial infarction; in-hospital fatalities within seven days after discharge, and within 30 days after surgery for coronary artery bypass grafting; 30-day in-hospital operative mortality for colorectal cancer; and 30-day operative mortality for stomach surgery, oesophageal surgery, pancreatic surgery, stem-cell transplantation, hip replacement, and percutaneous coronary intervention. Korea monitors mental-health care through a linkage of mental hospital in-patient data to prescription medicines data to produce the prescription rate of atypical anti-psychotics for schizophrenia. Through a linkage of mental hospital in-patient data to hospital in-patient data, Korea calculates the rate of readmission within 30 days of discharge from hospital for schizophrenia. Through the linkage of primary care data to prescription medicines data, outcomes of prescribing patterns including overlapping or inappropriate prescribing are monitored in Korea. Indicators include the rate of prescriptions of four-or-more component anti-hypertensive medications, parallel administration of diuretics, prescription of not-recommended parallel therapies, prescription days, and continued prescription for hypertension. For diabetes patients there is a set of monitored indicators including the rate of overlapping prescriptions; the rate of prescription of four-or-more component anti-diabetics, medication cost per administration day; and days of continued prescription. Korea also links the cancer registry data to mortality data to assess the relative survival of cancer patients and links long-term care data to survey data on the activities of daily living to estimate the percentage of patients with reduced activities of daily living.
Project approval	The Quality Assessment of National Health Insurance Benefits is conducted by HIRA under the requirements of the National Health Insurance Act. Data linkage projects are approved by a deliberation committee of HIRA on a project-by-project basis and are evaluated according to the requirements of the Privacy Protection Act.
Data and data linkage	Data linkages are conducted by HIRA and depend on the Resident Registration Number which is issued at birth and is used throughout the health care system. HIRA receives data from other government sectors, such as death data from the Ministry of Public Administration and Security.
Protection of data privacy	HIRA has internal guidelines on the protection of data security and confidentiality including specific guidelines related to data linkage. HIRA's data security and protection of data privacy are subject to audit by both the Ministry of Public Administration and Security and the National Intelligence Service. Data analysis takes place only within a designated area and by designated employees within HIRA. HIRA employees are trained in data security and privacy protection on a regular basis. External non-profit academic researchers or researchers in public-good organisations may apply to the deliberation committee for approval to access de-identified personal health data. When approved, analysis must take place only within a designated area within HIRA. Requests for access to data to prepare educational materials or to contribute to a thesis would not be approved.
Study results and future directions	Through data linkages, HIRA is able to report on the quality of services provided by physicians, clinics, hospitals and long-term care providers. These statistics are used to report on the quality of services for particular patient groups, including diabetic, heart and cancer patients. HIRA also reports on expenditures by disease categories and can therefore examine efficiency.

Table 2.8. **Sweden: Quality and efficiency assessments of clinical guidelines**

Study title	Open comparison and assessment (of clinical guidelines)
Lead organisation	National Board of Health and Welfare, Sweden.
Project description	In Sweden, there are quality and efficiency assessments of areas of care that are subject to national guidelines including cardiac and stroke care, care for four types of cancer, dental care, diabetes care, and mental health care. Generally there are clinical care guidelines developed for diseases involving large groups of patients. Clinical care guidelines are reviewed every 4-5 years. A panel of experts is convened to review and prioritise new treatments that could be incorporated into clinical care guidelines. This committee also reviews and prioritises health care quality indicators that could be developed to measure the quality and efficiency of care. These indicators require data linkages. Indicators for cardiac and stroke care were the first to be undertaken and results have been published (Socialstyrelsen, 2010). Assessments are now underway for psychiatric care, diabetes care and dementia care. The assessment takes place three-to-four years after the introduction of the clinical care guideline. For the first assessment, records for cardiac care patients were linked to health care encounters to assess how processes of care may have changed as a result of the introduction of the guidelines and to also examine results in terms of patient health. For example, the study looked at patient survival after a heart attack and the history of medications prescribed to the patients after the acute event. If, for example, a medication is found to have generated complications, its use may be given a lower priority when the care guidelines are revised.
Project approval	The government has given the National Board of Health and Welfare the mandate to assess and compare areas of care and to develop the indicators needed to assess the clinical care guidelines. As the National Board of Health and Welfare is authorised to collect and to process personal health data, no further research ethics approval was required for the project.

Table 2.8. **Sweden: Quality and efficiency assessments of clinical guidelines** (cont.)

Study title	Open comparison and assessment (of clinical guidelines)
Data and data linkage	The first published study involved the linkage of data for cardiac care patients in the National Quality Register to the Patient Registry. The National Quality Register is focused on the treatment of cardiac conditions. This linkage of the quality register to the patient registry enabled examination of all of the health care encounters of cardiac patients. This is particularly important when examining the effectiveness of medications, as they may have unintended health consequences. For example, a patient may be given blood-thinning medicine in response to a cardiac condition and then be admitted to hospital for gastric bleeding. The hospitalisation is not a cardiac event, but may be a complication of the medication given because of a cardiac condition. It is only through data linkage that a more complete picture of patient outcomes of care emerges. In Sweden, every person has a Personal Identity Number that is used for social security and health care and the use of the identifier is mandatory. Linkages using the PIN are of high quality. There are some data coverage issues, particularly for recent immigrants who do not yet have a permanent residence status and thus may be given a different temporary number for each health care encounter. Further, some quality registers have high patient coverage (85-90% of patients) while others have lower coverage (as low as 60%). Low coverage can bias study results. In Sweden, there are 21 county councils that govern health care. The government reaches out to these councils to implement health care guidelines and the councils work with their hospitals to participate. Participation in quality registers is voluntary and some councils work hard to gain the participation of hospitals including offering financial incentives. Others do not place the same priority on gaining high hospital participation. To participate in a quality register, a hospital would need to dedicate some staff time to data reporting.
Protection of data privacy	Patient participation in registries is mandatory. However, if patients wish to have their data removed from a registry they may appeal to the Board. Information on the registries maintained by the board is posted for patients to read in patient wards and health care centres. Quality registers in Sweden have initiated a process of patient consent and ask consent to use personal health data for research or statistical purposes. There is a specific unit within the National Board of Health that is permitted access to identifiable data and who undertake data linkages. Linked files then have identifying numbers removed before they are provided to individuals within the board for analysis. Data analysts never see identifiable data. De-identification involves removing names, personal identity numbers, addresses and full birth dates. Analysis files may contain a study number which has been assigned in place of the personal identity number. Data that has been linked for the health care quality assessment project is retained for six months and then it is destroyed. Data is stored in a locked and secure building using computers that have been protected from unauthorised access. Only employees granted access to the data can use the data and all use is tracked by a security officer. Data confidentiality rules are applied to prevent residual disclosure of patients, particularly from hospitals with very few cases. New employees receive training on data confidentiality and security and on their legal responsibilities related to the data. Data used for these assessments is not available to researchers external to the National Board of Health and Welfare. External researchers would need to approach the quality registers for access to their data.
Study results and future directions	The government has requested this project to assess the impact of the clinical guidelines and the results of the assessment are taken seriously. The conduct of the assessment itself has lead to quicker adoption of the guidelines because results are reported for each hospital by name and the media and the general public have the opportunity to examine how hospitals are performing. Hospitals who don't participate in the quality register are also named. The whole process of undertaking the assessment has been beneficial for both introducing and effectively implementing new policies. The coverage of the registers is improving and they are better now than they were five years ago. Data linkages are expected to be used more often in the future and to expand to new areas, such as to education and to social care. This would enable examination of differences in access to care and in health care quality for different groups within the population.

Table 2.9. **Switzerland: Understanding the life expectancy of a nation**

Study title	Swiss National Cohort
Lead organisation	Consortium of university researchers and the Federal Statistical Office, Switzerland.
Project description	The Swiss National Cohort (SNC) is a long-term, census-based, multipurpose cohort and research platform. It is based on the linkage of individual data from the 1990 census to the 2000 census and then the linkage of this data to mortality records from 1991 up to 2008 (Spoerri et al., 2010). It permits a better understanding of the socio-economic and socio-demographic characteristics of mortality and life expectancy and forms a baseline cohort from which additional data may be linked for specific research studies, such as to the cancer registry, the childhood cancer registry and survey data.
Project approval	The SNC began as a pilot project with the Federal Statistical Office (FSO) to evaluate if data linkage would be feasible. Given feasibility was determined; the university research team successfully obtained a grant to undertake the project from the Swiss National Science Foundation. The university consortium then entered into a contract with the FSO. The next step was to obtain research ethics board approval in each of the Swiss Cantons. The Federal Data Protection and Information Commissioner evaluated the project and provided a letter indicating that the project plan reflected good practices for data privacy and confidentiality protection. Once the baseline cohort was established, there have been requests to link other data files to the baseline cohort for specific studies. For each new linkage proposal, the FSO grants approval and, if approved, a module contract is drafted. . Whenever there is a linkage of data to the baseline cohort for an approved project, the data is deleted when the project is completed.

Table 2.9. **Switzerland: Understanding the life expectancy of a nation** (cont.)

Study title	Swiss National Cohort
Data and data linkage	The core of the SNC is census and mortality data, both of which are in the custody of the Swiss FSO. The FSO provides the SNC team with de-identified data. This de-identification includes the removal of names and addresses. Other identifiers remain on the file including dates of birth, nationality, marital status, sex and municipality. There is no national identifying number that could be used to conduct linkages in Switzerland and the researchers use probabilistic techniques to link the data using these less direct identifiers. Overall the quality of the linkage is quite good with more than 90% of deaths linked to the Census. For younger age groups, such as those aged 20 to 40, however, data quality is less good due to their increased likelihood to live alone, to marry, to separate and to move residence. Data quality is also higher where the date of death is closer to the date of the administration of the census. Quality problems can bias study results and the research team prefers to be responsible for the probabilistic linkages necessary to build the cohort.
Protection of data privacy	The Swiss census is mandatory and there is no requirement to obtain consent for the linkage of this data to mortality data. Additional linkages to the regional cancer registry data are conducted with patient consent. The protection of data security is part of the negotiated agreement between the SNC team and the FSO. Elements of the agreement include that the data cannot be shared with a third party, that the data cannot be linked to another file without approval and that any research results destined for publication will be first reviewed by the FSO. Researchers who will have access to the data files are identified by name. The data is stored on a secure computer. Tru-crypt software is used to encrypt data on any mobile devices, such as lap-top computers, in the event of theft or loss. SNC researchers only have access to the databases and variables they need to conduct their projects. When the SNC project was first established, the FSO inspected the SNC facilities. Researchers external to the SNC team can request access to the data and, if their proposal is accepted, they must sign a contract with the SNC team. The contract limits them to the databases and variables within the databases they need for their project, describes how the data must be securely stored and protected.
Study results and future directions	The study provides a population denominator for the cancer registry to enable calculation of the incidence and prevalence of cancer in Switzerland. The cohort also enables the study of cancer types, causes of death and life expectancy by socio-economic variables and other population characteristics available from the census. The cohort is on-going and a next step will be to link it to the new registry-based population census for Switzerland that has replaced the questionnaire-based census. The registry-based census will provide more current information but will not have the same details on the population's socio-economic characteristics as did the questionnaire-based census. The SNC cohort team will need to explore linkages to survey data. There is future potential to extend the cohort to health insurance data to enable the study of health care quality and outcomes. The research team would like to have access to higher quality patient identifiers for more successful linkages, such as encrypted names. Whether access to higher quality patient identifiers would be possible, and indeed, whether access to the same identifiers currently used by the SNC team will continue, depends on the evolution of legislation. There is a new law under development to create a national cancer registry from the existing ten regional registries. This law has the potential to influence privacy protection requirements that may have implications for the future work of the SNC cohort team.

Table 2.10. **United Kingdom, England: NHS Information Centre for Health and Social Care**

Study title	NHS Information Centre for Health and Social Care
Lead organisation	National Health Service, United Kingdom.
Project description	The NHS Information Centre for Health and Social Care collected, processed, linked, analysed and published national information for health and social care communities in England (National Health Service Information Centre for Health and Social Care, 2011). Under the Health and Social Care Act of 2012, by April 2013, it will become an executive non-departmental public body entitled the Health and Social Care Information Centre (HSCIC) and it will have broader responsibilities, including assuming data collection responsibilities previously held by other arms-length bodies (Department of Health, 2012). It will become a single national repository for data for secondary purposes, including holding and linking person-identifiable data where approved and necessary. At the time of this OECD study in October 2011, the Information Centre was both producing tabulations from hospitalisations data (HES) and conducting limited data linkages on behalf of clients. Clients included government departments, academic researchers and commercial interests.
Project approval	At the time of this OECD study, for data linkages, all requests must have had the approval of the Secretary of State for Health, who made these decisions on the advice of the UK National Information and Governance Board (NIGB) Ethics and Confidentiality Committee before the Information Centre could accept to undertake the linkage for the client. A key requirement of NIGB was that the project was in the public interest. The Information Centre itself had been approved by NIGB to conduct data linkages without patient consent when the linkage was among health care administrative databases. This NIGB approval was renewed annually and the Information Centre was required to continue to justify retaining the databases in its custody. All clients of the Information Centre entered into a written data release agreement with the Centre.

Table 2.10. **United Kingdom, England: NHS Information Centre for Health and Social Care** (cont.)

Study title	NHS Information Centre for Health and Social Care
Data and data linkage	At the time of this OECD study, the Information Centre was the custodian of the hospital commissioning dataset and mental health in-patient data and its data linkage service focused on linkages involving Hospital Episode Statistics (HES). The Information Centre received data from the central registry of the NHS, mortality data from the Office of National Statistics and data from the Cancer Registry. The Information Centre linked databases using the NHS number. Where unavailable, other identifiers were used to assign an NHS number to a file before linkage using both deterministic and probabilistic techniques. After data linkage, the NHS number was removed from the linked file and replaced with a study number that had no other meaning. Also removed from the file were full dates of birth, postal codes and any local patient identifying numbers. The execution of the data linkage by the Information Centre could be quite efficient. For example, for a project where all data files had NHS numbers and an established linkage algorithm was then able be used, the client may have received their results in less than one week. Generally the quality of linkages to hospitalisation data (HES) was quite good with 90% or more of clinical trial cohort participant records successfully linked. Projects where NHS numbers were not as available had been less successful.
Protection of data privacy	The collection of patient-level hospital records occurred without consent. Patients had the right, however, to refuse to have their data used for public health research. This was a rare request and, when it did occur, the Information Centre took steps to ensure the patient's records were suppressed. Patients were informed of the uses of their data thorough governmental websites and also, depending on the project, through posters in health care facilities. Researchers who had a cohort of data they had collected, such as from a clinical trial, may have requested to the Centre to link their cohort to follow the patients for subsequent hospitalisations, cancers and deaths. If the cohort was collected with the informed consent of participants, the Information Centre could approve the project and proceed. If the cohort was not collected with the consent of participants, the project must have first been approved by NIGB. Researchers requiring approval of NIGB should have planned for a six-month delay between the first submission of an application and a decision. NIGB met bi-monthly and it was typical that a researcher received questions and must revise and resubmit their application. External researchers providing a cohort of data to be linked would be able to re-identify cohort members, even though the NHS numbers are removed from the linked files. Data transfers to and from the Information Centre used a secure web transfer system. The Information Centre had a security policy which was required for its annual approval by NIGB and the security of the Centre was reviewed by security experts in the Department of Health. The computer system was protected by a firewall. Employees of the Centre only had access to data files required for their job and computers were password protected. Employee data access permissions were reviewed annually. Access logs were kept and were monitored to ensure that employees were still using the files they had approved access to use. Employees had on-line training in data protection annually that included a test that must be passed.
Study results and future directions	The data linkage service provided by the Information Centre was relatively new at the time of the OECD study and it had not yet been widely publicised. Centre staff expected that requests for data linkage services would grow in the future in response to greater awareness.

Table 2.11. **United Kingdom, England and Wales: Birth outcomes studies**

Study title	Linkage of birth data to delivery records from hospital data (1) and estimation of gestation-specific infant mortality statistics (2)
Lead organisation	1) Government of Wales. 2) Office for National Statistics, England and Wales.
Project description	Two data linkage projects are underway in the United Kingdom to improve understanding of infant health. 1) The linkage of birth data to delivery records from hospital data was undertaken by the Welsh Government to reconcile inconsistencies between multiple sources of birth data for Wales, each of which had content missing from the other. The objective is to arrive at a better, more comprehensive and more consistent picture of maternity outcomes (Welsh Government, 2010). 2) In 2002, a new system was implemented to allocate National Health Service (NHS) numbers at birth in England and Wales. The linkage of NHS birth notifications with birth and death registration records enables statistics on births and infant deaths by population characteristics, such as gestational age and ethnicity (Moser et al., 2008).
Project approval	1) The study was approved by the Caldecott Guardian who is responsible for access to and use of all data in the custody of the NHS Wales Informatics Service (NWIS). 2) The study was approved by the National Information and Governance Board which is a national research ethics board that renders decision on projects requiring the linkage of personal health data where patient consent to linkage has not been obtained. Application materials must correspond to the eight principles of data privacy protection within the UK Data Protection Act and must include a justification for each variable within each dataset that would be required for the study; evidence of the benefits to policy of the study; a literature review that demonstrates the project's contribution to knowledge; and a description of how data security will be protected. It took about 40 days to receive a decision from NIGB once the application for approval had been submitted.

Table 2.11. **United Kingdom, England and Wales: Birth outcomes studies** (cont.)

Study title	Linkage of birth data to delivery records from hospital data (1) and estimation of gestation-specific infant mortality statistics (2)
Data and data linkage	1) NWIS helps to administer the health system and is the custodian of health care administrative data. NWIS is responsible for undertaking data linkages related to health care for the government of Wales. Linkage requests submitted to NWIS require at least a six month lead time before the linkage needs to take place. For this project, birth records from the Child Health System that registers births were linked to birth and delivery records within hospital data. The NWIS first pseudonymised the NHS number using a similar algorithm for both databases to be linked. The NWIS then performed the linkage using the encrypted number. In cases where a deterministic match on the encrypted number was unsuccessful, the NWIS used other identifiers, such as the mother's date of birth to clarify matches. While the quality of the linkage was high, with about 98% of infants linked to their delivery record, some issues with the underlying data were discovered as a result of the data linkage. These included that the health numbers recorded for infants from a multiple birth can become switched between the hospital record and the birth registration. 2) This study involves the linkage of birth notifications in the custody of the NHS to birth registrations and death records in the custody of the Office for National Statistics (ONS). The ONS undertook the data linkage. The linkage was deterministic and depended on the NHS number. For records that could not be linked deterministically, a probabilistic matching was undertaken using the date of birth of the mother and the infant and the postal code. The NHS data was of good quality and over 99% of live births were successfully linked. The undertaking of the linkage, however, did uncover a few data quality issues. For example, some local areas had incomplete data and some had incompletely recorded ethnicity. The ONS was able to report these findings back to the NHS which helped to further improve the quality of the NHS data.
Protection of data privacy	1) In Wales, a child health record book is given to new parents at the birth of a child or at the first physician visit in the ten days following a birth. The book contains a paper that explains to parents that the birth record will be held in a national database. There is no option to opt-in or to opt-out. The NWIS conducted the data linkage on behalf of the Wales Office for National Statistics (ONS). There is a secure web-based transfer of data between NWIS and the ONS. Within the ONS, the data are then stored on a protected network. Only a few approved persons within the ONS have access to the linked data for analysis purposes, and the analysis file has been de-identified. The ONS follows both the Welsh Government standards for information protection and the ONS code of practice. The ONS also has ISO 27001 status which confirms that it conforms to this international standard for data security. Staff members obtain training and subsequent refresher training on data security and confidentiality. Access to the data has never been requested by researchers external to the ONS. 2) As NIGB has recognised in the approval of the project that patient consent is not practical for the more than 700 000 live births occurring annually in England and Wales, it has accepted that the ONS informs patients of the use of their data. ONS produces a poster that is put up in birth and neo-natal units within health care facilities and distributes a leaflet to new parents. The poster and leaflet describe the ONS and its mandate, the data that will be collected and how it will be used and present some recent findings from the data. The ONS removed the NHS number from the linked file provided to ONS staff for analysis. The analysis file retained, however, the date of birth and the postal code as both were required for the study. The postal code was used to include in the analysis variables representing area deprivation from another data source. Access to the analysis file was restricted to a small number of approved ONS staff members and their names were provided to NIGB. The analysis file is stored on a server that is separate from the server used to perform the data linkage and analysts never have access to the identifiers used to perform the linkage. Staff members are provided with training and with regular reminders about data security and confidentiality. There are internal security audits.
Study results and future directions	1) The new maternity service in Wales has recognised that there is insufficient information on maternity outcomes. Rather than launching new data collection, data linkage was piloted as an alternative approach to reconcile databases of births to arrive at a better overall picture of maternity outcomes. Whether or not to continue this data linkage on a regular basis is still to be determined. 2) In the past, the main indicator of poor birth outcomes was infant mortality. Today, infant mortality rates are low and there is interest in better understanding outcomes for low birth-weight babies. The data linkage provides the only database that enables monitoring of low birth-weight babies in relation to their gestational age and enables reporting of birth outcomes by the age of the mother, by ethnicity, and by location to enable better targeting of programmes to support healthy infants. The study began as a pilot and now continues as an annual project.

Table 2.12. **United Kingdom, England: Mapping pathways across health and social care – Torbay Care Trust**

Study title	Mapping pathways across health and social care
Lead organisation	Torbay Care Trust, United Kingdom (England).
Project description	Torbay Care Trust is an integrated health and adult social care organisation responsible for providing and commissioning services for the population of Torbay, England which is about 140 000 people. The trust engaged the firm MedeAnalytics to develop a data management system that links patient records across health and social care databases to produce pathways of services and their associated costs on an on-going basis (Health Service Journal, 2011). This information is then used to evaluate and improve services which cross jurisdictional boundaries. Included in the information system are patient level records from acute care hospitalisations and all contacts of adult patients with community-based services (ancillary care, home care and nursing homes), All social care services that are fully or partially reimbursed by the Trust are included within the information system.
Project approval	The Trust executive approved the linkage of data for this project.
Data and data linkage	The databases included in the project are largely within the custody of the Torbay Health Trust which is either directly providing the services or is commissioning the services. The acute care hospitals in Torbay are the only other data custodians contributing records to the database. Linkage is possible because these hospitalisation records contain the NHS numbers for patients. The patient records shared with the Torbay Care Trust are the same records also shared with the NHS, as part of hospitals' mandatory data collection. Data linkage is deterministic using the NHS number. Torbay is unique in requiring an NHS number for all patients who receive social care services. When the data system was first developed, Torbay had to invest in cleaning up its databases to ensure complete and correct NHS numbers were available. Older records had patient identifying numbers that were unique to the service provider's IT system and did not have an NHS number. Torbay has now over 99% of records for social care with an NHS number. One of the means of achieving such a high proportion has been efforts to ensure that GPs include the patient's NHS number on referrals to social care services. A unique identifying number is essential to the project and the analytical value of the database was well worth the costs associated with assigning NHS numbers to older records. The database also contains dates of birth and information on the locality of the patients and their GPs.
Protection of data privacy	The analysis of the patient records is within the mandate of the Trust for the administration of its programs. Patients are made aware of the uses of their data as part of the face to face assessment that occurs when patients first enrol in social care services. The project uses a web-based system to upload and download data that is encrypted and password-protected. Torbay Care Trust uploads patient records to the system that are accessed by MedeAnalytics who prepare the analysis ready database which is then used by the Trust for analysis over a secure network. Within the Trust, only a small number of named individuals have access to the linked database. When MedeAnalytics was selected to assist the Trust to develop its data infrastructure, the data security protections of MedeAnalytics were checked. Trust staff receives training in IT governance and protection of data confidentiality. Data security protection is also explicitly part of employees' job descriptions. Staff members are only able to receive a computer account necessary to access the database if they have been recommended by the Deputy Minister. An information governance team within the Trust ensures that data security and privacy protections remain strong. The Trust has not experienced a breach of data security. If a breach occurred, the matter would be the responsibility of the Information Governance Officer within the Trust. As the database is fairly new, there has only been one request from an external researcher to analyse the data. The executive team of the trust evaluated the proposal and the project was approved. The data analysis for the project was conducted by the Torbay care staff.
Study results and future directions	The linkage of health and social care data has given a new perspective on the costs of disease management. The linked data has shown that when both health and social care expenditures are considered together, the costs of caring for patients experiencing events such as a hip fracture or stroke, are much higher and require a much longer care period than had previously been appreciated. This has raised the importance of prevention efforts to identify and support high-risk patients to avoid acute events. The data has also informed the Trust about the full picture of costs associated with caring for patients and has provided the empirical evidence needed to avoid shunting costs from one area of care to another, particularly when budgets are being reduced. Even though Torbay is a small community, analysis of its linked data has had an impact on public policy at a national level. The national government had discussed moving funds from social care services to acute care services to commit acute care providers to being responsible for their patients in the 30 days after their discharge. While this initiative was in response to a need to combat readmissions, analysis of the linked data from Torbay showed the potential negative impact on social care services that could result. The national roll-out of the policy was halted in favour of testing the policy in a few pilot locations. The Trust now has three years of linked data and, is planning to benefit from this growing resource to identify health services with better patient outcomes and that are more efficient and to introduce measures of health care quality. Future directions for the Trust include incorporating data on primary care services from General Practitioner's offices into the database which will improve understanding of how GP services form part of health care pathways. A challenge will be to engage GP's participation. Over the past five years it has become easier for the Trust to link and analyse personal health records. The availability and use of NHS numbers has been a key factor. The services of MedeAnalytics have made it easy for the Trust to harness the power of their patient records to extract information for decision making. The first year of the project involved a lot of testing, and as a result of confidence in the quality of the data, it is relied upon for policy and commissioning decisions. A concern for the future is that recent NHS emphasis on the use of pseudonymisation when data is first collected could have the consequence of making data linkages impossible as the sharing of data with common unique identifiers is a necessary prerequisite for linkage. Another challenge is the lack of standardisation of service definitions and coding across health care Trusts in the United Kingdom. Thus it is very difficult to compare social care services across Trusts. The only benchmarks for Torbay are in the acute-care sector where comparability is possible.

Table 2.13. **United States: Understanding health care users and health outcomes**

Study title	Linkages of population health surveys to death and medical care records
Lead organisation	National Center for Health Statistics, United States.
Project description	The National Center for Health Statistics has a data linkage group who is building a repository of surveys that are ready to support linkage projects through harmonising content and standardising variables across different surveys and survey waves (Centers for Disease Control and Prevention, 2012). Two key projects have been undertaken. 1) The linkage of survey data to the National Death Index (NDI) and 2) the linkage of survey data to data on health care for Medicare and Medicaid recipients from the Centre for Medicare and Medicaid Services (CMS).
Project approval	The NCHS is authorised by law to collect and process a broad range of statistics on illness and disability of the population of the United States. Data linkages are approved by the Research Ethics Board of the NCHS. The linkage of survey data to CMS data was first proposed by the CMS and the Social Security Administration (SSA) in response to a Congressional request in 2000. This project required the development of the first interagency agreement of its kind and involving four federal entities, the NCHS, the CMS, the Social Security Administration and the Department of Health and Human Services. The Agreement makes reference to the legal authorities under which each of the entities is able to share data to undertake the project. Each of the two projects is on-going and there is no set date where the linked data would be destroyed. Project (1) is updated every 3-4 years as part of the data programme of the NCHS. The Interagency agreement enabling Project (2) is updated and signed annually by all of the agencies involved.
Data and data linkage	The NCHS is the custodian of the survey data and the death index data involved in data linkages. The CMS is the custodian of Medicare and Medicaid enrolment and claims data. The Social Security Administration is the custodian of the SSA benefit history data. Linkages of population health survey data to the National Death Index are conducted probabilistically using seven matching criteria including a combination of Social Security Number; date of birth; first, middle or last name; and/or father's last name. The linkage of population health surveys to CMS data are conducted in three steps using a deterministic linkage method. First the NCHS prepares a file containing SSN, names and dates of birth from the population health surveys to be linked. This file is sent to the Social Security Administration (SSA) who links the file to their own databases to correct any errors in the SSN for the survey respondents. The NCHS file that has corrected SSNs is then sent by the SSA to the CMS. The CMS conducts a deterministic linkage of the NCHS file to Medicare and Medicaid records based on SSN, Medicare identification numbers and dates of birth. Once the health care records have been linked to the NCHS file, the SSN and Medicare identification numbers are removed from the file by the CMS, leaving only an NCHS assigned identity number and the file is returned to the NCHS for subsequent analysis.
Protection of data privacy	Consent requirements have changed over time. All potential survey respondents are mailed a letter about the survey that explains that survey data may be linked to other health records. During the interview, respondents are asked to provide their Social Security Number and their Medicare identification number, if they receive Medicare benefits. More recently, the NCHS has asked respondents to provide the last four digits of their identification numbers. If they do not provide the numbers, they are asked if their data may be linked to other health data without the identification numbers. The change in the consent process has resulted in an improvement in the proportion of survey records eligible for linkage, from 45% of the records for the 2006 National Health Interview Survey to 86% of the records for the 2009 administration of this survey. Death data may be linked to other data holdings without the prior consent of the decedents or their surviving family. Researchers outside of government may submit a research proposal to access linked data files within the NCHS Research Data Centers (RDC) or at the NCHS headquarters. The RDC are secure facilities for data access that are maintained by the NCHS throughout the United States. Research proposals are evaluated by NCHS staff unless the proposal involves genetic data. In that case, the proposal is reviewed by the NCHS research ethics board. Researchers are only approved to access data files and variables that are required for their project and names, SSN and Medicare identification numbers are not provided. Exact dates are provided only if their inclusion is necessary for the project. The linkage of survey data to death data is provided to external researchers through a public-use micro data file. This file has been de-identified, including perturbations of the data to avoid indirect identification. No public-use micro data file is available for the linkage of survey data to Medicare and Medicaid records. The health care administrative data is more sensitive as it pertains to living subjects. NCHS staff signs yearly affidavits attesting to their agreement to protect data confidentiality. Staff members also receive yearly training on data security.
Study results and future directions	The linkage of the NCHS survey data to health care administrative data (Medicare and Medicaid) is being repeated. The process is proceeding more quickly this second time as the Interagency agreement needs only to be updated. The survey file linked to the CMS records is a complex file to analyse as the histories are inclusive of different types of health care from pharmaceutical use to physicians and to hospitals and the observations are affected by changes in eligibility for CMS programmes over time. Despite these challenges there are a significant number of analytical projects underway with the data currently and growing interest in using the data to examine the effectiveness of health care (Looker et al., 2011; Gorina and Kramarow., 2011). The linkage of survey and death data has been used to investigate policy-relevant topics such as the characteristics of individuals who have committed suicide and socio-economic disparities in life expectancy (Denney, 2010; Dray-Spira et al., 2010). The NCHS is working on ways to make linked data easier to analyse including on-line tutorials for complex issues, such as the necessity to re-weight data to reduce the impact of non-response and linkage biases on study results.

Table 2.14. **United States: Kaiser Permanente Center for Health Research**

Study title	Center for Health Research
Lead organisation	Kaiser Permanente.
Project description	Kaiser Permanente is a closed-panel health care maintenance organisation (HMO) with eight sites and 8.5 to 9 million members in the US states of Hawaii, Oregon, California, Ohio, Washington, DC, and Maryland. As a closed panel HMO, Kaiser members tend to see Kaiser doctors and Kaiser doctors tend only to treat Kaiser patients. Within this HMO, an electronic medical record system has been implemented. Kaiser has seven research centres conducting public-domain research analysing patient-level data (Kaiser Permanente Center for Health Research, 2011). The research group is semi-autonomous from the medical group that provides direct patient care. The research arm is a non-profit entity.
Project approval	Kaiser uses an internal review board (IRB) to evaluate proposals for access to patient-level data. Each Kaiser site is identified under the US Health Information and Protection of Privacy Act (HIPPA) as a covered entity and must abide by HIPPA requirements. As a result, each site has a separate IRB and has developed its own process for application submission and approval. When a research project is proposed that would benefit from data from more than one site, a separate application must be submitted to the IRB of each site involved. It has taken effort to coach physician researchers to submit proposals to the IRB and now that processes are established, many research projects do involve multiple sites.
Data and data linkage	Kaiser has an extensive and complete array of health care data for Kaiser patients at the level of person-encounters and use of services. This includes service dates and products, including pharmaceuticals. What can be lost are health care encounters and purchases outside of the system of the health care organisation. Kaiser implements initiatives that increase adherence and minimise data loss. For example, it operates a robotic pharmacy for prescription re-fills that mails re-fill to claimants. Kaiser members are offered a financial incentive to use the robotic pharmacy. In this way, it is possible to measure adherence to prescription medicines. Kaiser patients receive a unique record number that they keep for life. This record number is used to link patients across databases. As a private company, there is no public access to data on Kaiser patients. However, Kaiser researchers may enter into collaborations with external researchers in other organisations or universities. For example, there is a current project to estimate medical care costs at the end of life for cancer patients with researchers at Henry Ford, Seattle and Group Health. The project will compare costs for all cancer cases from 2000 to 2008 in the cities of Detroit, Seattle and Denver. A virtual database was established to provide all of the researchers involved with access to patient-level data. Kaiser has been bio-banking biological samples and tissues from since 1964 and it is the oldest of the stored tissues that now have the greatest value for research into the genetic factors that have resulted in disease in patients today. For example, it may take 20 years or more of exposure to tobacco smoke, dust, and air pollution to develop disease and it is only with a comprehensive analysis that the relative influence of different potential risk factors be estimated.
Protection of data privacy	Personal health data is not available for research until the patient has provided informed consent. The Kaiser membership agreement explains to patients, or family members of patients, that when the agreement is signed they are providing consent to research with their medical records and with any biological samples or tissues. Any member who declines to consent is tracked and their data is suppressed from research studies. In Oregon, state law requires patient consent for the collection of genetic information for research. The reach of the law is broad as even gender or race may be considered genetic information. To ensure compliance with this new law, Kaiser administered a document to all members asking if they would decline to have their data used for research. About 10% of members did decline. There is a separation of duties at Kaiser Permanente. There is a separate directory space on the Kaiser computer network where employees who conduct data linkages work. The unique record number used to link databases is removed from linked files provided to researchers for analysis. There are audit trails that track who within the organisation have access to personal health information and to spot intruders and to prevent attacks on its data security. This monitoring takes place on a 24/7 basis. Facilities were data are stored are secure and can only be accessed by authorised employees. Guests must be escorted at all times. There are hierarchies of access to data at Kaiser with individuals only approved to access data required for their job. Servers and files are protected from unauthorised access. Identifiable data may not be removed from a secure facility. Researchers may have access to de-identified data for research, however, the researcher must log into a secure server and all keystrokes are encrypted. All employees sign an affidavit to protect data confidentiality annually and there is on-line training annually for employees on the protection of data security and confidentiality.
Study results and future directions	Kaiser has accumulated 50 years of expertise in conducting research with patient-level data and linkages. Kaiser, with its EMR system and bio-bank, is on the forefront of research with linked data with new research areas including genetics, genomics and personalised medicine. Bio banking is expensive and complex, requiring a system to barcode samples and storage in temperature-controlled environments; however, it represents one of the most promising avenues for new research. For example, a new study at Kaiser involving the linkage of stored samples and health care records is investigating if certain prescription medicines for mental illness are linked to producing genetic mutations in people. Other new opportunities on the horizon include the use of devices to measure risk factors, such as accelerometers to measure physical activity and devices to measure the environment around individuals, such as air quality and noise.

Summaries of further examples of policy-relevant data linkage projects

Country	Study title	Project description
Australia	Care pathways for older patients with chronic diseases	The Australian Institute of Health and Welfare explored care transitions for older people with dementia, cardiovascular disease, arthritis and musculoskeletal conditions. Records for all people aged 65 and older who were assessed under the Aged Care Assessment Program were linked to data for six major aged care programs and to mortality data over a four-year period. The linked data enabled examination of care pathways and the factors influencing different care paths. Of particular interest were the entry into and the time to entry into residential care and how this may have been influenced by the use of community care (AIHW, 2011).
Australia	Study of the health effects of exposure to low-dose radiation from CT scans in childhood	This study, led by researchers at the University of Melbourne, with data linkage undertaken by the Australian Institute of Health and Welfare, explored whether exposure to low-dose computerised tomography scans in childhood increases the risk of cancer. Records of all children aged 0 to 19 who received medical services between 1985 and 2005 in the Medical Benefits database were linked to the Australian cancer registry and death databases. The cancer incidence of those exposed to CT scans was compared to that of the non-exposed of similar age and sex. Results will be compared with those of parallel studies in the United Kingdom and the United States to inform international guidelines for CT scan use in childhood.
Belgium	Studies of health care quality and outcomes for cancer patients	The Belgian Cancer Registry has several projects underway where data linkages are helping to generate new information about the quality of care and health outcomes of cancer patients. These include a linkage of breast cancer screening results and the cancer registry to measure the quality of screening through the identification of the occurrence of interval cancers. A second project involves the continuous linkage of cancer registry data with nomenclature (medical procedures and pharmaceutical data) and vital statistics. This analysis will produce indicators of care quality including cancer survival and variability in treatment practices. The registry has also elaborated indicators of the quality of oncology care for breast and testicular cancer that could be implemented within cancer centres (Stordeur et al., 2011; Vlayen et al., 2011).
Belgium	Disease registries for cystic fibrosis and neuromuscular diseases	Two projects are underway within the Scientific Institute of Public Health to develop disease registries for cystic fibrosis and neuromuscular diseases. To create the registries, patients with these two conditions who were treated in expert centres would be followed up for subsequent health outcomes.
Denmark	Monitoring of cancer pathways	This project of the National Board of Health reports on wait times in cancer treatment pathways.
Finland	Drug and pregnancy project	Through the linkage of a number of registers this project evaluates patterns of medication use during pregnancy to estimate the effect of drug use on pregnancy outcomes. Results enable monitoring of the safety of medications used during pregnancy (Artama et al., 2011).
France	Monitoring health care use and expenditures	France has developed a national insurance information system including a permanent sample of beneficiaries (SNIR-AM) to create a national picture of health care consumption and expenditures. Longitudinal data for patients are available for the current year and the previous two years. The database is used to study certain chronic diseases where there is a 100% reimbursement rate and certain prescribed medicines (Tuppin et al., 2010). This linked data has been used to study implantation of pacemakers and cardioverter-defibrillators; hospitalisation rates for low-income subjects with full health insurance coverage; and the use of the medication Benfluorex among Diabetic patients and the occurrence of valvular heart disease.
Germany	Quality of health care of patients after hospital discharge for myocardial infarct	A project is being planned to assess the quality of care of patients discharged from hospital for a myocardial infarct through the linkage of claims data from AOK Berlin-Brandenburg and clinical data from the Berliner Herzinfarktregister.
Israel	Quality of health care projects	The Ministry of Health in Israel is undertaking data linkage projects to monitor quality of health care in order to determine health policy in specific areas. These projects include examination of post-operative clinical complications, re-hospitalisations and mortality. The projects are on-going in several areas: colon surgeries, craniotomies, fractures of neck of femur and appendix (Simchen et al., 2011). Another study is exploring mortality among psychiatric patients in order to improve community mental health care (Haklai et al., 2011).
Korea	Annual cancer statistics	The National Cancer Centre established a National Cancer Incidence Database incorporating: the Korea Central Cancer Registry, a medical review survey, eleven population-based regional cancer registries, and site specific cancer registries. The centre reports nationwide cancer statistics, including incidence, mortality and survival rates, and their trends (Jung et al., 2010).
Norway	Social inequalities in health	The Norwegian Institute of Public Health is working to describe trends in social inequality in Norway from 1960 to the present through the linkage of mortality and population records. The project has described socio-economic inequalities in mortality for children and adults by cause of death and also socio-economic inequality in life expectancy (Næss et al., 2007)
Singapore	National Chronic Disease Management Programme	The national programme evaluates the quality of primary care providers by examining health care providers' adherence to recommended care processes, as well as their success in preventing hospitalisations related to those diseases. The programme encourages patients with chronic conditions to work closely with their doctors to avoid acute exacerbations or complications that could lead to hospitalisations while encouraging doctors to follow evidence-based disease management protocols (Ministry of Health, 2011).
Sweden	Quality and Efficiency in Swedish Health Care: Regional Comparisons 2010	This project uses data from approximately 30 health data and health care quality registers to generate statistics to openly compare processes and outcomes of health care (Socialstyrelsen, 2012).

Summaries of further examples of policy-relevant data linkage projects (cont.)

Country	Study title	Project description
United Kingdom	National Cancer Intelligence Network	This network is a UK-wide initiative to drive improvements in standards of cancer care and clinical outcomes by improving and using information collected about cancer patients for analysis, publication and research (Morris et al., 2010 and 2011; Lambert et al., 2011).
United Kingdom	Hospital Episode Statistics linkage to mortality	This project links mortality data from the UK Office of National Statistics to hospital episode statistics from the NHS Information Centre for Health and Social Care in order to add a unique anonymised patient identifier to the mortality database. This variable will help to perform analysis of hospital patients who have subsequently died (NHS Information Centre for Health and Social Care, 2011).
United Kingdom	Cancer survival	This project produces statistics on cancer survival for England and for the United Kingdom. The UK results are provided to the OECD for the Health at a Glance publication (Office for National Statistics, 2011).

Bibliography

AIHW – Australian Institute of Health and Welfare (2011), "Pathways in Aged Care: Do People Follow Recommendations?", *AIHW Bulletin*, No. 88, Cat. AUS 137, Canberra.

Altman, B.M. and S.P. Gulley (2009), "Convergence and Divergence: Differences in Disability Prevalence Estimates in the United States and Canada Based on Four Health Survey Instruments", *Social Science and Medicine*, Vol. 69, No. 4, pp. 543-552.

Artama, M., M. Gissler, H. Malm and A. Ritvanen (2011), "Nationwide Register-based Surveillance System on Drugs and Pregnancy in Finland 1996-2006", *Pharmacoepidemiology and Drug Safety*, Vol. 20, No. 7, pp. 729-738.

Canadian Institute for Health Information (2012), "Pathways of Care for People with Stroke in Ontario", Ottawa, https://secure.cihi.ca/estore/productFamily.htm?locale=en&pf=PFC1695, accessed 9 October 2012.

Centers for Disease Control and Prevention (2012), National Center for Health Statistics Data Linkage Activities, www.cdc.gov/nchs/data_access/data_linkage_activities.htm, accessed 10 October 2012.

Commission Technique d'Échantillon Permanent au Conseil Général de l'INAMI (2011), *Échantillon Permanente Steekproef 1/19*, Annexe – CGSS 2011/097, Belgium, www.riziv.fgov.be/information/fr/sampling/pdf/report.pdf, accessed 6 April 2012.

Denney, J.T. (2010), "Family and Household Formations and Suicide in the United States", *Journal of Marriage and Family*, Vol. 72, No. 1, pp. 202-213.

Department of Health and NHS Informatics (2012), *Informatics: The Future – An Organisational Summary*, www.dh.gov.uk/health/2012/07/informatics-future/, accessed 18 February 2013.

Di Iorio, C.T., R. Andány et al. (2010), "Privacy Impact Assessment Report", EUBIROD Consortium.

Di Iorio, C.T., F. Carinci, M. Brillante, J. Azzopardi, P. Beck et al. (2012), "Cross-border Flow of Health Information: Is 'Privacy by Design' Enough? Privacy Performance Assessment in EUBIROD", *European Journal of Public Health*, Epub May 4, IF: 2.313.

Di Iorio, C.T., F. Carinci, J. Azzopardi, V. Baglioni, P Beck et al. (2009), "Privacy Impact Assessment in the Design of Transnational Public Health Information System, the BIRO project", *Journal of Medical Ethics*, Vol. 35, No. 12, pp. 753-761.

Dray-Spira, R., T.L. Gary-Webb and F.L. Brancati (2010), "Educational Disparities in Mortality Among Adults with Diabetes in the U.S.", *Diabetes Care*, Vol. 33, No. 6, pp. 1200-1205.

DUQuE (2011), "Deepening Our Understanding of Quality Improvement in Europe", www.duque.eu, accessed 25 April 2012.

EUBIROD (2010), *WP5 Data Collection: Privacy Impact Assessment Report*, www.eubirod.eu/documents/downloads/D5_2_Privacy_Impact_Assessment.pdf.

EUBIROD (2011), www.eubirod.eu/index.html, accessed 25 October 2011.

EUROCARE (2011), www.eurocare.it, accessed 25 April 2012.

EuroHOPE (2012), www.eurohope.info/, accessed 10 October 2012.

EURO-PERISTAT (2011), www.europeristat.com, accessed 25 April 2012.

Gorina, Y. and E.A. Kramarow (2011), "Identifying Chronic Conditions in Medicare Claims Data: Evaluating the Chronic Condition Data Warehouse Algorithm", *Health Services Research*, Vol. 46, No. 5, pp. 1610-1627.

Gulley, S.P. and B.M. Altman (2008), "Disability in Two Health Care Systems: Access, Quality, Satisfaction and Physician Contacts Among Working-age Canadians and Americans with Disabilities", *Disability and Health Journal*, Vol. 1, No. 4, pp. 196-208.

Häkkinen, U. (2011), "The PERFECT Project: Measuring Performance of Health Care Episodes", *Annals of Medicine*, Vol. 43, Suppl. 1, pp. S1-S3.

Häkkinen, U., A. Malmivaara and R. Sund (2011), "PERFECT – Conclusions and Future Developments", *Annals of Medicine*, Vol. 43, Suppl. 1, pp. S54-S57.

Haklai, Z., N. Goldberger, N. Stein, I. Pugachova and I. Levav (2011), "The Mortality Risk Among Persons with Psychiatric Hospitalizations", *Israel Journal of Psychiatry and Related Sciences*, Vol. 48, No. 4, pp. 230-239.

Health Insurance Review and Assessment Service (2011), "Quality Assessment Service", Seoul, *www.hira.or.kr/eng/activity/01/04/activity01_04.html*, accessed 30 April 2012.

Health Service Journal (2011), "HSJ Best Practice Awards 2011", *www.hsj.co.uk/journals/2011/11/21/o/c/i/HSJBP2011.pdf*, accessed 6 April 2012.

IARC – International Agency for Research on Cancer (2011), *Cancer Incidence in Five Continents*, World Health Organization, monograph series, *www.ci5.iarc.fr*, accessed 25 April 2012.

Institute for Clinical and Evaluative Sciences (2011), Toronto, *www.ices.on.ca/index.html*, accessed 30 April 2012.

Jung, K.-W., S. Park, H.-J. Kong et al. (2010), "Cancer Statistics in Korea: Incidence, Mortality and Survival in 2006-2007", *Journal of Korean Medical Science*, Vol. 25, No. 8, pp. 1113-1121.

Kaiser Permanente Center for Health Research (2011), *www.kpchr.org/research/public/default.aspx* accessed 30 April 2012.

Krishnakumar, N., J.V. Tu and D.S. Lee (2011), "Why Are Implantable Cardioverter Defibrillator Outcomes in Practice Different from Clinical Trials?", *Cardiac Electrophysiology Clinics*, Vol. 3, No. 4, pp. 511-520.

Lambert, P.C., H. Moller et al. (2011), "Quantifying Differences in Breast Cancer Survival Between England and Norway", *Cancer Epidemiology*, Vol. 35, No. 6, pp. 526-533.

Looker, A.C. et al. (2011), "Hip Fracture and Risk in Older U.S. Adults by Treatment Eligibility Status Based on New National Osteoporosis Foundation Guidelines", *Osteoporosis International*, Vol. 22, No. 2, pp. 541-549.

Ministry of Health (2011), "Medisave for Chronic Disease Management Programme (CDMP) – The Third Year", Singapore, *www.moh.gov.sg/content/moh_web/home/Publications/information_papers/2010/medisave_for_cdmp-thethirdyear.html*, accessed 30 April 2012.

Morris, E.J. et al. (2010), "Comparison of Treatment and Outcome Information Between a Clinical Trial and the National Cancer Data Repository", *British Journal of Surgery*, doi: 10.1002/bjs.7295.

Morris, E.J. et al. (2011), "Thirty-day Postoperative Mortality After Colorectal Cancer Surgery in England", *Gut*, doi: 10.1136/gut.2010.232181.

Moser, K., K. Stanfield and D. Leon (2008), "Birthweight and Gestational Age by Ethnic Group, England and Wales 2005: Introducing New Data on Births", *Health Statistics Quarterly*, Vol. 39, pp. 22-31.

Næss, Ø. and A.H. Leyland (2010), "Analysing the Effect of Life Course Area of Residence in Multilevel Epidemiology", *Scandinavian Journal of Public Health*, Vol. 38, Suppl. 5, pp. 119-126.

Næss, Ø., B.H. Strand and G. Davey Smith (2007), "Childhood and Adulthood Socioeconomic Position Across 20 Causes of Death. A Prospective Cohort Study of 800 000 Norwegian Men and Women", *Journal of Epidemiology and Community Health*, Vol. 61, pp. 1004-1009.

National Health Service Information Centre for Health and Social Care (2011a), *The Health and Social Care Information Centre Annual Report and Accounts 2011/12*, *www.official-documents.gov.uk/document/hc1213/hc03/0332/0332.pdf* accessed 18 February 2013.

National Health Service Information Centre for Health and Social Care (2011b), "Linked ONS-HES Mortality Data", *www.hesonline.nhs.uk/Ease/servlet/ContentServer?siteID=1937&categoryID=1299*, accessed 30 April 2012.

Obi, N., A. Waldmann, V. Babaev and A. Katalinic (2011), "Record Linkage of a Large Clinical Practice Patient Cohort with the Cancer Registry Schleswig-Holstein", *Gesundheitswesen*, Vol. 73, No. 7, pp. 452-458.

Office for National Statistics (2011), "Index of Cancer Survival for Primary Care Trusts in England – Patients Diagnosed 1996-2009 and Followed Up to 2010", *Statistical Bulletin*, 13 December.

Peltola, M., M. Juntunen, U. Häkkinen et al. (2011), "A Methodological Approach for Register-based Evaluation of Cost and Outcomes in Health Care", *Annals of Medicine*, Vol. 43, Suppl. 1.

Simchen, E., I. Weiss Salz, A. Ekka-Zohar, L. Freedman et al. (2011), *The National Project for Quality Measures in Israeli Hospitals, 1st Report: General Surgery*, Ministry of Health, Jerusalem.

Socialstyrelsen (2010), *Open Comparison and Assessment 2009 – Cardiac Care*, Stockholm, www.socialstyrelsen.se/publikationer2010/2010-9-2, accessed 30 April 2012.

Socialstyrelsen (2012), *Quality and Efficiency in Swedish Health Care 2010*, Stockholm, www.socialstyrelsen.se/Lists/Artikelkatalog/Attachments/18336/2011-5-18.pdf, accessed 30 April 2012.

Spoerri, A. et al. (2010), "The Swiss National Cohort: A Unique Database for National and International Researchers", *International Journal of Public Health*, Vol. 55, pp. 239-242.

Spoerri, A., M. Egger and E. Von Elm (2011), "Mortality from Road Traffic Accidents in Switzerland: Longitudinal and Spatial Analyses", *Accident Analysis and Prevention*, Vol. 43, No. 1, pp. 40-48.

Stordeur, S., F. Vrijens et al. (2011), *Quality Indicators in Oncology: Breast Cancer*, KCE Reports 150C, Brussels.

Tuppin, P., J. Drouin, M. Mazza et al. (2011), "Hospitalisation Admission Rates for Low-income Subjects with Full Health Insurance Coverage in France", *European Journal of Public Health*, Vol. 21, No. 5, pp. 560-566.

Tuppin, P., A. Neumann, E. Marijon et al. (2011), "Implantation and Patient Profiles for Pacemakers and Cardioverter Defibrillators in France (2008-2009)", *Archives of Cardiovascular Diseases*, Vol. 104, No. 5, pp. 332-342.

Tuppin, P., L. de Roquefeuil, A. Weill et al. (2010), "French National Health Insurance Information System and the Permanent Beneficiaries Sample", *Revue d'Épidémiologie et de Santé Publique*, Vol. 58, No. 4, pp. 286-290.

Van Eycken, R., K. Haustermans et al. (2000), "Evaluation of the Encryption Procedure and Record Linkage in the Belgian National Cancer Registry", *Archives of Public Health*, Vol. 58, pp. 281-294.

Van Klaveren, R.J., M. Oudkerk et al. (2009), "Management of Lung Nodules Detected by Volume CT Scanning", *New England Journal of Medicine*, Vol. 361, pp. 2221-2229.

Vlayen, J., F. Vrijens, K. Beirens et al. (2011), *Quality Indicators in Oncology: Testis Cancer*, KCE Reports, Vol. 149, Brussels.

Wahlbeck, K., J. Westman, M. Nordentoft et al. (2011), "Outcomes of Nordic mental health systems: Life Expectancy of Patients with Mental Disorders in Denmark, Finland and Sweden 1987-2006", *British Journal of Psychiatry*, Vol. 199, No. 6, pp. 453-458.

Welsh Government (2010), "Adding Value to the Analysis of Welsh Birth Data, 2008", http://wales.gov.uk/docs/statistics/2010/101215addingvalueen.pdf, accessed 30 April 2011.

Further reading

Canadian Institutes of Health Research (2002), *Secondary Use of Personal Information in Health Research: Case Studies*, Ottawa.

Chappel, A. (2011), "Multi-payer Claims Database (MPCD) for Comparative Effectiveness Research", Presented to the NCVHS Full Committee Meeting, 16 June 2011.

Coleman, M.P., D. Forman, H. Bryant et al. (2011), "Cancer Survival in Australia, Canada, Denmark, Norway, Sweden, and the United Kingdom, 1995-2007 (the International Cancer Benchmarking Partnership): An Analysis of Population-based Cancer Registry Data", *The Lancet*, Vol. 377, No. 9760, pp. 127-138.

Faeh, D., J. Braun, S. Tarnutzer and M. Bopp (2011), "Public Health Significance of Four Cardiovascular Risk Factors Assessed 25 Years Ago in a Low Prevalence Country", *European Journal of Cardiovascular Prevention & Rehabilitation*, doi: 10.1177/1741826711430282.

Faeh, D., S. Tarnutzer, J. Braun, and M. Bopp (in press), "Individual and Combined Impact of Traditional Risk Factors on Cardiovascular Mortality in Switzerland", *European Journal of Cardiovascular Prevention & Rehabilitation*.

Gill, L.E. (1999), "Ox-Link: The Oxford Medical Record Linkage System", Record Linkage Techniques – 1997 Proceedings of an International Workshop and Exposition, National Academy Press, Washington.

Gissler, M., M. Artama, A. Ritvanen and K. Wahlbeck (2010), "Use of Psychotropic Drugs Before Pregnancy and the Risk for Induced Abortion: Population-based Register-data from Finland 1996-2006", *BMC Public Health*, Vol. 30, No. 10, p. 383.

Goldacre, M. (2002), "The Value of Linked Data for Policy Development, Strategic Planning, Clinical Practice and Public Health", Symposium on Health Data Linkage Proceedings, Australian Government Department of Health and Ageing, Sydney, pp. 95-98.

Karmel, R., P. Anderson and A. Peut (2009), "Pathways Through Aged Care: A First Look", *Bulletin* No. 73, AIHW Cat. No. AUS 116, Canberra.

Malm, H., M. Artama, M. Gissler and A. Ritvanen (2011), "Selective Serotonin Reuptake Inhibitors and Risk for Major Congenital Anomalies", *Obstetrics and Gynecology*, Vol. 118, No. 1, pp. 111-120.

Paulinski, D. (2011), "ASPE/CMS Multi-payer Claims Database", Presented to Academy Health ARM, 14 June 2011.

Piro, F.N., Ø. Næss and B. Claussen (2007), "Area Deprivation and its Association with Health in a Cross-sectional Study: Are the Results Biased by Recent Migration?", *International Journal for Equity in Health*, Vol. 6, No. 10.

Spycher, B.D., M. Feller, M. Zwahlen et al. (2011), "Childhood Cancer and Nuclear Power Plants in Switzerland: A Census-based Cohort Study", *International Journal of Epidemiology*, Vol. 40, No. 5, pp. 1247-1260.

Sund, R. (2008), "Methodological Perspectives for Register-based Health System Performance Assessment – Developing a Hip Fracture Monitoring System in Finland", Stakes, National Research and Development Centre for Welfare and Health, *Research Report* No. 174, Helsinki.

Weill, A., M. Paita, P. Tuppin et al. (2010), "Benfluorex and Valvular Heart Diseases: A Cohort Study of a Million People with Diabetes Mellitus", *Pharmacoepidemiology and Drug Safety*, Vol. 19, No. 12, pp. 1256-1262.

Westman, J., M. Gissler and K. Wahlbeck (2011), "Successful Deinstitutionalization of Mental Health Care: Increased Life Expectancy Among People with Mental Disorders in Finland", *European Journal of Public Health*, Vol. 22, No. 4, pp. 604-606, doi: 10.1093/eurpub/ckr068, Epub 2011 Jun. 9.

Strengthening Health Information Infrastructure for Health Care
Quality Governance
Good Practices, New Opportunities and Data Privacy Protection
Challenges
© OECD 2013

Chapter 3

National health information infrastructure

National information infrastructure appears strong with all 19 countries reporting national hospital in-patient, mortality, health survey and population data and all countries reporting using some data to regularly monitor health care quality. Further, all report having legislation that speaks to the protection of the privacy of personal information. Following patients through the care pathway, and from one database to another, requires patient identifying information. More than one-half of countries report that their national personal health databases do contain unique patient identifying numbers. Countries are divided, however, with about one-half engaged regularly in data linkage studies to monitor health care quality.

This chapter presents the findings of the 2011/12 OECD study of 19 countries regarding the availability of personal health databases at the national level, the sharing of data across national public authorities, national infrastructure for data linkages and analysis, regional and health care network infrastructure for data linkages, and regular uses of linked data for national health and health care monitoring and research.

The statistical data for Israel are supplied by and under the responsibility of the relevant Israeli authorities. The use of such data by the OECD is without prejudice to the status of the Golan Heights, East Jerusalem and Israeli settlements in the West Bank under the terms of international law.

National information infrastructure is quite strong across the countries participating in this study. All have the legal authority to collect identifiable personal health data and all are collecting identifiable personal health data at a national level. Countries also report no limitation in law affecting the retention of personal health information for their unlinked databases. All countries are legally able to analyse the data they have collected to monitor the public's health and to conduct research.

Many pursue data linkage studies on a regular basis and a number regularly monitor health care quality and the performance of their health system through data linkages. Challenges to pursing data linkage studies, however, relate to multiple data custodians and the consequent necessity of the sharing of person-level data across different public authorities.

National databases

There is a strong underlying infrastructure for analysis of personal health data within the countries participating in this study (see Annexes A and B). All 19 participating countries have national inpatient hospitalisation data, national mortality data; national population health surveys and a national census or a national population registry (see Annex D, Table D.1). Seventeen have a national cancer registry and mental hospital in-patient data. Sixteen countries have national data for primary health care and formal long-term care. Less common are national data collections on prescription medicines (14) and patient experiences (11). Ten countries have reported one or more other databases that are important to their national data infrastructure. These include emergency care data; clinical quality databases; data on births and congenital anomalies; retirement and disability pension claim data; disease management programme data; sickness fund data; dental care registries; immunisation registries; cancer screening data; and registries for diseases other than cancer.

All countries use their national databases to regularly report on health care quality (Table 3.1, Table D.2). Seventeen countries benefit from their inpatient hospitalisation data and 16 countries benefit from cancer registry data and mortality data to monitor health care quality. Fourteen countries report using mental hospital in-patient data and 13 countries report using population health survey data for health care quality monitoring. Twelve countries monitor health care quality using primary health care data and eleven use prescription medicines data and formal long-term care data. Ten benefit from population census or population registry data (in conjunction with health information). Nine countries benefit from patient experiences data to monitor health care quality and the same number also use other important databases to complement their programme of health care quality monitoring.

Seventeen countries have national data at the level of individuals for mortality (Table D.3). Such data can be organised in a database where each row of the database represents an individual. This type of data is a prerequisite for detailed analysis of risk factors or determinants of health and health care outcomes and is a prerequisite for data linkage. Sixteen countries have individual-level records in their hospital in-patient data, cancer registry data, population health survey data and population census or population registry data. Fourteen have individual-level data for mental hospital in-patients, 13 have this data for primary care and formal long-term care and twelve have this data for prescription medicines. Seven have individual records for patient experiences.

Table 3.1. **Number of countries reporting linkable data and reporting data use**

	Hospital in-patient data	Primary care data	Cancer registry data	Prescription medicines data	Mortality data	Formal long-term care data	Patient experiences survey data	Mental hospital in-patient data	Population health survey data	Population census or registry data
National database available...	19	16	17	14	19	16	11	17	19	19
Contains records for patients or persons	16	13	16	12	17	13	7	14	16	16
Contains a UPI that could be used for data linkage	14	12	13	12	14	11	1	12	11	11
Contains other identifying variables that could be used for data linkage	14	12	16	12	16	12	3	15	11	15
Is used for data linkage studies	14	10	13	12	15	11	1	8	10	11
Is used regularly for data linkage studies	12	8	11	10	15	6	1	7	7	11
Is used regularly for data linkage studies to *monitor health care quality*	12	4	11	7	12	4	1	5	4	4

Note: The data custodian should be a national authority and data should be included even when it does not cover 100% of the nation.
Source: OECD HCQI Questionnaire on Secondary Use of Health Data, 2011/12.

StatLink ⟶ http://dx.doi.org/10.1787/888932796644

Countries were asked to report for all data available at a national level; even it does not cover 100% of the nation. While the impact of population coverage is minor in some countries, it can introduce significant biases in others. For example, some national databases in Canada are available for a limited number of provinces. In this case, the databases do not reflect the regional diversity of the country but do reflect the heterogeneity within the provincial populations. In the United States, national data on health care encounters may be limited to particular sub-populations, such as individuals enrolled in Medicare (elderly persons) or Medicaid (lower-income persons) health insurance programmes or military veterans. In this case, the data is not representative of the underlying heterogeneity of the population.

National infrastructure for data linkage and analysis

Record linkage involves linking two or more databases using information that identifies the same patient or the same person.* An example would be linking patient records in a hospital database to any death records for the same persons in a mortality database in order to identify patients who died following treatment. A specific type of record linkage, often referred to as deterministic linkage or exact matching, involves using

---

* Other privacy sensitive uses of personal health data could include the linkage of data for patients to records for close biological relatives or disclosure of aggregated data at a level so detailed that it is possible to identify an individual in more than one database without having first undertaken a data linkage.

a unique identifier or set of identifiers to merge two or more sources of data. In health linkages, the identifier used is often a unique patient identifying number or UPI. When a unique patient identifying number is consistently applied and recorded with few errors, this type of record linkage yields the highest quality and most accurate results, at the lowest cost in terms of person-hours.

Sixteen countries reported a national number that uniquely identifies patients (Table 3.2). In 13 countries, the number is used for health care encounters and other governmental purposes, such as social security and taxation. The United States reports the Social Security Number (SSN) as a unique identifying number that can distinguish patients in public health care programmes such as Medicare and Medicaid. The SSN, however, is not used generally for health care encounters in the United States and is therefore not a national identifying number for health care services. In three countries, Canada, Portugal

Table 3.2. **National number that uniquely identifies patients and the main uses of this number**

	Name of the unique identifying number	Main uses of the identifying number
Belgium	INSZ NISS	INSZ NISS is a national person identifier (national number) used for various purposes, such as health care, social security, and tax.
Canada	Health Card Number	The provinces and territories assign a health card number that is a unique patient number for all publicly funded health care encounters. There is also a unique Social Insurance Number assigned nationally for tax and social security purposes that is not used for health care.
Denmark	CPR N.R. (Central Person Register Number)	Used for "everything" in relation to national and local governments including health care. Also banks and other business identifications, etc.
Finland	Personal Identity Code	The personal identity code is used in practically all data collections in public services, such as health care, social welfare services, education, justice, etc.
France	Numéro d'identification au répertoire (NIR)	Persons born in metropolitan France and overseas departments are registered on the national directory for the identification of natural persons (RNIPP) and are assigned a registration number (NIR). The NIR is used by medical authorities for the issuance of a "carte vitale". The NIR is also used for social security.
Italy	TS number	TS number contains both a health number and a tax file number and has nearly universal coverage of the population. It is managed through a publicly owned private company, SOGEI that could be considered as a trusted third party.
Israel	ID number	The ID number is used for tax, social security, education, health, licensing, banking and other identified activities.
Korea	Resident Registration Number	Resident Registration Number (RRN) is assigned to each individual upon his/her birth and contains various information including birth date, gender and location of birth. RRN is used in virtually all aspects of life, including economic activities, for personal identification in various documents and communications in Korea.
Malta	Identification Number ID No	ID No is a unique identification number used throughout the country for all purposes including electoral lists, taxation, social security, etc. It is based on the registration number at the Public Registry.
Norway	National Identification Number	The National Identification Number is used for tax, social security, health records, banking and other purposes.
Poland	PESEL	PESEL number is assigned to all citizens at birth; permanent residents; temporary residents with stays of two months or longer; applicants for an identity card; and other persons where regulations require it.
Portugal	Número de Utente do Serviço Nacional de Saúde	This number is used throughout the country for access to national health service care and benefits.
Singapore	National Registration Identity Card Number (NRIC)	NRIC is used for identification, government procedures, and some commercial transactions (e.g. the opening of a bank account).
Sweden	Personnummer (Personal Identity Number)	Personnummer is the main identifier used for all official purposes in Sweden (tax, social welfare, health care, living conditions, education and so on).
United Kingdom	NHS number Scotland also has the Community health index (CHI) number	Everyone registered with the National Health Service in England, Scotland and Wales is issued a unique NHS number. The NHS number is not used for tax/social security purposes. In Scotland, the CHI system was set up for administrative purposes to track patients registering with GPs.
United States	Social Security Number	The SSN is issued to US citizens, permanent residents, and temporary (working) residents and its main purpose is for taxation.

Source: OECD HCQI Questionnaire on Secondary Use of Health Data, 2011/12 and, for Italy, follow-up telephone interview, October 2011.

and the *United Kingdom*, the identifying numbers are exclusive to the provision of health services and are not used for taxation and social security. In *Canada*, the provincial HIN will change when individuals move province and there is no linkage of old to new HIN numbers across provinces. As a result, record linkage studies that depend on the health insurance number might be affected by inter-provincial mobility. UK respondents to the telephone interview for this study were not sure if the NHS number issued to UK residents is a unique number that would be maintained when an individual moved within the United Kingdom or if it would change if an individual moved country within the United Kingdom, producing a similar bias to that experienced in Canada.

Fourteen countries reported a unique identifying number for patients exists currently within their national hospitalisation databases and mortality databases and that this number could potentially be used for data linkage (Table D.4). Thirteen countries reported the same conditions for their cancer registry and twelve for their primary care data, prescription medicines data and mental hospital in-patient data. Eleven reported the same conditions for their formal long-term care data, population health survey data and population census or registry data. Only one country, however, had a unique identifying number that could be used for data linkage of patient experiences data.

France reports the use of different unique patient identifying numbers and that this is a barrier to some data linkage projects. The identifying numbers used by hospitals may vary across hospitals and are different from the identifying numbers used for medical insurance. France has been working on establishing a national identifying number for medical records and this development was approved by law in 2007. Such a number would enable patients to be assured that when electronic medical records are exchanged among providers; health care providers are receiving the correct record for them. Medical insurance records, however, currently depend on a different unique identifier, the NIR, which is the country's social security number. The NIR was considered to be too sensitive to be used for electronic medical records. Options being explored to overcome the difficulty of linking databases include the establishment of a third party who could hold the key that would enable health insurance records with an anonymised NIR to be linked with medical records with the new health identifying number. Another possibility would be to have the insurance system adopt the same identifying number as that used for medical records. Data protection, health insurance and other authorities are working together to determine the best solution.

There are new developments in three countries that have not been able to use a unique identifying number for record linkages, *Switzerland*, *Germany* and *Japan*. The current process in Switzerland involves the health care providers in the Swiss Cantons, who have access to patient names, dates of birth and sex, to create an encrypted identifier that cannot be reversed to reveal the identity of a person. The same algorithm is applied throughout the country and through time and is provided to the Federal Statistical Office (FSO) who uses it to enable data linkages. The algorithm has limitations. In particular, it does not account for name change, which creates a systematic bias in the data, particularly for women, where changes in marital status may result in name changes. There is a unique Social Security Number (SSN) in Switzerland that could potentially be used for data linkage in the future in an encrypted form. Recently, the Swiss Federal Statistical Office (FSO) sought an opinion of the Swiss national Office of Data Protection to determine if the FSO had the legal authority to process data using the SSN. The determination was that this use is in compliance with the health insurance law and could be in compliance with the law authorising the FSO, if the FSO amends the ordinance that accompanies its authorising legislation that specifies the data that the FSO is collecting. The FSO is pursuing this change in its ordinance. In *Japan*, there is a current proposal to introduce a uniform identifying number for tax and social security purposes, including health care. In *Germany*, a health insurance number, incorporating a unique and unchangeable code for identifying insured persons, is already mandatory within the health insurance system. This number has also been used to support data exchange. In future, this health insurance number is likely to be used in all areas of care provision, once the electronic health card (eGK) has been introduced throughout the country.

Other variables in a database can also be used to link records through a process of exact matching or through probabilistic matching. For probabilistic matching, a set of possible matches among the data sources to be linked are identified. For example, identifying information such as names, dates of birth and postal codes, may be used to assess potential matches. Then statistics are calculated to assign weights describing the likelihood that the records match. A combined score represents the probability that the records refer to the same individuals. Often there is one threshold above which a pair is considered a match, and another threshold below which it is considered not to be a match. This technique is used when an exact match between records across databases is not possible, or when data capture errors have caused deterministic matches to fail.

More countries reported having a set of identifying variables within their databases that could be used for record linkage than reported having a unique patient identifying number (Table D.5). These variables included names, dates of birth, addresses or postal codes, sex, and dates of events. Not all of these identifying variables are available on all of the data, but all of the data have at least some of these identifiers. Sixteen countries reported having a set of identifying variables within their cancer registry and mortality databases. Fifteen reported these variables within their mental hospital in-patient data and within their population census or registry. Fourteen reported these are part of their hospital in-patient data. Twelve reported these within primary care, prescription medicines, and formal long-term care data and eleven reported these within population health survey data. Only three reported such identifiers within patient experiences data.

In Australia, data linkage and data integration are predominantly undertaken through probabilistic means involving a set of potential identifiers, such as name, birth date, sex, and sometimes address. While the two large national health insurance databases [under the Medicare Benefits Schedule (MBS) and the Pharmaceutical Benefits Scheme (PBS)] have Medicare numbers, these numbers have not generally been used for linkage as the number is often not available on other databases and there are legal restrictions to its use. Specifically, there are legal restrictions concerning the linkage of MBS data to PBS data. Hospitalisation data in Australia at the national level are held by the Australian Institute of Health and Welfare. National hospitalisation data lack personal identifying information to permit data linkage, although state government data sets may hold this information. Hence, any project requiring access to identifiable hospitalisation data in Australia requires seeking access to hospitalisation data from the relevant Australian State. In 2010, Australia introduced unique patient identifying numbers, however participation in e-health is not compulsory and the use of e-health numbers for data linkages has not been approved.

Sub-national infrastructure for data linkage projects

In some countries, data linkage is commonly undertaken at the level of regions, states or within specific networks of health care organisations. Networks of health care organisations, such as the US health care organisation network Kaiser Permanente, offer a broad range of health care services and can conduct research where patient data is linked across the different health care facilities they operate.

Eleven countries reported sub-national data linkage activity at the state or region level (Table D.6). *Canada* reported regular health-related data linkage activity across all the major types of health data in nine of the ten Canadian provinces and involving a unique patient identifying number, the provincial Health Information Number. Canada also reported that these provinces have a broader range of projects using data linkage because the provinces have access to more detailed and comprehensive data than is available nationally.

Similarly, *Australia* reported data linkage centres in almost all Australian States and Territories, where data linkage projects are being conducted with a broader array of health and social data than is possible at the national level. Also, a wider array of databases at the state level contain unique person identifying numbers that can be used to support data linkages and data integration. States have been better positioned to advance research based on data linkage due to less complex legislative and organisational restrictions than exist at the national level. The Population Health Research Network, with funding from the Australian Government, is building the infrastructure for record linkage in all states and territories and also at the national level.

Germany reported data linkage project activity at the state level involving cancer registry, mortality, population health survey and other data. Examples include projects related to the development of a mortality index in Bremen State; sickness fund data linkages in Hessen; and linkages involving population health surveys in Augsburg and Essen. The states of Bremen and Hessen are undertaking health-related data linkage studies on a regular basis. These state-level linkages benefit from unique patient identifying numbers. Also, legal provisions allow data from a "morbidity-oriented risk adjustment scheme" of the statutory health insurance system, conducted at the state level, to be analysed at the federal level for health services research and to advance the health insurance system. *Portugal* and *Japan* reported sub-national infrastructure for data linkages within cancer registries.

Sweden also reported data linkage activity within some of the 21 county councils, such as the Skåne Region and the West Region and that these regions are able to undertake a broader range of data linkage activities than can be undertaken at a national level. For example, the West Region has a primary care register that may be linked.

The *United States* reports that each state (plus DC) has a wide variety of data users, data sources and products and may well be undertaking data linkage projects. Further, states have Social Security Numbers that might be used to facilitate linkages along with Medicaid identifiers. Whether or not the states are undertaking a broader range of data linkage activities than are taking place at the national level cannot be determined without an extensive survey. However, the medical and health services literature shows a wide variety of research studies by government, academia, health care quality organisations and industry in the United States.

The *United Kingdom* also reports sub-national data linkage activity in the region of Tayside Scotland. This local area does not, however, have a broader range of data linkage projects than are possible at the national level in Scotland. Data linkage activity was also reported for the Torbay Care Trust in England (see Case study 11).

Seven countries, *Belgium, Canada, Germany, Israel, Portugal, Singapore and the United States* reported networks of health care organisations conducting data linkage projects with their own data (Table D.7). Belgium reported this activity within networks of hospitals. Germany reported this activity for several statutory health insurance funds such as Barmer-GEK, AOK and the Bremen Institute for Prevention Research and Social Medicine, BIPS. Israel reported this activity within four national health funds: Clalit, Leumit, Maccabi and Meuhedet. Portugal reported this activity within Integrated Delivery Services. The United States reported this activity among large health care insurers including Kaiser-Permanente, Puget Sound, Harvard Health Plan and others. *Singapore* reported that public health care providers undertake this type of work on an ad hoc basis.

Data linkages for public health research and health care quality monitoring

Most countries with variables within their national databases that would permit data linkages have conducted data linkage projects. Overall, most countries reported record linkage projects involving mortality data, hospital in-patient data, cancer registry data, and prescription medicines data (Table D.8). Half of the countries also reported record linkage studies with all other major types of data, with the exception of patient experience surveys where data linkage has occurred in only one country.

Fewer countries reported undertaking data linkage studies on a regular basis, such that a project was usually underway (Table D.9). Only mortality data was used regularly to support data linkage project in most countries (15 countries). Twelve countries regularly undertook data linkage studies with hospital in-patient data and eleven countries with cancer registry data and population census or registry data. Less common were regular data linkage studies with primary care data (eight countries); population health survey data (seven countries); mental hospital in-patient data (seven countries); and formal long-term care data (six countries). Only one country reported regular data linkage activity with patient experience data.

Figure 3.1. **Number of countries reporting national data used to conduct record-linkage projects on an occasional and on a regular basis**

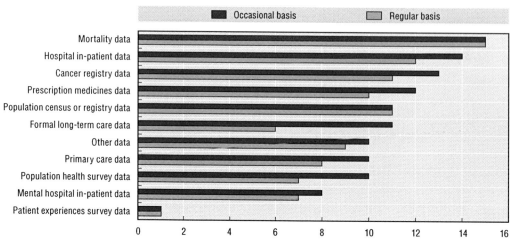

Source: OECD HCQI Questionnaire on Secondary Use of Health Data, 2011/12.

StatLink ᴍᴤᴘ http://dx.doi.org/10.1787/888932796606

Seven countries have a regular occurrence of data linkage projects involving many national databases (Denmark, Finland, Israel, Korea, Sweden, the United Kingdom and the United States). In all but one of these countries, a unique patient identifying number is available to facilitate the linkages (Tables 3.1 and 3.3). The United States relies more on sets of patient identifying information to establish links. Australia, Belgium, France and Switzerland also undertake projects involving the linkage of several databases on a regular basis. Belgium and France have greater ability to conduct these linkages using a unique patient identifying number, while other identifiers are more often used in Australia and Switzerland. Belgium, Canada, Malta and Norway conduct regular data linkage projects with some databases and use a unique identifying number to undertake the work. Norway (nine databases), Singapore (seven databases), Malta (seven databases) and Portugal (four databases) have national databases with patient identifying numbers and/or other patient identifiers, but engage in data linkage on a regular basis with one-half or fewer of the available databases. Germany, Japan and Poland all have databases with variables that could be used to undertake data linkage projects, but none do so regularly with any of these databases.

Countries are divided, with just over one-half engaged regularly in national data linkage studies to monitor health care quality involving their hospital-inpatient, cancer registry and mortality data and less than half of countries with their prescription medicines data (Table 3.1, Table D.10). Regular linkage studies to monitor the quality of primary health care, mental hospital in-patient care and formal long-term care remain relatively rare, with only 4-5 countries reporting undertaking such work.

Finland reports that hospital in-patient data is linked to formal long-term care data on a regular basis to get complete information on institutionalised care; cancer registry data is combined with mortality data to complete the data with all cancer cases; and data on deaths is combined with the Medical Birth Register and the Register on Congenital Malformations to get more exact information on perinatal and infant deaths. To monitor health care quality, examples include combining registers to get information on the consequences of the use of medicines during pregnancy on the health of newborns; to benchmark hospital health care quality performance for major diseases and medical conditions, such as stroke and very premature births; and to monitor life-expectancy among patients with severe mental health disorders who have been hospitalised. This last project was a multi-country study with other Scandinavian countries.

Table 3.3. **Distribution of the regular occurrence of health-related record linkage projects by availability of databases with patient identifiers**

	Most national data with a unique patient identifying number (UPI)	Most national data with other patient identifiers	Some national data with a unique patient identifying number (UPI)
Data linkage projects on a regular basis…			
With 7+ national databases	Denmark, Finland, Israel, Korea, Sweden, United Kingdom	United States	
With 5-6 national databases	France, Belgium	Australia	Switzerland
With 3-4 national databases	Canada, Malta, Norway		
With 2 national databases	Singapore		Portugal
None		Japan	Poland, Germany

Source: OECD HCQI Questionnaire on Secondary Use of Health Data, 2011/12.

Israel reports regularly conducting projects involving linkages of mortality data to cancer registrations, long-term care data, mental hospital inpatient data and to data from the census of population. A number of indicators are regularly estimated in order to monitor health care quality. These include 30-day mortality rates after admission to hospital and after procedures within hospital; rates of rehospitalisation; and deaths after discharge from mental health hospitals. Also regularly undertaken are survival analysis and analysis of leading causes of death using linked databases.

Korea reports an extensive programme of regular health care quality monitoring using data linkages. Indicators from the linkage of hospital in-patient data to mortality data include 30-day case fatality for acute myocardial infarction and 30-day post-operative mortality for major types of surgery. Linkages of mental hospital in-patient data to hospital in-patient data enable monitoring hospital re-admissions for mental-health patients; and further linkage to prescription medicines data enable monitoring health outcomes of prescribing to mental-health patients. Outcomes of prescribing patterns in primary care are monitored through linkage of prescription medicines and primary care databases. Korea also links the cancer registry data to mortality data to assess the relative survival of cancer patients and links long-term care data to survey data on the activities of daily living to estimate the percentage of patients with reduced activities of daily living.

Sweden also reports a comprehensive programme of data linkages that facilitate health care quality monitoring including regular linkages of all registers to mortality data; linkages of patient registry data to the prescribed drug register; and the cancer register to the patient register. *Denmark* reports a similar data linkage capacity including linkages to more than 50 national clinical quality databases.

The *United Kingdom* has the most comprehensive suite of national data among the countries that participated in this study; however, the coverage of these databases is often limited to one or two of the member countries. In Scotland, hospital in-patient data, cancer data, mental hospital in-patient data and mortality data are maintained as a permanently linked database. Prescription data has only recently become available at record level with a UPI in Scotland and will now be regularly linked. Population health survey data is used regularly in research linkages in Scotland. Scotland reports using linkage to monitor outcomes of health care including HEAT targets, such as monitoring readmissions and deaths among coronary heart disease patients. In England, hospital data is linked to mortality data on a monthly basis. England monitors hospital standardised mortality ratios that will be replaced, in future, with a summary hospital-level mortality indicator (SHMI). Cancer incidence data in England is routinely linked to mortality, hospital treatment (surgery and radiotherapy) and, for a proportion of the population, to primary care data. Birth notifications are linked to birth registrations (e.g. to determine prematurity) and to death registrations in England and the cancer registry is linked to mortality data. England produces a 30-day post-operative mortality rates for patients following colorectal cancer surgery. In England and Wales, the ONS Longitudinal Study (LS) has linked a 1% sample of the population census in 1971, 1981, 1991 and 2001 across censuses and to births, deaths and cancer registrations. The study can be used to understand the distribution of health outcomes by census population characteristics as well as changes in characteristics and health outcomes over time. Wales has linked births to hospital delivery records; and the cancer registry to mortality data. The linkage of hospital in-patient data to other databases is under development.

The *United States* reports the regular creation of files linking hospital records, the cancer registry and the population census to mortality data; and population health survey records to mortality data and to health care records for Medicare and Medicaid enrolees. National health care quality monitoring from data linkages includes cancer survival rates, 30-day mortality following in-patient hospitalisations, and infant mortality.

Australia reports that mortality data are linked to cancer registry and diabetes registry data on a regular basis. Data from the population census (conducted every five years) is also regularly linked to mortality data in order to assess under-reporting of Indigenous status on mortality records. Data from the Australian and New Zealand Dialysis and Transplant Registry are linked with mortality data to produce estimates for end-stage kidney disease in support of monitoring quality of care. None of Australia's regularly published Health Performance Indicators, however, currently involve the linkage of administrative databases. There are pilot projects underway that may lead to linkage-based indicators in future. *France* reports regularly undertaking data linkage of primary care data to data on in-patient hospitalisations and to health survey data. France is developing health care quality indicators and does not yet regularly link databases for this purpose.

Switzerland reports the linkage of hospital in-patient data, mental hospital in-patient data, formal long-term care data, mortality data and the population census. *Singapore* reports linking data on hospitalisations to both primary care data and to mortality data on a regular basis for policy analysis. Singapore also uses data linkages to develop regular health care quality monitoring indicators including annual rates of 30-day mortality inside and outside of hospital following hospitalisations for acute myocardial infarction and stroke.

In *Belgium*, hospital data is regularly linked to hospital expenditure data; and cancer registry data is linked to mortality data, to health insurance nomenclature, to hospital in-patient data and to cancer screening. Databases on cystic fibrosis and neuromuscular disease patients are linked to the population register to capture year of birth, district, sex and deaths. Belgium reports data linkages to produce process and outcome indicators for breast, testicular, and rectum cancers with on-going work on oesophagus and stomach cancers. Linkage has also been used to assess GP performance. Belgium also maintains a linked sample of health insurance records to monitor health care consumption and expenditures.

Canada also has a number of national databases that are regularly linked using a unique health care identifying number administered by each province. Hospital in-patient data are often linked to other types of health care including emergency room visits; and population health surveys are routinely linked to in-patient hospitalisation data and to mortality data. At the provincial level, data linkage activity to inform about population health and health care quality is extensive.

Norway regularly undertakes linkages of data from the cancer registry to mortality data and data on prescription medicines to data on hospital in-patients. Data linkages are also used to regularly monitor health care quality. Indicators include annual rates of five-year relative survival after four types of cancer and annual rates of diabetes-related lower extremity amputations. *Malta* regularly links data from the cancer registry to mortality data. Also regularly linked are data on hospitalisations to data within the cancer registry, the congenital abnormalities register and to mortality data. Cancer survival rates are regularly reported to monitor quality of care. *Portugal* reports regularly undertaking projects linking primary care and prescription medicines data.

Strengthening Health Information Infrastructure for Health Care
Quality Governance
Good Practices, New Opportunities and Data Privacy Protection
Challenges
© OECD 2013

Chapter 4

National electronic health record systems

Countries are moving forward to develop databases from electronic health records for monitoring and research. Twenty-two of twenty-five countries report a national plan or policy to implement electronic health records and 20 report starting its implementation. Eighteen national plans include the secondary use of the data. Thirteen countries are using data from electronic record systems to monitor public health, eleven countries to conduct health research and nine countries to monitor patient safety. Barriers to creating and analysing databases from electronic health records reported by countries include concerns with current legislative frameworks, particularly as they apply to data privacy protection (16 countries); problems with the quality of data within EHRs (14 countries); and resource constraints to database creation (nine countries) and to the de-identification of data to protect privacy (seven countries). Data quality concerns include a lack of clinical terminology standards; improper coding; missing data; and variable quality across health care providers.

This chapter reports findings from the 2011/12 OECD study of 25 countries regarding current uses of electronic records in physician offices and hospitals; national plans to implement electronic health record systems; implementation of national systems; the development of minimum datasets; the use of structure and terminology standards to code data; the status and technical challenges of database creation from electronic health records; and current uses of data from electronic health records including public health, patient safety and health system performance monitoring.

The statistical data for Israel are supplied by and under the responsibility of the relevant Israeli authorities. The use of such data by the OECD is without prejudice to the status of the Golan Heights, East Jerusalem and Israeli settlements in the West Bank under the terms of international law.

Electronic health record systems in some countries enable patients to have an electronic record of their key characteristics and health concerns, as well as their history of encounters with the health care system and the treatments that they have received from a variety of health care providers. This record can then be shared with new health care providers to support provision of the most appropriate care. The existence of such records opens a promising new frontier for advancing patient care, in the same way that advancements in the use of information technologies have revolutionised most other industries.

The goals of such systems include improving the quality and safety of care for individual patients, as well as facilitating optimal care pathways and promoting efficiency in the use of health system resources. It is not difficult to see the benefit of sharing records to avoid medical errors. This is particularly evident during emergencies; when patients may be unable to speak for themselves and thus unable to alert health professionals to their underlying medical conditions, current medications and allergies. It is also evident that when multiple physicians and professionals are treating the same patient, sharing a patient's medical history would help to prevent adverse health outcomes from inappropriate treatment combinations and would help to avoid unnecessary repetition of clinical tests.

The ideal electronic health record system would have the attributes of accuracy, completeness, comprehensiveness, reliability, relevance, timeliness and accessibility. These are also the attributes of a well-functioning statistical system. This is not surprising given an electronic health record system is essentially the same: a very large and complex system that is gathering, compiling, organising, and reporting data.

As countries move toward realising a national electronic health record system that meets all of these desirable attributes; there is an increasing possibility of benefiting from the system to build databases to monitor and to conduct research to improve the health of the population and the quality, safety and efficiency of health care. At the same time, wherever the implementation of the electronic health record system is inadequately addressing one or more of these desirable attributes; it may be difficult or impossible to benefit from the system to evaluate whether or not health care quality and safety are improving.

The scope of the effort to implement national electronic health record systems is daunting for governments in all countries. Essential elements include development of national plans; enactment of new legislation to launch the effort or to manage particular elements, such as the protection of information privacy; development of governance mechanisms; development of standards for both semantics and for the interoperability of electronic health records across different health care settings; engagement of regional authorities, insurers and health care providers in the effort; liaison with private industry for infrastructure and software; development of certification for software vendors; training efforts and public education; and considerable budgetary support.

It is perhaps not surprising that, as a result of the difficulty of transforming an industry as complex as the provision of health care, early work toward electronic health care system development often did not include consideration of the potential of electronic health record systems to support national monitoring and research to improve population health and the quality, efficiency and performance of the health care system.

The challenge countries face however, is that assessment of the usability of electronic health records for statistical purposes cannot wait until after the implementation of electronic health record systems. This is because decisions taken during the implementation may result in a system that is poorly suited to the generation of high quality and useable statistics. The better course of action is to critically evaluate the electronic health record system plan and its implementation today, so that the deployment can yield the data needed to advance population health, efficient and effective health systems and patient safety tomorrow.

Use of electronic medical and patient records in physician offices and hospitals

All countries participating in this study (see Annex C) reported that at least some primary care physician offices, medical specialist physician offices and hospitals are capturing information on patient diagnosis and treatment electronically (Table D.11). For this study, an electronic medical record (EMR) or electronic patient record (EPR) is a computerised medical record created in an organisation that delivers care, such as a hospital or physician's office, for patients of that organisation. EMR and EPR are provider or organisation centric and allow storage, retrieval and modification of patient records.

Most countries were able to report an estimate of the proportion of primary care physician offices capturing patient data electronically. Twelve countries reported high penetration of electronic medical records among primary care physician offices, with 80% or more having adopted EMRs. Many countries were also able to report an estimate of the proportion of medical specialist physician offices capturing patient data electronically. Generally, countries with a high penetration of use among primary care physician offices, reported large proportions of medical specialist physician offices capturing patient data electronically. Many countries were also able to report the proportion of hospitals capturing in-patient diagnosis and treatment information electronically. Among them, nine countries reported all hospitals using electronic patient records including *Austria, Denmark, Estonia, Finland, Iceland, Israel, the Netherlands, Sweden and the United Kingdom*. Annex E provides additional information about the adoption and use of electronic medical and patient records in the countries participating in this study.

National plans and policies to implement electronic health records

Most countries have a national plan or a national policy to implement electronic health records* (Tables D.12 and D.13). Such plans commonly include elements of governance of the process and the establishment of standards. Countries are divided, however, on whether or not current plans extend to secondary uses of data from these systems. More than half of the countries participating in this study have included public health monitoring (15 countries); health system performance monitoring (15); and supporting physician treatment decisions by enabling physicians to query the data to

* Table D.13 provides web-links to plans or policies to develop national electronic health record systems.

inform themselves about previous treatments and outcomes for similar patients (14). Many countries also intend to benefit from the data for research (13); patient safety monitoring (12); and facilitating and contributing to clinical trials (10), such as enabling the follow-up of clinical cohorts to measure treatments and outcomes over time.

Eight countries, *France, Indonesia, Korea, Mexico, Poland, Singapore, Slovakia, and the United States,* have a national plan or policy to implement electronic health record systems that includes all of the secondary uses of personal health data investigated in this study.

Korea reported that the implementation of a national EHR project was part of a 2005 National Health Information Infrastructure Plan under the provisions of the Framework Act on Health and Medical Services. The availability of budget to execute the plan was an initial problem, however dimensions of the plan are now underway including computerisation of public health and medical institutions; development of a national health information infrastructure master plan; proliferation and management of information standards and enactment of necessary legislation; development of a national health information system; and development and implementation of a pilot project for a national e-health service. A national interoperability roadmap was established for *Mexico* in 2008 with implementation phases underway. The roadmap is updated annually.

Five countries, *Belgium, Finland, Estonia, Portugal and the United Kingdom* report that their national plans or policies will include most of the secondary uses of personal health data explored in this study.

Belgium reports that public health monitoring is not yet incorporated into EHR plans at the federal level; however, it is already part of the functionalities of certified EHR systems. The semantic interoperability layer will need to be completed for wide adoption of public health reporting and for the use of electronic records to facilitate and contribute to clinical trials. Similarly, patient safety monitoring will be developed but priority is currently placed on the deployment of the EHR system and developing trust in it. Data from EHR systems will contribute to supporting physician treatment decisions through use cases, such as for nephrology. The monitoring of health system performance and research to improve patient care, health system efficiency or patient health are usually undertaken with social security and sentinel site databases rather than data from electronic health records.

Finland has an established set of national registers that are used for all of the secondary data uses included here. There is already implementation of systems to extract data from the electronic health record system to update the registers. To support physician treatment decisions, however, there are local and regional applications but no national level data extraction for this purpose. National plans, however, include the implementation of this feature in all regions. Both national registers and local and regional EHR systems are used for research. At the national level, however, current legislation does not permit direct access to records in the national EHR system for research purposes. There are policy discussions to consider revisions to the legislation to enable this research.

In the *United Kingdom*, England reports that virtually all of the secondary analysis activities are included in the EHR plan. The tracking of cohorts or groups of patients to facilitate clinical trials is not part of the original plan but it was added as an activity later. Scotland reports that it is likely that data from EHRs will be used to support most of the secondary analysis activities included in this study; however, they are not all explicitly mentioned in the high level strategy.

Portugal is planning to undertake public health monitoring, monitoring of health system performance and patient safety, and research to improve population health and health system performance through analysis of data from electronic health records. Concerns with the quality of the information within the EHR system have lead to a decision to not plan to use the data to facilitate or contribute to clinical trials or for physician queries to support treatment decisions.

Iceland and Slovenia have plans to use data extracted from electronic health records for public health and health system performance monitoring. In *Slovenia*, other secondary data uses explored here are expected to be in scope for inclusion when more detailed national plans are drafted. The national EHR has not yet been implemented in Slovenia and currently only local EMRs are in place. In *Iceland*, national disease registries that are not based on EHR data are currently used for research and surveillance purposes.

In the primary care sector in *Denmark*, data from EHR systems is used to support physician treatment decisions by enabling examination of treatments given to similar patient groups. There are no other secondary uses of data from EHR systems. Databases in Denmark are prepared from completion of forms or extraction of data from health information systems and are used for all of the secondary purposes examined here. For clinical trials, the trial will collect its own data or obtain data from local area surveillance systems.

Israel, Japan, Spain and Switzerland have not included secondary uses of data from electronic health records within their national development plans or policies.

Canada does not have a national plan or policies for secondary data use from electronic records. Planning to increase secondary uses of data from EHR systems within provinces and territories has been underway, including efforts to develop a shared vision for secondary data use in Canada and efforts to expand the scope of the national EHR funding plan to also include secondary uses of data. No uses of data from the national EHR system were reported for *Israel*. At present, most secondary data uses explored here are undertaken by analysing data from electronic medical records of hospitals and HMOs.

Japan introduced a personal EHR called "My Hospital Everywhere" in 2010 to be implemented by 2013. This EHR is intended only for the personal use of patients and their health care providers and therefore is not available for secondary analysis. The national plan aims to promote the effective use of national insurance claims data to improve quality and efficiency and enables this patient-level data to be used for research purposes under strict conditions. The national plan also calls for the development of a multi-hospital data base entitled the "Japan Sentinel Project" that will be developed from electronic patient records in order to ensure drug safety.

In *Spain*, autonomous communities develop regional policies for their own EHR systems. Co-ordination efforts ensure that regional developments support national plans. There are no plans to extract data from electronic health records for analysis. Spain has established hospital and primary care databases, health system activity registries, safety events registries, and special studies for monitoring and research.

Switzerland has placed first priority on the establishment of the national EHR and secondary uses of data may be a next step. This will be explored by the Swiss Federal Statistical Office which is responsible for health care statistics with anonymised data.

There is no national plan or policy to implement EHRs in *Germany, the Netherlands or Sweden*. *Germany* noted governmental support for e-health services, such as the introduction of an electronic health card and an associated telematic infrastructure. In Germany, however, health care providers are mainly responsible for the design, implementation and use of electronic health records following medical guidelines and quality requirements. The *Netherlands* reported that the Ministry of Health has put much effort into developing a national law that would enable the creation of a national exchange point for the sharing of electronic patient information. Although the initiative was already far developed, the Senate voted unanimously against the law in 2011. As a result, there is no national policy currently; however, several stakeholders intend to re-launch the initiative on an opt-in basis. *Sweden* has a decentralised health care system with 20 county councils and 290 municipal councils responsible for providing adequate care services and for developing, quality-assuring and financing all care activities. While the Swedish e-Health Strategy co-ordinates national EHR implementation, county and municipal councils are responsible for their own EHR implementations.

Implementation of a national electronic health record system

Twenty countries participating in this study have implemented or are starting to implement a national electronic health record system. In accordance with the definition used in this study, such a system refers to the longitudinal electronic record of individual patients that contains or virtually links together records from multiple electronic medical and patient record systems which can then be shared (interoperable) across health care settings. It aims to provide a history of contact with the health care system for individual patients.

Fourteen countries are aiming toward a system where patient's electronic records may be both shared among physician offices and between physician offices and hospitals; and where these records can exchange information about current medications, laboratory test results and medical imaging results. These systems can result in a unified longitudinal patient record. Six countries are restricting the scope of the national electronic health record to only some of these dimensions.

Fifteen countries (Austria, Estonia, Finland, France, Indonesia, Israel, Poland, Portugal, Japan, Singapore, Slovakia, Spain, Sweden, Switzerland and the United Kingdom) reported implementing either a single country-wide electronic health record system or an integration of regional EHR systems permitting some records to be exchanged nationally. The national EHR implementation is new among all of these countries, with only a few countries reporting a small proportion of practices having implemented the national EHR within the past four years. The exceptions are Estonia, where implementation also began within the past four years, but where a majority of physicians offices and hospitals have implemented the national EHR system and Israel, where sharing of electronic records was established a decade ago within certain HMOs.

Japan's "My Hospital Everywhere" project enables patients to store and access their electronic medical records which may then be retrieved by health professionals anywhere in the country. The Japan Sentinel Project networks a dozen large medical centres as well as large national hospital chains with 40-50 hospitals to share electronic medical records to monitor drug safety.

Sweden's national electronic health record system is a shared national patient summary record. Similarly, *Israel's* national system will allow HMOs and Hospitals to share summary records on admission and discharge.

Austria is introducing a country-wide system involving virtually linked data through the use of IHE (Integrating the Healthcare Enterprise) recommendations to facilitate interoperability.

Singapore is implementing a single country-wide EHR system to achieve its vision of "One Singaporean, One Health Record". A document exchange solution EMRX was implemented in 2004 which enabled the exchange of some medical information across public health care institutions. The National EHR (NEHR) is a more robust system which stores data in structured formats and is standards-based. It builds upon existing systems and allows extensions beyond the public sector coverage. It extracts and consolidates into one record, clinically relevant information from patients' encounters across the public and private health care system throughout their lives, and enables authorised health care providers to improve the overall quality of care rendered to patients at different points of care. *Portugal* is developing a single country-wide system called the Portuguese Health Record (Plataforma de Dados de Saude, PDS). Data exchange between hospitals and physicians is already in place in the Northern Region which covers about 45% of the population. The system shares information across levels of care and builds an evolving patient summary record over time that is controlled by the patient's general practitioner. This system includes all of the dimensions of record exchange investigated here (see Table D.14). The remaining four regions will be connected in 2012.

Slovakia aims to complete nation-wide implementation by 2014. *Indonesia* has introduced an information exchange among six hospitals and intends to extend this implementation nationwide.

Switzerland reported undertaking a step-by-step integration of regional EHR systems in the direction of achieving a national EHR system in the future. A new national law sets certification requirements that must be respected by communities of health care providers in order for them to share records with other communities. The law aims to ensure that regional systems will be interoperable.

The *United Kingdom* has different electronic health record systems across member states. England is implementing a single summary record for emergency care. About one-quarter of providers have implemented the English EHR system over the past four years. Scotland is making available a single summary record from primary care physicians for use in medical emergencies. Scotland also makes some systems available to its regions, but it is a regional decision whether or not to implement them. Scotland reports that each system has a different implementation date and participation rate.

Poland reported beginning to implement a patient account as a single system accessible to patients over the Internet that would include laboratory test results and prescription medicines. For other dimensions of electronic health record implementation, the regions are organising the effort.

Spain is establishing a central national node as a hub for messaging services between health services providers in each territory. Territorial nodes act as concentrators of EHR contents from diverse systems. The health care authority in each territory will manage its integration platform (node). Nine document types have been identified for inclusion in the national system, which is only a portion of the documents that may be available within local systems.

In *Denmark,* the implementation of electronic health records is a regional responsibility. The regions have a goal of achieving five coherent EHR landscapes. Regional

EHRs will be able to access read-only information from national data sources. This system will be implemented from 2012 onward. Some features of the Danish EHR system have been implemented, including physician receipt of laboratory test results (85%), sharing of medications information among physician offices and hospitals (50%), and physician sharing of medications information with other physician offices (30%).

Similarly, the implementation of EHR systems is a provincial and territorial responsibility in *Canada*. Each of Canada's 13 provinces and territories has an electronic health record deployment project underway. Deployment ranges from 0-100% as defined by a mix of six core elements of electronic health record systems. Canada Health Infoway estimated that at least 50% of Canadians had these core elements available to them as of March 2011. Some provinces and territories provide primary care physicians with access to electronic repositories of patient information about laboratory tests, medications, and digital images and some receive discharge and clinical notes from hospitals.

In *Belgium*, the exchange of data is organised at a regional level. Belgium is using a federal reference directory, a national unique patient identifying number and common standards and rules to ensure the interoperability of regional systems and to achieve national coverage. Some health care providers have already implemented the regional systems. The sharing of information within regional EHRs is recent with some functionality implemented one year ago.

In *Iceland*, there is not yet a national electronic health record system. Patient data is exchanged among health care providers and, for laboratory test and medical images, within each health region, excluding the capital area.

In *Korea*, there is no national electronic health record system. Public health centres however, have been adopting the electronic health record system developed as a result of the Public Health and Medical Institution Informatisation Project over the past few years and are now at 100% participation.

In *Mexico*, the four main health care institutions, providing primary and tertiary care, have electronic patient records. A master patient index for three of these institutions is under development in 2012. The architecture of an interoperability platform was designed in 2010 but is not yet implemented. States and other institutions within Mexico have plans to implement interoperability mechanisms.

Minimum data sets

Countries were asked if their national EHR plan included the identification of a defined set of data that could be shared among physicians treating the same patients. This dataset may be called a "minimum data set" and it is intended to support standardisation and sharing of a core set of key information. The existence of a minimum dataset also has important implications for a country's ability to extract consistently defined data from electronic health records to build a national database, should they wish to do so.

Eighteen countries reported having defined a minimum data set for the sharing of electronic patient data (Table D.15). For all of these countries, the minimum dataset would contain patient identifiers, such as a unique patient identifying number and/or a set of identifiers, such as names, addresses and dates of birth; clinically relevant diagnostic concerns, such as chronic conditions and allergies; unique identifiers for health care providers; and patient demographic information, such as dates of birth and sex. Seventeen countries will also include current medications and 16 will include patient clinically relevant procedures, such as surgeries, screening tests and laboratory results. Nine also reported including patient clinically relevant physical characteristics, such as body mass; and ten reported including clinically relevant behaviours, such as smoking and alcohol use. Fewer countries indicated including patient socio-economic data or clinically relevant psychosocial or cultural issues, such as caregivers or stressful events.

Denmark implemented a minimum dataset in conjunction with the EU epSOS project in 2010. It is a common electronic journal for primary and secondary care. This e-journal will include ICD10 coded diagnosis, episodes of care, and treatments, including coded surgery interventions. All patients in Denmark currently have at least some of the elements of the minimum dataset in their electronic record. There is only one minimum data set specification. It is, however, in pilot testing in 2012 and may be subject to change. Also being pilot tested this year is an electronic journal that patients can view. It will contain all of their health care contacts, laboratory tests and medications.

Denmark is also piloting in 2012 the development of a common medications list for patients that will be exchanged among physician offices and hospitals through a common medications database. A database of medications dispensed by private pharmacies (outside hospitals) is already accessible to physicians and hospitals. In Denmark, information on diagnosis from hospital discharges and outpatient clinics is coded using ICD10 and collected in a national repository that is accessible to all hospitals and patients.

Switzerland reported first specifying a minimum dataset in 2009. In addition to the minimum dataset content explored in Table D.15, Switzerland includes within its minimum dataset: blood group, date of transfusion, immunisation status, dates of transplantation, allergies, diseases and disabilities, an address to contact in case of emergency and information on the patient's insurance provision. Fully 90% of patients have an electronic record containing this minimum dataset which is related to the adoption of smart cards.

Singapore first specified a national minimum dataset in 2011; however, in a short time it has been able to implement the dataset for 90% of patients. *Belgium* implemented a minimum dataset in 2003 and about 5% of patients currently have an electronic record containing this dataset. *Indonesia* reported a minimum dataset that was specified in 1996. There is no data on the proportion of patients with an electronic record containing these dataset elements. These three countries all report that there are no other minimum dataset specifications in use.

In the *United Kingdom*, England reported establishing a minimum dataset called the national summary record for the sharing of patient information electronically to support unscheduled (emergency) care. The NHS number will be used to uniquely identify patients. While patient demographic information is not included in the summary record, it is possible to look up the information from the national demographics file. Patient clinically relevant procedures are a possible future addition to this summary record. This minimum dataset was first specified in 2006 and 25% of patients now have a summary record. This minimum dataset and transactions standards for it have been agreed upon for England and there are no other minimum dataset standards in use.

Scotland has specified 14 sets of information to be made available through a clinical portal. Only one minimum dataset has been agreed upon for all patients, which is a patient summary dataset to support emergency care. The minimum dataset was first specified in 2004. Other datasets are published in the NHS data dictionary and are also specified by professional bodies for disease-specific or specialty domains. Scotland is focussing on clinical record headings to define how content can become interoperable.

Finland specified a minimum dataset for sharing information that is planned to be implemented by law by 2014. The current implementation level differs across the country. In addition to the elements identified in Table D.15, Finland has also introduced additional information, such as health risk factors, within its minimum dataset. While socio-economic data is not included in the minimum dataset, it can be linked to the minimum dataset from other data sources when this information is required.

A minimum dataset was first specified by the Clalit HMO in *Israel* in 2002. This minimum dataset was then adopted nationally in 2012. At present, about one-half of patients in Israel have an EHR containing this minimum dataset. *Estonia* first specified a minimum data set in 2008 and reports that 68% of patients have an electronic health record containing this minimum data set.

In the *United States*, there is no single "minimum dataset" that all providers would be required to capture for the purposes of populating an EHR and there are different specifications in use. Health care providers who adopt a certified EHR system, however, may qualify for a financial incentive associated with meeting "minimum use" requirements in accordance with the 2010 HITECH Act. Such certified systems use an established patient summary record format for the purpose of supporting patient transitions among different health care providers. The elements within the summary record relate to standards of care recognised internationally. The information on procedures (such as surgeries, screening tests and laboratory results) included in a patient summary record will vary by patients and their clinical circumstances. In the United States, information on patient socio-economic characteristics is considered valuable for population health and health care decision making, but there is some cultural sensitivity to their inclusion in the patient summary record. There is no data on the proportion of patients with a summary record.

Canada recommends that provinces and territories adopt standards for specifications of a minimum set of data that are based on the internationally recognised HL7 standard for the exchange of information among physicians and hospitals that was recommended in 2002; and pan-Canadian standards for the content of primary health care electronic medical records, that were recommended in 2009. Adoption of these standards by the provinces and territories is voluntary and each province or territory defines their own content for their minimum dataset based on business requirements and the data available from existing EMR systems vendors and hospital information systems vendors operating within their jurisdiction. In addition to promoting interoperability and vocabulary standards, Canada Health Infoway is developing toolkits for both vendors and jurisdictions to use when implementing and managing differences in standards and terminologies. There is no data yet on the proportion of patients covered by a minimum dataset adhering to the standards.

Korea reports the specifications of a minimum dataset are shared among public health centres. This dataset was established in 2008 and the minimum dataset has been fully implemented among these centres, covering 70% of patients. *Mexico* specified the minimum dataset at a national level in 2010; however, the large federal institutions were already using their own minimum information specifications. They are now working toward adoption of the common national specifications. These main institutions estimate that about 30% of patients have an electronic record meeting the national minimum information specifications.

Spain specified a minimum dataset in 2010 and the data set has been incorporated within the electronic health records of an estimated 27% of patients. In addition to the data elements noted here, Spain includes other items within the minimum data set. These include information on risk of domestic violence or child abuse; advanced directives; participation in clinical research studies; and an option to restrict access to clinical information. A minimum dataset was also established for *Sweden* in 2010 and less than 10% of patients were reported to have an electronic health record containing this dataset at the time of the survey. A minimum dataset was recently specified in Portugal (2012) and no patients' electronic records contain it yet. There are no other minimum dataset specifications in use.

The minimum dataset for *Slovakia* is being developed in 2012 and a pilot project to implement it will be part of the second phase of eHealth implementation beginning in 2013. There are no other minimum dataset specifications in use. *Austria* has not yet developed a patient summary record, although it is being designed. There are currently other specifications for minimum datasets in use. *Japan* has also not yet developed a minimum dataset. A taskforce of the IT headquarters within the Cabinet proposed in May 2011 to introduce a minimum dataset within the next few years. The proposed minimum dataset would contain all of the items included for Japan in Table D.15.

In *Poland,* the National Centre for Health Information Systems (CSIOZ) is responsible for developing propositions for the minimum dataset which is planned to be specified by 2014. CSIOZ intends to implement results and standards of the EU epSOS project and is awaiting decisions of the EU Digital Agenda for 2020. Poland does have a current problem of multiple specifications for a minimum dataset, including data required by the NHF and also other datasets connected with specific health problems (such as cancer and mental diseases). The National Centre for Health Information Systems is working to solve problems of inconsistency of regulations and requirements.

France reports no minimum dataset specification as part of the national electronic health record and there are also no other sets of minimum dataset specifications in use. In France, patients specify the elements of their electronic documents to be shared. There is also no minimum dataset in *Germany*. Datasets are defined by organisations of health care professionals and are mostly specific to the care situation. There are, however, some similarities across datasets in terms of patient identification, and reporting diagnosis and medications used in communication of reports and discharge letters. The probable existence of more than one specification for a minimum dataset is not viewed as a problem. *Slovenia* has also not specified a minimum dataset.

Structured data elements within electronic records

One of the early worries about the usability of data within electronic health records for patient care was the use of free flowing text. Early implementations of electronic records provided physicians with essentially an electronic means to record clinical notes. As interest in sharing records grew, so did the need to ensure that health care providers could access, and quickly and accurately interpret, a record created by another health care provider. The use of structured data entry that follows clinical terminology standards emerged as a solution.

In this study, less than half of countries participating have succeeded in implementing a system where all electronic health records have key data elements that are structured and follow a clinical terminology standard, such as diagnosis, medications and laboratory tests. Most countries, however, report that at least some of their electronic records have reached this level. Less common is the use of terminology standards for medical imaging results, surgical procedures and patient characteristics, behaviours and psychosocial or cultural needs.

The use of structured data that follows a common terminology standard enables data to be analysed using statistical techniques. Countries with more than one terminology standard in use would need a reference to map data from one standard to another, in order to build databases and conduct analysis. Many countries are contending with the use of multiple standards for the same data element. This is because legacy systems may no longer conform to current national standards or to the recommended version of a national standard. It is expensive for health care providers to upgrade their systems when national standards change and it can also be difficult to persuade vendors of legacy systems to upgrade them, if there are no incentives or penalties in place. Where data is unstructured, and where statistical analysis is desired, the use of human coders or sophisticated technologies would be needed to create structured data.

Thirteen countries indicated that diagnosis information is entered into all electronic health records in a structured manner using a terminology standard; eleven indicated the same for medications information; and ten for laboratory test results (Figure 4.1, Table D.16). The number rises to 21 countries reporting structured data for diagnosis, medications and laboratory test results, when countries who reported some or most records will have elements entered in a structured format are also considered.

Less frequently reported is the use of structured data for other types of information in electronic health records. Eight countries reported that all electronic health records will have structured data for medical image results, surgical procedures and socio-economic information. Five countries indicated that all records have structured elements for physical characteristics, such as body mass, and health behaviours, such as smoking and alcohol

Figure 4.1. **Number of countries reporting elements are structured using clinical terminology standards**

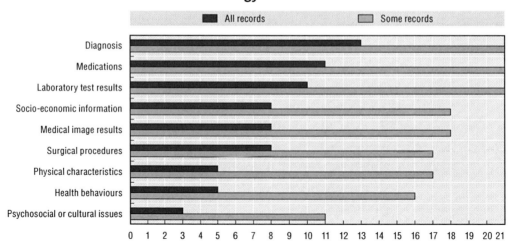

Source: OECD HCQI Questionnaire on Secondary Use of Health Data: Electronic Health Records, 2012.
StatLink http://dx.doi.org/10.1787/888932796625

use. Three countries reported all records to have structured data for psychosocial or cultural issues.

In *France*, all elements of the electronic health record are structured; however, free text can be added by the patient in a box called "patient's personal expression". This enables patients to contribute content to their records. France has not experienced barriers to the introduction of one set of national terminology standards. *Estonia* also reports that structured data is used for virtually all of the data elements investigated here. It took time to get all standards to be used and, further, it is resource consuming to ensure that the standards used are kept up-to-date.

All elements of the electronic health record in *Slovakia* are structured elements, with the exception of some unstructured entry of socio-economic data. The country-wide deployment of the national electronic health record will resolve existing inconsistencies in terminology standards in current use. Slovakia has experienced some resistance from the medical community to the terminology standards adopted for the national system.

Denmark also relies on structured data elements for key components of its electronic health record, with some records containing unstructured data for socio-economic status, physical characteristics, behaviours and psychosocial or cultural issues. A recent initiative is the introduction of a common electronic medications list. This list has been implemented in three regions in Denmark and will be used in all regions by the end of 2012. The common list will be shared between hospitals and primary care and medical specialist physician offices through a National Common Medication Database. In Denmark, there is a distinction between the terminology standards in use in primary and secondary care. The introduction of national terminology standards is challenging because it is costly to change systems using existing classifications and terminology.

Iceland also relies on structured data for key components of its electronic health record. Iceland reported that there is a problem of inconsistency in terminologies across the country. For example, both NCSP and NCSP-IS codes are being used to code surgical procedures. Further, local coding systems for disease symptoms are in use in some settings. *Israel* reports that inconsistencies arise in terminology standards when national standards, such as ICD-9-CM, are modified at the local level. Israel plans to introduce ICD-10 and SNOMED, however, there are barriers to overcome, including the costs to change legacy systems.

Singapore reported a mix of structured and unstructured elements, with medical imaging and surgical procedures entered as free text. There are different electronic medical record systems with different localised content and nomenclature across clusters of hospitals in Singapore. A national consensus is being worked on for a nation-wide implementation of standards in several areas, including laboratory test results and medications.

Indonesia has only structured data elements in electronic health records, with the exception of allowing the capture of clinical notes. Hospitals in Indonesia have adopted HL7 standards however primary health care is using different standards which vary by local area. The use of different standards is a barrier to interoperability.

In *Japan*, the "My Hospital Everywhere" project listed the data elements to be included in electronic health records. The first phase would implement pharmaceutical data, and the second phase, laboratory data and discharge summaries. Image data, such as CT and MRI results, were not recommended for inclusion because of the size of the files. Instead, reports of findings from these images would be recorded by doctors. The terminology standards that may be adopted by Japan have not yet been set. There is a concern that Japan's current coding system for insurance claims may not be consistent with the content of the electronic health records.

Results reported for *Korea* refer to the standards for electronic health records in public health centres. These standards were developed through the Public Health and Medical Institution Informatisation Project. These standards are not yet used by private sector hospitals and there is no policy to motivate them to adopt these standards, particularly given the risks they would incur in changing from their existing standards. Some networks of health organisations in Korea are sharing clinical information electronically using their own proprietary standards. A pilot project lead by the Seoul National University Bundang Hospital, involves 35 clinics in Seongnam City and Yongin City in the sharing of patient information electronically including diagnosis, laboratory and medical imaging results, and prescription medications. Data transfer and semantic standards are being used including HL7 CDA for data transfer, ICD for diagnostic coding, DICOM for images, specific codes for laboratory tests and medications, and fee codes.

In *Belgium*, there is one set of clinical terminology standards in use for electronic health records. There have been some difficulties in introducing the national standards, including that the SNOMED-CT based on the Belgian CMV is under development and will be incorporated into the EHR semantic requirements once it is completed. Syntactic and contextual interfaces also need to be developed for electronic record systems, in order to increase the adoption of the national terminology standards.

Finland also has one set of standards for electronic health record terminology, with all records having structured diagnosis, laboratory tests and medical images elements, and most records having structured elements for medications and surgical procedures. A difficulty in the introduction of national standards includes addressing concerns of clinicians about the usability of the terminology. It is important for vendors to work toward strategies that enable clinicians to more easily enter structured data.

There are inconsistencies across *Austria* in the terminology standards used for electronic health records. It is a national commitment to address this discrepancy, however, the costs of migrating to new standards is a barrier to change.

Slovenia notes that there are inconsistencies between electronic record systems across the country in the terminology standards used. Providers of software solutions have been using different information models and datasets. Effort is underway at the national level to establish a common set of standards and terminologies. Challenges to progress include insufficient knowledge and financial resources. *Spain* reported that state law to establish a minimum data set was published on September 10, 2010 and has been in force since March 3, 2012. The law concretely defines standards used in clinical reports across the country; however, local implementation still lacks sufficient resources to complete the effort. While there are no terminology standards for surgical procedures within the national EHR, this information is provided through an alternative dataset.

Portugal reports that there are inconsistencies in the clinical terminology standards used across the country and that there are difficulties introducing national terminology standards, including insufficient awareness of the value of standardising terminology and the costs associated with changing existing IT systems.

Poland is still in a phase of analysis in advance of making final decisions on the use of terminology standards. Despite the use of an official terminology for laboratory results that is supported by the Association of Laboratory Medicine, there remain local discrepancies in the terminology used across laboratories in Poland. Regional projects are underway to reach a decision on standards for laboratory results. Poland also notes experiencing pressure from the lobbying efforts of companies advocating the adoption of particular terminologies.

In *Canada*, health care is a provincial and territorial responsibility and the 13 jurisdictions have the flexibility to adopt their own standards. As a result, different versions of standards are being implemented by jurisdiction. This is partly the result of differences in existing legacy hospital and clinical information systems, which may pose barriers to the adoption of new versions of standards. The use of structured data is inconsistent across levels of care and provincial and territorial jurisdictions. There are multiple vendors of electronic medical record systems and hospital information systems in Canada. As a result, structured data for diagnosis is not consistently available, but is more available in the acute care sector. The same inconsistency applies to other data elements as well. In some cases, laboratory test results and medical imaging results may be attached to the record as a PDF document. Some jurisdictions have, however, implemented a local laboratory information system and/or a drug information system that captures structured data. Other barriers to the introduction of national terminology standards in Canada include the complexity of the SNOMED-CT reference sets, encouraging and managing change at the level of health care providers, and the ability of vendors of legacy systems to incorporate terminology standards into their products.

The *United States* reported working to sensitise health care providers to the importance of capturing data in structured fields, such as medications and diagnosis. Anecdotal reports indicate that these key fields are sometimes still entered as free text in some electronic record systems. The United States is also working to ease the use of structured fields for many data elements. Socioeconomic characteristics and clinically relevant psychosocial or cultural issues may be entered by physicians as free text in some electronic record systems. There are multiple vendors of electronic record systems in the United States. The capabilities of the systems vary according to the target end user of the system, with products for clinicians more likely to have structured data elements for medications and laboratory results, while products targeted to public and private payers may not have structure for clinical elements. The federal government has mandated the use of terminology standards in medical records and these are the standards reported here (Table D.17). As a result, there is no inconsistency across regions in the clinical terminology standards used.

There are no semantic requirements for the electronic health record system in *Switzerland*. Information may be contributed in a structured or an unstructured format. Also, the terminology standards used differ across health care providers. The different needs and priorities of users of electronic records would make it difficult to introduce national terminology standards.

In *Sweden*, no terminology standards are being used today on a national level for documentation in the EHR, but the national strategy is to increase the use of standardised terminologies. The aim is to use SNOMED CT as a terminology standard on a national level, but the implementation of SNOMED CT is still under development. In connection with the

Swedish strategy for eHealth, the National Board of Health and Welfare is responsible for the development and management of the national information structure and the interdisciplinary terminology for health and social care, including SNOMED CT. The aim of the Swedish national strategy for eHealth is to ensure efficient information supply in health and social care. The National Board of Health and Welfare will, within the strategy, assume overall national and strategic responsibility for making individually based patient and user information clearer and more easily measurable and accessible. The work involves defining and describing the content of appropriate health and social care documentation. The interdisciplinary terminology includes concepts and terms that have been agreed on a national basis and published in the Board's terminology database, statistical classifications and coding systems that have been agreed on a national and international basis and the Swedish translation of the clinical terminology SNOMED CT. The interdisciplinary terminology provides the tools for information that is created around an individual and his/her health to be described in a uniform and clear manner. The detail and structure of SNOMED CT creates conditions to meet the various activities' requirements of concepts and terms in electronic records. The interdisciplinary terminology also provides the bio psychosocial model contained in the ICF, which is used to describe functioning, disability and health.

In the *United Kingdom*, England has implemented a standard for key elements of the electronic record including medications, diagnosis, laboratory tests, medical images and surgical procedures. There are differences in the use of consistent standards, however, between primary and secondary care in both England and Scotland. There is no business case in Scotland for decision makers to accept a single terminology standard or to change existing systems. There is also no agreement among stakeholders as to which terminology will suit all domains. At present, local READ codes are used in primary care and in some secondary care settings. ICD and OPCS codes are used for in-patients in secondary care settings. SNOMED-CT and ICF are both being considered for future use.

In *Mexico*, electronic records for patients began to be introduced about 15 years ago. At that time there were no regulations to govern the adoption of EHR systems. As a result, health care providers implemented terminology or vocabulary that suited their business requirements, including the adoption of different international standards across providers. A barrier to the introduction of national terminology standards is the training of professionals to use new vocabularies correctly.

Terminology standards in use

There is considerable variety across countries in the terminology standards used for electronic health records. Some countries lean more toward the adoption of international terminology standards, while others rely more on national coding systems (Table D.17). Diagnosis is one element where there seems to be greater harmony across countries, with 19 reporting the use of ICD-10 codes and five reporting SNOMED codes. Thirteen countries are using DIACOM standards for the electronic storage of medical images. There is also some consistency in the use of international standards for laboratory tests and medications, with 13 countries using LOINC codes for laboratory results and twelve using WHO ATC codes for medications.

In addition to mapping to the code sets reported in Table D.17, *Finland* is also using ISO standards for medical aids and for languages and countries; *Mexico* is mapping to the WHO

International Classification of Functioning (ICF); *Belgium* is undertaking projects to harmonise SNOMED CT to WHO and local coding requirements; *Korea* is mapping the Korean Standard Terminology of Medicine (KOSTOM) codes to Unified Medical Language System (UMLS) codes; and *France* is mapping primary care encounter codes to SNOMED vf 3.5 and DRC. *Finland* reports that a national code server is used to provide a large range of codes and to assist with data harmonisation.

Unique identifiers within EHR systems

Unique identifiers are crucial to the development of longitudinal electronic health records, in order to ensure that the data within the record is complete and accurate for patients, as they move among health care providers, health insurers, and regions within their country and over time. They are also important for statistical purposes to identify unique patients and to conduct, where approved, linkages of data across more than one data source. It may also become increasingly important to identify the health care professionals entering data into electronic health records, for purposes of ensuring and validating the completeness and accuracy of the record and for statistics related to quality, efficiency and performance.

Belgium, Estonia, Finland, France, Iceland, Indonesia, Korea, Poland, Singapore, Slovakia, Slovenia, Sweden, Switzerland and the United Kingdom (England) report both a unique national identifying number for patients that will be used to ensure the identity of patients to build their electronic health record; and a unique identifying number for health care professionals entering data into electronic health record systems.

Poland will use the PESEL number, which is granted to citizens at birth and to all legal inhabitants, to establish the unique identity of patients to build electronic health records. Poland also assigns a unique ID number to health care professionals including, physicians, nurses, dentists, laboratory specialists and other regulated medical professionals. This ID will be used to establish the identity of medical professionals entering data into electronic health records. A registry of health care providers provides a unique ID number for health care facilities.

In the *United Kingdom*, a unique identifying number for patients and providers is being used for electronic health records in England. In Scotland there are unique identifying numbers for primary care physicians. There are also unique ID numbers for doctors and nurses in secondary care, but these numbers are not routinely used in electronic patient record systems. In *Sweden*, the use of a unique health care provider ID number within electronic health records is not yet fully developed at the national level.

Denmark, Germany, Israel, Portugal, Spain and Mexico report a unique identifying number of patients within electronic health records, but not yet for health care providers. *Denmark* has an ID number for authorised doctors, nurses and midwives but it is not used in local electronic medical records and is only partly used for some centralised services. Denmark is working on how to implement the general use of this authorising ID in electronic records. *Germany* reports a unique identifying number for patients that may be used for electronic records. There is no ID for health care professionals entering data into electronic records; however there are certificate numbers on health professional's membership cards. *Mexico* has a unique identifying number for patients and will use the national population code to identify health professionals; however the identification of health professionals is not mandatory for electronic health records. In *Israel*, the identification of the health provider is done within the EMR of the organisation the provider belongs to. There is no data entry within the EHR and therefore no need for a provider ID. In Spain, a national registry for health care professionals is under development. In *Portugal*, there are identifiers for the professional group entering data into the record (doctor, nurse, etc.).

Austria is developing a unique ID for both patients and health professionals. The patient ID will be an amalgamation of a national and local numbers and will be used to create a patient registry. The e-Government plan for Austria also includes a unique ID number for health care providers and a registry of providers will also be created.

The *Netherlands* does not have a unique identifying number for patients, but does have other identifying variables that may be used for research requiring data linkage. There is a unique identifying number for health professionals in the Netherlands which is used for health insurance claims. *Japan* has an identifying number for patients but because it is composed of names and dates of birth it is not able to uniquely identify persons.

There is no national unique patient or health care provider identifying number in *Canada*. Patients have a unique health insurance number within each of the provinces and territories. Health care providers are also uniquely identified within each jurisdiction. Regulatory bodies within each jurisdiction manage the identity numbers. Each jurisdiction is defining their own approach to the use of identifiers within electronic health records.

The *United States* does not have a unique patient identifying number and the expenditure of government resources to develop such a number is prohibited by law. Patient summary records and medical records contain patient identifiers: names, addresses and dates of birth that can be used for confirmation or probabilistic data linkage. Health care provider identifying information is not required for every summary record for exchange. There is a national provider identifier system for providers reimbursed for public health care programs and the same system is available and widely used by private health care insurance and care providers.

Smart cards

Smart cards contain an embedded microprocessor that can assist with secure identification of patients and providers to ensure accurate health records and can enable patients to have secure access to services or records on-line. Some countries may include or consider future inclusion of elements of a patients' minimum data set directly within the card, which can serve to assist patients with emergency care.

Belgium, Estonia, France, Israel (partial implementation), *Spain, Slovenia, Switzerland* and the *United Kingdom* (England) have introduced smart cards for both patients and health professionals. Switzerland notes that 80% of mandatory insured persons already have a smart card. Similarly, in *Spain*, about 80% of patients are now covered by a smart card (citizens' dni-e). The distribution of smart cards to providers in Spain is underway. *Israel's* HMOs have introduced smart cards for patients and health care providers. In the United Kingdom (England), the number of patients with a smart card is still low.

Germany has distributed smart cards to patients and smart cards for health professionals are available. *Portugal* has introduced smart cards for patients in some services and is considering the introduction of smart cards for health professionals. *Finland* and *Sweden* have introduced smart cards for health professionals, but not for patients.

Poland plans to implement an electronic ID for patients and health professionals. *Austria* is also introducing smart cards for patients. The *Canadian* province of British

Columbia will introduce a smartcard for patients in 2012 that will enable patients to securely access their health records on-line. Other Canadian provinces are conducting pilot studies of the introduction of smartcards for patients and providers.

Status and technical challenges of database creation from electronic health records today

Twelve countries are using data from electronic health record systems to build databases that can be used for health care monitoring and research and four are planning to do so in the future (Table D.19). A potential challenge within some countries will be the legal and policy frameworks to build national databases involving a large number of database custodians. While many countries report a small number of data custodians, Belgium, Spain, Sweden, the United Kingdom and the United States report more than 20.

Most countries participating in this study (16 countries) cite legal issues as a barrier to the creation and analysis of databases from electronic health records. These challenges will be explored further in the next chapter.

Fourteen countries are also sufficiently concerned with the quality of data within electronic health records to identify this as a barrier to database creation. Other barriers include lack of financial resources or technically skilled personnel to create databases (nine countries), or to de-identify the data to protect patient's data privacy (seven countries).

The complexity of the development, analysis and de-identification of databases, as well as the complexity of assuring requirements of data privacy protection are correctly addressed, may motivate some jurisdictions to identify one or more third parties to assume complex responsibilities. In this study, only three countries have signalled the use of a third party, separate from government, insurance and practitioners, to take responsibility for the creation of databases from EHR records and to undertake data de-identification. Four countries have identified a third party to approve or decline requests for access to data.

Finland reports extensive information infrastructure of person-level health data in established registries. Finland has begun to extract data from electronic health records to populate these registries beginning with the creation of a primary care registry (AvoHilmo). Challenges to database creation include that the register keeper needs to have a legal status and that resources to develop databases are not always sufficient.

Iceland's Directorate of Health has developed a set of registries that rely on data collected from EHR systems. These include national registries for cancer, births, contacts with primary health care centres, patients, prescription diseases and communicable diseases that are all in the custody of a small number of organisations. In *Iceland*, concerns reported include that data are frequently not coded in a timely manner, there is a lack of internal data quality audits within each health care institution and there are financial barriers to building capacity to de-identify databases from EHR records.

Sweden reports over 100 clinical research databases and quality of care registries that depend upon electronic health records. National health databases, such as the National Patient Register, in Sweden also rely upon some elements within electronic health records. As a result, there are more than 20 custodians of databases created from EHR systems. Sweden has reported concerns with the quality of EHR data that may limit database creation and challenges due to a lack of resources to create databases.

In *Slovenia*, data elements within EMRs (such as chronic disease risk factors) are exported to national health databases. Data elements within the EHR system related to quality of care, such as prevention efforts, are exported to national registries, such as the registries of chronic disease risk factors and cardiovascular disease. Custodians of databases from electronic records include the National Institute of Public Health and clinical organisations for particular databases and registries (i.e. oncology, cardiovascular disease). Challenges to database creation in Slovenia include national level shortages of skills and funding and the lack of structured clinical data.

Korea's Public Health and Medical Institution Informatisation Project involves the creation of databases of laboratory test data, procedures, medications, injections, physical therapy, and causes of diseases. Vaccination history is monitored in co-operation with the Korea Centre for Disease Control and Prevention. National health examination data are shared with the National Health Insurance Corporation. Korea has reported concerns with the quality of EHR data that may limit database creation.

In the *United Kingdom*, there are several databases that have been created from data from electronic health records including, in England, the Secondary Uses Service, the Renal Registry, Cancer Registries and research databases; and in Scotland, the SCI Diabetes Disease Register, GP IT Systems – Quality Outcomes Framework data, GP Practice Team Information (PTI), Primary Care Clinical Information (PCCIU), and other disease registers. More than 20 organisations are in custody of databases developed from electronic health records. Challenges to the development of databases from electronic health records include records that are not sufficiently complete or coded and are, therefore, difficult to analyse. In Scotland, this problem is noted to be gradually reducing with improved coding. There are also concerns with the potential disclosure of confidential information and ensuring that appropriate safeguards are in place.

Portugal reports that a central database with data from electronic records for all cases admitted to public hospitals is currently being used to monitor health care management and health care quality. Electronic records are also populating databases related to prescribing and to other smaller disease-specific registries. Overall there are a small number of custodians of these databases including the Central Administration of the Health System and scientific societies. In Portugal, there are concerns with the quality of data entered into electronic records that limit database development.

Canada reports that a few national chronic disease databases have been created, such as the Canadian Centre for Health Information's Canadian Primary Care Sentinel Surveillance Network (CPCSSN). This database is Canada's first multi-disease electronic record surveillance system which has been created to monitor a set of key chronic diseases. To create this database, data is extracted from primary care physician offices' electronic medical record systems for a subset of providers and their patients. Some provinces and territories have created jurisdictional research data centres where databases may be analysed that have been created from electronic health record systems. At a national level, the Canadian Institute for Health Information creates national databases for monitoring health system performance and patient safety and for research. Data submitted by provinces and territories to develop these database may derive from jurisdictional electronic health record systems.

The National Health Fund in *Poland* has created a large database from electronic records related to reimbursement purposes. This data had been poorly used for statistical or research purposes, however, two years ago several disease registries, including a cancer registry, we prepared from extractions of sub-sets of this larger database. Co-ordination remains an issue, as the roll out of the national EHR is a large project composed of many local initiatives. There is also the challenge of critical opinions to the creation of databases that are not always based on knowledge or experience.

At a regional level in *Spain*, some authorities are establishing data marts or data repositories from EHR systems to support public health, health system management, evaluation and other uses. Data from EHR systems has had limited use for research, and most research studies have been at a local level. There are more than 20 custodians of databases from EHR systems in Spain involving regional health authorities and local custodians. Spain reports challenges to database creation from electronic health records that include concerns with the quality of data; the use of diversified formats, vocabularies and terminologies; lack of support for standardised terminologies; strong bureaucracies and the lack of written policies to support applicants seeking access to data; and ICT providers who may charge health care providers or researchers for access to data for secondary uses.

France is not yet building databases from electronic health records, but intends to do so as this is part of the final phase of the national EHR strategy. There is currently a collaboration project of the National Institute for Cancer and ASIP Santé to build a database of shared oncology records. There will be only one data custodian to develop the databases. French law protects the privacy and security of personal health data and limits analysis of electronic health records to research purposes. *Estonia* is currently implementing database creation and is regularly using data from the national electronic health record system for public health monitoring. *Slovakia* is also planning to build databases from electronic health records in future.

In the *United States*, various providers and professional organisations have implemented clinical data registries. The extent to which these registries are populated with data extracted from electronic health records is not known. The Office of the National Co-ordinator is working to enable and promote the availability of EHR-based submissions to clinical registries and quality measurement systems that are sponsored or otherwise supported by the government. In terms of the technical feasibility of building databases from electronic health records, standards and applications remain in development that will be needed to implement distributed query. Standards and implementation specifications for the routine production and reporting of both quality measures and clinical data registries are in development. Further, some clinical data elements are captured in ways that may require normalisation to compile records across multiple providers. The United States Office of the National Co-ordinator for Health Information Technology (ONC) is engaged in or sponsoring research to increase the ease of routinely capturing health and clinical data in standard formats and with standard terminologies that could eventually reduce the need for normalisation.

Denmark has established an extensive system of established registries that rely on forms completed by health care providers or extractions from existing health information systems to populate them. Considerable will and financial resources would be needed to move away from the current system to a new approach where extractions from electronic health records would populate key databases. Within *Israel*, data is collected for analysis from hospitals and HMO provider EMR systems and not from the HER system.

Singapore reports that variability in the quality of EHR records across institutions; the policy and guidelines needed for data de-identification; the need to establish data governance; the duty of care of users of electronic health records; the acceptance of users and other privacy-related issues, are all challenges that need to be addressed to build and analyse data from electronic health records. In *Switzerland*, challenges to the development of databases from electronic health records include a lack of structured data in electronic medical and health records and limitations to interoperability.

In *Germany*, personal medical data is only to be used for the purposes for which it was originally collected and electronic health data is collected for medical care. Direct access to electronic health record data for other purposes is restricted and only possible when explicitly allowed by law. An example is data extraction for billing purposes. Certain datasets, however, may be extracted in a controlled way and used for other purposes within the constraints of the Data Protection Act. These constraints are not barriers as they are necessary regulations to protect patient's privacy. For the monitoring of health care quality in Germany, the approach has been to extract data from electronic medical records within individual health care organisations. Such data are anonymised or pseudonymised for approved research projects and the approach has been to have national procedures for the creation and management of pseudonyms. To evaluate the complete care process, data linkage at the level of individual patients may take place for approved projects, with merging based on a common pseudonym.

Estonia also expects challenges to database creation from electronic health records. These include a lack of human resources to create databases and concerns with both the quality and patient coverage of discharge letters within the records (epicrises). *France* reported that it is still too early to determine if there may be resource or data quality barriers to database creation.

Canadian jurisdictions have been focussed on deploying their electronic health record systems and this effort has required a greater need for IT resources that are skilled in the development of databases. As well, potential data users will increasingly need to be skilled in data and analytics. These skill sets are still growing in Canada. Existing investments in legacy systems and the ability of health care providers to incorporate clinical terminology standards continues to be a challenge for all jurisdictions and their EHR vendors. While there are standards for interoperability, these standards are still evolving as they relate to data capture (such as structure, format, terminology and coding). Lack of standardisation will impact on the ability to use electronic health records for large-scale analysis.

There will be challenges in the *Netherlands* to the development of databases from electronic health records. These relate to issues of data privacy and ownership of data. Further, monitoring and research often lacks resources, not only to appoint researchers but also to support the use of the data. Past experience has shown that health care providers, who will be the custodians of the data, do not easily allow access to data for projects conducted by research institutes. A further difficulty is that, until now, the possibility of building databases for research from electronic health records was not taken into account in the development of electronic health records.

Analysis of data from electronic health records for statistical purposes and evaluations of data usability

Many countries (11) have already implemented a process to evaluate the usability of data from electronic health records for statistical purposes and many (13) are already regularly using data extracted from electronic health records for some aspects of national monitoring or research about population health and health care services (Table D.20). Thirteen countries reported regular use of electronic health records for public health monitoring; eleven countries reported use for research; and nine countries reported regular use for patient safety monitoring. Less common was regular use for health system performance monitoring (seven countries); supporting physician treatment decisions (six countries); and facilitating or contributing to clinical trials (four countries).

Finland reported undertaking continuous work to evaluate the usability of data from electronic health records. This work is necessary because the structure of the records and of the registries is being standardised. Finland conducts analysis of electronic health records on a regular basis in order to conduct infectious disease surveillance, monitoring patient safety, and supporting physician treatment decisions by enabling physicians to query data. Finland is working toward the use of electronic health records from primary care to monitor the performance of the primary care system. For secondary care, existing registers are used for this purpose. Research to improve patient care, health system efficiency or population health care is conducted in Finland typically only on a local or regional level from electronic health records. At a national level, existing registries are analysed for these purposes.

Slovenia is currently using data from electronic health records for public health monitoring, such as monitoring the number of patients with chronic diseases and risk factors for patients with certain chronic disease types; and for health system performance monitoring, such as tracking office visits of patients with certain chronic diseases and monitoring overall usage of primary, secondary and tertiary care. Electronic records have also been used in Slovenia to monitor patient safety and to conduct research, however, not on a regular basis.

Electronic health records are regularly used in *Sweden* for secondary analysis across all of the dimensions explored here (see Table D.20). National clinical databases of patient problems, medical interventions, and outcomes after treatment; and the National Patient Register of hospital in-patient and outpatient care, form the backbone of Sweden's national monitoring and research infrastructure from electronic health records.

In *Poland*, there is already experience in the development of disease registries from electronic medical records including databases for acute cardiac episodes, haemophilia patients and cancer screening, as well as pilot testing of drug utilisation reports and some published research and data quality evaluation. In Poland, a research project has compared the quality of data from electronic health records with data from the services reimbursement system for the building of a cancer registry. This research has explored the quality of the data to study treatment patterns and outcome measures for cancer care.

The *United Kingdom* is evaluating the usability of data from electronic health records for analytical purposes in both England and Scotland. England, for example, is looking at the ability to re-use SNOMED coding for analytical purposes. England reports capturing central summaries of patient encounters from primary care physician offices as part of an initiative to monitor primary care quality and patient outcomes (Quality and Outcomes

Framework). These summary care records are available for all of England to authorised users. Scotland reports extracting data from the Scottish Care Information system to populate a diabetes reporting system for Scotland. Scotland reports extracting data on hospital in-patients to contribute diagnosis and treatment information to a morbidity database for Scotland. Data from electronic health records currently contribute to public health monitoring in the United Kingdom, including the generation of reports on a practice by practice basis. Electronic records from the reimbursement system in England and from the General Practice system in Scotland are used to monitor health system performance. Data from electronic health records is also used to support physician treatment decisions, such as a cardiac clinical audit in England, and to contribute to research projects involving clinical trials. Other types of research projects with electronic health records may also be approved, including data linkage to undertake risk stratification.

Belgium reported intending to establish a process to evaluate the usability of electronic health records but not until the semantic interoperability layer has been largely deployed. Public health monitoring and monitoring of patient safety are not yet included in the national plan for the EHR, however, it is part of the functionalities of the EHR that have currently been certified. The semantic interoperability layer will need to be first deployed before wide adoption of the use of EHR data for public health monitoring. While Belgium monitors health system performance and conducts research to improve patient care, health system efficiency and population health, data originate mainly from social security records and sentinel sites rather than from electronic health records. Electronic health records are used to support physician treatment decisions by enabling queries to look at groups of patients; such studies are limited to specific use cases, for example, a study of nephrology. EHR records may also be used in future to facilitate and contribute to clinical trials, but such uses will not be possible before the semantic interoperability layer is deployed.

The *United States* is developing, at a national level, methods and mechanisms to collect data from electronic health records for the purposes of quality measurement, patient safety monitoring, surveillance and public health purposes. These methods and mechanisms are in development and are not yet in nationwide use. As part of these methods and mechanisms, data validation and other quality assurances will be undertaken to ensure that the quality of the data is sufficient to support the purposes for which it is being collected and analysed. Methods and mechanisms for supporting physician treatment decisions, by enabling them to query data to examine care and outcomes for similar patient groups, have been implemented in some provider systems in the United States. The methods, mechanisms and governance structures needed to implement this as a national norm have not yet been established. Infrastructure, methods and mechanisms to support the use of data from electronic health records for population health and health services research have not been established at the national level.

At the national level in *Canada*, no data from electronic health records is being used on a regular basis for secondary analysis. However, there is a Primary Health Care Voluntary Reporting System at the Canadian Institute for Health Information where physicians may volunteer to submit data from electronic medical records which is analysed and reported back with key indicators. A supporting electronic tool also allows physicians to query their own data and drill down to understand trends. The Canadian Institute for Health Information also develops and maintains national databases of patient records from existing information systems that are used to report on many aspects of health and health care. As previously noted, jurisdictions within Canada may further develop the secondary uses of data from electronic heath records. Some have implemented public health care quality reporting.

In *Portugal*, electronic health records contribute, in a limited way, to public health monitoring and to health system performance monitoring through analysis of the hospital in-patient and prescribing components of the electronic health record system. There is also progressively greater use of electronic records from primary care for these purposes. Quality of care indicators are also developed from electronic records. These data sources have also been used for research projects.

In *Singapore*, the evaluation of the usability of data from electronic health records for the development of databases and data analysis is part of the national EHR project; this includes key patient indicators (KPI) and metrics. *Switzerland* has established a process for the evaluation of the usability of electronic health records to contribute to cancer registration, but has not explored other usability dimensions. *Slovakia* and *Estonia* have included in their plans for their national EHR systems to both evaluate the usability of data to develop databases and have planned to conduct secondary analysis of data from electronic health records. *Iceland* reported progress toward the creation of a national patient data warehouse from EHRs where data quality evaluation processes will be included. Iceland is currently regularly using data from its EHR to build registries, as previously noted, and to monitor communicable diseases.

Korea reported that the Public Health and Medical Institution Informatisation Project established the process for the evaluation of the usability of the electronic health record data to develop and analyse databases. Although vendors of EHR systems offer tools for database development and analysis, there are governmental controls as all analysis of EHR data from the project is performed by two authorities, the Korea Health and Welfare Information Service and the Ministry of Public Administration. The Security and National Information Society Agency also manages and controls personal information security.

Currently, EHR data is used in *Indonesia* to develop national health profiles and for research. *Indonesia* notes that the process for procurement for EHR systems is used to require evaluation of the usability of data from the EHR system for the development and analysis of databases. *Japan* notes that national claims databases may be approved for use for public health monitoring and for research currently.

Strengthening Health Information Infrastructure for Health Care
Quality Governance
Good Practices, New Opportunities and Data Privacy Protection
Challenges
© OECD 2013

Chapter 5

Protection of privacy in the collection and use of personal health data

Cross-country variation in the use of personal health data is linked to differences in risk management in the trade off between risks to individual patient privacy and risks to public health and the good governance of health systems. Informed consent has become the pillar for protecting individual's autonomy. The requirement to obtain patient consent is often either impossible or impracticable when studies involve the linkage of national historical databases. There is significant variation across countries in granting an exemption to patient consent requirements for projects within the public interest. Among the 19 countries participating in this part of the study, ten countries report that an exemption to patient consent requirements is possible under existing law; while seven countries report that an exemption is not possible without introducing new authorising legislation. There are also concerns with compliance with the legality and appropriateness of sharing data between government authorities that either prevent data linkages (four countries) or result in lengthy and complex negotiations (four countries).

This chapter discusses the OECD guiding principles for the protection and transborder flow of personal data and cross-country differences in the application of these principles found in these OECD studies, including in the conduct of data linkage activities, the sharing of data and in the development of data from electronic health records.

The statistical data for Israel are supplied by and under the responsibility of the relevant Israeli authorities. The use of such data by the OECD is without prejudice to the status of the Golan Heights, East Jerusalem and Israeli settlements in the West Bank under the terms of international law.

All 19 countries responding to the OECD study of the secondary use of personal health data report legal and policy restrictions on the collection and use of personal health data that reflect the importance of the protection of data privacy and confidentiality (see Annexes A and B). This chapter is not in any way exhaustive of the full legal frameworks in place within countries. What it presents, instead, are the views of officials responsible for data protection and of health researchers that were developed from their personal experience of working within their legal frameworks to make decisions about or to undertake projects requiring the secondary use of personal health data.

Risk management in any decision-making process involves identifying the risks and evaluating their potential costs and benefits (ISO, 2009). It does not imply avoiding all risks, but making an informed decision under uncertainty. Uncertainty is unavoidable in decision making about the collection and use of personal health data. Nonetheless, avoiding or delaying decision making carries its own risks, in terms of compromising patient safety and the quality of health care. To protect the population from the spread of infectious diseases, many countries have weighted the risks and have incorporated terms within their legislative frameworks to make explicit the need for some loss of individual data privacy in the event of a disease outbreak. For the monitoring of the quality and safety of health care, the weighing of risks in decision making about legislative frameworks has not always received the same attention. Figure 5.1 presents a schematic view of the continuum of risk associated with the collection and use of personal health data in relation to two key outcomes: the protection of individuals' data privacy and monitoring and reporting on the safety and effectiveness of health care.

On the one hand, the collection and use of personal health data presents a number of important risks to the privacy of individuals. These risks relate to the potential harms to individuals that could result from the misuse of their personal health information. Losses to individuals can be severe and can include financial and psychosocial harms. Financial harms can result from discrimination in health insurance or employment. Psychosocial harms could include embarrassment, stigma and loss of reputation, resulting in isolation and stress. Disclosures of personal data can also increase individual's risk of experiencing identity theft. Less discussed, but of social relevance, is also the risk of loss of public confidence in government and its institutions that could result from misuses of individuals' personal health records, including a loss of confidence in the health care system.

On the other hand, there are significant risks to individuals and to societies when health information assets are not developed, or are unused or are very difficult to use. Societies lose the opportunity to monitor and report on their population's health and the quality and safety of health care services. This elevates the risk of individuals experiencing inefficient, ineffective and even harmful health care. Societies also lose the opportunity for research and innovation to improve health and health care outcomes, which can improve well-being, productivity and the efficient use of public resources.

Figure 5.1. **Continuum of risk associated with the collection and use of personal health data**

	Individual data privacy				
No risk				High risk →	**Risks to individuals** / **Risks to societies**
No data	No data sharing, no data linkages	Best practices in data sharing, linkage and analysis – protection of individuals' data privacy	Data use with weak privacy protection practices	Data use with weak privacy protection practices and incentives to misuse the data	• Identity theft • Discrimination • Mental health harms • Financial harms / • Political risks • Loss of confidence in government and its institutions

	Patient safety and health system performance				
No risk				High risk →	**Risks to individuals** / **Risks to societies**
	Best practices in data sharing, linkage and analysis – regular programmes of monitoring and research	Limited data sharing and data linkages – some monitoring and research	No data sharing, no data linkages – little monitoring, little research	No data – no monitoring, no research	• Less safe and even harmful health care • Inefficient or ineffective health care / • Lost innovation in health care • Lost efficiency and lost mechanisms to manage expenditures of public funds • Loss of life, loss of quality of life

Source: Author for the OECD.

In the context of the collection and use of personal health data, the core challenge is for countries to identify and weigh the tradeoffs among data risks and data utilities. This balance is reflected in Figure 5.1 diagram one as the point where best practices in data collection, linkage and analysis are identified and implemented, providing the optimum risk/return trade-off. This trade-off will be specific to the context of individual countries.

Variations in risk management lead to differences in OECD country practices

This study (see Annexes A and B) found that all 20 participating countries have enacted legislation that relates to the protection of personal information and have procedural requirements to protect personal information. Some countries have identified health data as an area that requires explicit legislative protection. Study results, however, point to variation across countries in the application of data privacy protections and to opportunities for all countries to improve in this regard.

These differences were generally attributed to risk management in four key areas which are further discussed in this and in the next chapter:

- use of personal health data when obtaining patient consent is impossible or cost prohibitive,
- sharing of identifiable personal health data among government authorities,
- approval of projects involving the linkage of personal health data, and
- use of personal health data for multi-country projects.

Guiding principles and legislation

All countries report a legislative environment with specific pieces of legislation that relate to the protection of personal information in general and, for some, additional legislation specific to health data protection. New legislations and privacy policies have all been influenced by the 1980 publication of the OECD privacy guidelines and these guidelines are still recognised as representing "the international consensus on privacy standards and providing guidance on the collection of personal information in any medium" (OECD, 2009). The OECD guidelines emphasize that data collections are respectful of the protection of personal privacy when they follow the following eight guiding principles (Box 5.1):

1. collection limitation,
2. data quality,
3. purpose specification,
4. use limitation,
5. security safeguards,
6. openness,
7. individual participation, and
8. accountability.

These principles were subsequently reflected in the 1995 *Data Protection Directive* of the European Union that regulates the processing of personal information. In the European Union, a directive is a legal act that is required as a result of an EU treaty. Directives are binding for member states and each state is required to incorporate the directive into law within the time period specified in the directive.

Following the directive, European countries have implemented specific legislation relating to the protection of the privacy of personal information that complies with EU regulatory requirements. All of the European countries participating in this study report the existence of data protection legislation and an oversight body responsible for guidance and monitoring of this legislation in the form of a privacy or data protection office at the national level. While providing a unifying framework, the directive left considerable freedom to countries regarding whether to apply, restrict or extend the rules on processing sensitive data. In 2012, the European Union published a proposal for a new data protection regulation (European Commission, 2012). The new regulation makes clearer that the processing of sensitive data, without consent, can be allowed for statistical and research purposes. However, as with the first implementation of the directive, the proposal gives considerable room for countries to implement rules about sensitive data. Consequently, the possibility to seek an appropriate balance between health research and privacy/data protection interests is, and is likely to remain, left to implementation at national levels (Di Iorio, personal communication).

Among the non-European countries in this study, the *United States* reports a federal Privacy Act with data protection requirements for federally held personal data and the Health Insurance Portability and Accountability Act (HIPAA) which specifies data protection requirements for personal health data in the United States. *Canada* reports a federal Privacy Act with data protection requirements for personal data and a federal Personal Information and Protection of Electronic Documents Act (PIPEDA) with specific data protection requirements for the transborder movement of personal data linked to a commercial enterprise. *Australia* reports a national Privacy Act (1988), as well as the National Health Act (1953), the Health Insurance Act (1973) and the Aged Care Act (1987), which all have general and specific sections dealing with the privacy and security of personal health data.

Japan reports a Privacy Protection Act that governs the protection of personal information. *Korea* has a new Personal Information Protection Act enacted in 2011 that

> **Box 5.1. Guiding principles for the protection of privacy and the transborder flow of personal data**
>
> The OECD guidelines for the protection of privacy and the transborder flow of personal data outline eight guiding principles for national application:
>
> | | |
> |---|---|
> | 1. Collection limitation principle | There should be limits to the collection of personal data and any such data should be obtained by lawful and fair means and, where appropriate, with the knowledge or consent of the data subject. |
> | 2. Data quality principle | Personal data should be relevant to the purposes for which they are to be used and, to the extent necessary for those purposes, should be accurate, complete and kept up-to-date. |
> | 3. Purpose specification principle | The purposes for which personal data are collected should be specified not later than at the time of data collection and the subsequent use limited to the fulfillment of those purposes or such others as are not incompatible with those purposes and as are specified on each occasion of change of purpose. |
> | 4. Use limitation principle | Personal data should not be disclosed, made available or otherwise used for purposes other than those specified in accordance with Paragraph 9 except:
 a) with the consent of the data subject; or
 b) by the authority of law. |
> | 5. Security safeguards principle | Personal data should be protected by reasonable security safeguards against such risks as loss or unauthorised access, destruction, use, modification or disclosure of data. |
> | 6. Openness principle | There should be a general policy of openness about developments, practices and policies with respect to personal data. Means should be readily available of establishing the existence and nature of personal data, and the main purposes of their use, as well as the identity and usual residence of the data controller. |
> | 7. Individual participation principle | An individual should have the right:
 a) to obtain from a data controller, or otherwise, confirmation of whether or not the data controller has data relating to him;
 b) to have communicated to him, data relating to him within a reasonable time; at a charge, if any, that is not excessive; in a reasonable manner; and in a form that is readily intelligible to him;
 c) to be given reasons if a request made under subparagraphs *a)* and *b)* is denied, and to be able to challenge such denial; and
 d) to challenge data relating to him and, if the challenge is successful to have the data erased, rectified, completed or amended. |
> | 8. Accountability principle | A data controller should be accountable for complying with measures which give effect to the principles stated above. |
>
> *Source:* OECD (2009), *OECD Policies for Information Security and Privacy.*

specifies the requirements for the protection of personal data. This Act applies to individuals who manage personal information directly or who are responsible for the management of personal information as part of their duties whether they act as private individuals or are employed within public institutions, corporate bodies, and other organisations. The Act has stronger provisions regarding the use of personal health data and the consequences of its misuse. Previous legislation applied only to personal information in the custody of public bodies. As was the case with previous legislation, the new Act requires public agencies to be authorised by another law to collect and analyse personal health data. In *Singapore*, a new Personal Data Protection Act came into effect in January 2013. It regulates the collection, use, disclosure, transfer and security of personal data by organisations. In addition, the National Disease Registry Act specifies data protection requirements of personal data related to specific diseases that are collected by the National Registry of Diseases.

Sub-national legislations related to the protection of personal information or personal health information is reported for the states within the *United States*, the *Australian* states, and among the *Canadian* provinces and territories.

In addition to national data protection offices, Canada reports privacy commissioners within the ten *Canadian* provinces and the three *Canadian* territories; *Switzerland* reports an

Office of Data Protection within each of the 26 cantons; and *Germany* reports data protection authorities in each of the 16 states.

Most countries also report authorising legislations that relate to the work of health ministries, statistical offices and other public authorities that also specify requirements related to data protection. Some have legislations at a much finer level as well, such as enabling legislation for a particular disease registry.

Privacy principles in practice – country variation

The collection and use of personal health information follows the principles of privacy protection in all of the participating countries. All countries, however, have areas where the application of privacy protections could be improved. Also, and importantly, some countries have applied privacy principles in a way that unnecessarily impedes privacy-respectful health research in the public interest. In these countries, reforms could likely facilitate greater public benefit from health information infrastructure without deterioration in public confidence.

Health monitoring and research often requires the use of health care databases originally collected for the purpose of the administration of the health system or for direct patient care. Health monitoring and research uses may not have been considered when the data were collected and persons from whom the information was gathered were not, consequently, informed. These databases often represent thousands or hundreds of thousands of patients and re-contact to ask a consent question is either impossible and/or financially infeasible for a country. These realities can place health research in question of disrespecting collection and use principles of data protection. These principles include that personal health data should be collected in a fair manner where individuals are aware that the information is being collected and are aware of the purposes of the information collection; that the subsequent use of the personal information should conform to the same purposes and not deviate from them; and that individual data subjects should provide consent to any new use of the personal health information or the new use should be authorised in law.

In *Belgium*, the Privacy Commission grants authority to collect and use identifiable personal information without consent. After the introduction of the European Directive on the Protection of Personal Health Data, the Privacy Commission advised the Cancer Registry that it could no longer process identifiable personal health data and that the only way it could continue normal operations would be to draft authorising legislation and reapply for permission. The legislation authorising the Cancer Registry clarifies that patient consent is not required to create the registry nor to link or analyse the registry data. The years when the legislation was being drafted, and normal operations were suspended, involved degradation in the quality of the registry, coupled with a resource-intensive process to try to maintain quality.

In *Italy*, when the European Directive was first introduced, the possibility to conduct health research involving identifiable personal health data was reduced. Under the first Italian Data Protection Act that came into force in 1997, personal health data should be de-identified; and only if it was impossible to do so, should identifiable health data be processed. In 2004, a Data Protection Code was introduced that included a chapter on the specific case of data processing in the health sector. This defined categories of the processing of identifiable personal health data that would be considered in the substantial public interest. This code permits the processing of identifiable personal health data if the data subject has given consent or if law authorises the process. Currently, many Italian regions have legislation that authorises them to develop disease registries from health care data without consent and to use the data for research purposes. Further in 2011, the Privacy Guarantor, who is the data protection authority, gave a general authorisation to enable regions to process identifiable and sensitive health data for research purposes. National birth and death registries exist in Italy but it remains very challenging to build national disease registries in Italy because a national registry that consolidates data from regional registries would be constructed from regional data that was collected without informed consent. As in Belgium, any national registry in Italy would require its own authorising legislation to be approved by the data protection authority. While regions have been authorised to conduct research and analysis with registry data, there is a growing concern that the Privacy Guarantor may revoke this approval. This concern has put a chill on health research in Italy, as many regions are becoming reluctant to participate in research studies.

In *Germany*, data protection requirements are established partly on the Federal level and partly on the state (Land) level. The Federal Data Protection Commissioner is responsible for federal public sector entities and service providers in the social security administration as well as undertakings by private-sector commercial entities that fall under public laws. There are 16 states in Germany, each with a State Data Protection Commissioner. These commissioners are responsible for service providers of the social security administration at the state level. There is no national cancer registry in Germany. Each state sends data on all registered cancer cases to the Centre for Cancer Registry Data at the Robert Koch Institute on an annual basis. This Centre then analyses the data for completeness and to report results at a national level. The Centre also makes the data available for research by external scientists through a scientific-use file. Any amalgamation of data from states for research projects, particularly any linkage of cancer registry data with other data sources, requires each state's authority to proceed.

Portugal reports that that the sharing of data across data custodians is limited and data linkages are not allowed. In *Poland*, it is not possible for data custodians to share identifiable data containing the unique patient identifying number (PESEL) and data linkages involving the use of PESEL are not allowed. It is, however, possible to undertake probabilistic linkage involving other identifying information. However, in practice, the only project reported for Poland is a pilot study involving the linkage of the cancer registry to data on cancer screening.

In *Sweden*, *Denmark* and *Finland*, legislation enabling a range of health registries and social welfare registries is in place. This legislation makes participation in the registries mandatory and enables the identifiable data to be processed without informed consent. In *Sweden* and *Finland*, if a patient wants to have their personal data removed from a registry they may appeal to the national health authorities. Consent processes have changed with respect to health care quality registers in Sweden. In the past, patients were informed of the use of their data through information and brochures. Now, hospitals are asking patients for their consent to use their personal data for research or statistical purposes. In *Denmark*, a patient cannot request the removal of their data from patient registries. Patients may, however, ask that their contact information never be provided for research projects where they would be contacted to answer a survey. In *Finland*, the website of the

NIHW is used to communicate with the public about the data files that are prepared, where the data comes from and how the data is used.

In the *United Kingdom*, all data custodians must register their collections of personal data with the UK Information Commissioner, who is responsible for overseeing the Data Protection Act. Schedule 3 of the UK Data Protection Act lists conditions that may apply to justify the processing of personal health data without consent. These include that it is necessary for prevention, diagnosis, medical research, patient care or the management of the health care system. The Act outlines levels of consent requirements for circumstances where patient consent would not be required (such as the communication of information about communicable diseases to authorities) to circumstances where consent would always be required. The processing of personal health data falls between these two ends. Data linkages may be undertaken without obtaining patient consent when government has collected the datasets involved. The onus is on data custodians to communicate with the public about how their data is being used. For example, National Services Scotland (NSS) has information about data collection and use on their website including any privacy notices. The NSS is considering increasing this public communication to also include a description of when data projects are using identifiers or there are data linkages and who has been provided access to the data. Another example is within the Office of National Statistics, where posters are put up in birth and neo-natal units in health facilities and a leaflet is distributed to new parents that informs about the ONS, its mandate, the collection and the use of birth registration information including data linkages and some recent findings. Patients have the right to refuse to have their data used for health research. For example, the NHS Information Centre reports the rare occasion of a request to suppress a patient's hospitalisation records.

In the *United States*, the Health Insurance Portability and Accountability Act (HIPAA) applies to certain covered entities and governs when patient consent is required and when personal health data may be used without consent. Covered entities include health plans, health care clearinghouses and health care providers who electronically transmit health information in connection with transactions including billing and payment for services or insurance coverage. Under HIPPA, written consent of data subjects is required to use or to disclose identifiable personal health information unless this use is for public health purposes or the data custodian's internal review board or a privacy board has approved it (National Institutes of Health, 2011). For example, Kaiser Permanente is a covered entity and it meets HIPPA requirements for written consent by including the collection and use of personal information within the terms of the membership agreement that is signed by individuals joining the Kaiser health insurance plan.

In the *United States*, there is no central federal entity for granting approval of uses of personal health data. Each federal agency is required to adhere to common laws and to their own legal framework, and therefore to make a determination to approve projects involving the sharing or linking of their databases. The US National Centre for Health Statistics has its own authorising legislation that permits the collection and use of personal health data. NCHS has an Internal Review Board (IRB) that approves data collections and data linkages. For any linkages that would involve health care administrative records, such as records from the Centre for Medicare and Medicaid Services, HIPPA requires that the linkage must conform to the terms of the statement signed by enrolees in these insurance programmes. This statement described the uses of the data and represents the patient's written consent. For example, the linkage of health care administrative files and immigration files may be determined to be outside of the terms of the signed statement and therefore not permitted. For some surveys, such as the National Health Interview Survey (NHIS), the NCHS administers a question to respondents asking for the last four digits of their Social Security Number. Respondents who decline to answer the question are asked to consent to link their survey responses to other health care and vital event databases for statistical purposes. In the past, survey respondents were asked for their 9-digit Social Security Number but were not asked for permission to link their survey responses to other health data. Typically, only 45% of respondents to the NHIS would provide the number. Those individuals were assumed to have consented to data linkage and were the only records eligible for linkage. After the NCHS changed the process, the proportion of respondents with data eligible for data linkage projects grew to 86%. Further, for records where respondents have consented and the Social Security Number is missing or incorrect, probabilistic matches are now possible. The NCHS IRB may authorise an exemption for the linkage of data where patient consent has not been obtained.

In *Korea*, personal health data may be collected and used with patient consent and, where authorised by law, without patient consent. Under the National Health Insurance Act and the Cancer Control Act, personal health data is authorised to be processed without consent by public authorities. In *Singapore*, patient consent is required for uses of administrative data that are beyond direct patient care. For public policy purposes, this requirement is met by informing patients. For example, when a patient is admitted to hospital they are informed about the uses of their data. There is also information provided to patients making a claim under the national health insurance programme.

In *Canada*, the Personal Information and Protection of Electronic Documents Act (PIPEDA) was introduced in 2000. PIPEDA governs the sharing of electronic health records across jurisdictional boundaries when those records originate from a commercial source, which can include health care providers. Organisations covered by this federal Act must obtain the consent of individuals when they collect, use or disclose personal information unless they are authorised to do so by another law. The introduction of the Act created ambiguity as to the legality of health research activities involving administrative health data without the express consent of data subjects. The Federal Privacy Commissioner's office eventually made a determination that there could be secondary use of personal health information without patient consent in situations where the use of the data could be demonstrated to be in the public interest.

Some provinces have since introduced legislation governing the protection of personal health information. For provincial laws to supersede the federal PIPEDA, a prerequisite is that they must be similar in spirit. Ontario was one of the first provinces to introduce its own legislation, the Personal Health Information Protection Act (PHIPA), in 2004. PHIPA clarifies in law that certain prescribed entities are able to collect and use personal health data without patient consent. The Institute for Clinical and Evaluative Sciences (ICES) at the University of Toronto, for example, is a prescribed entity and receives identifiable data for research purposes from a variety of public authorities in Ontario and receives Ontario-specific identifiable data from Statistics Canada. ICES is authorised to process the data and it conducts research and publishes research based on data linkages. To receive data from the province of Ontario without patient consent, the Canadian Institute for Health Information (CIHI) also needed to become a prescribed entity under PHIPA. As other provinces introduce similar legislation, CIHI works with the provinces to ensure that the legislation will permit CIHI to continue to receive transfers of personal health data to build and use national databases for statistical and research purposes.

In *Australia*, the national Privacy Act, as well as state-level legislation, regulates the protection of privacy of personal information. As well, at both the national and the state levels, there are specific acts related to health that may have a bearing on health data use. Privacy law reforms were among the recommendations of the 2008 Australian Law Reform Commission. Further, the national government recently established a set of principles that cover the integration (linkage) of national data for statistical and research purposes. Beginning in 2012, organisations may apply to become accredited as an integrating authority and therefore become authorised to conduct data linkages in accordance with these principles. Requirements for accreditation include that the organisation is governed by authorising legislation that specifies penalties for any breach of data privacy and security. Australian legislation, however, restricts the circumstances under which the two large national administrative databases, under the Medicare Benefits Schedule and the Pharmaceutical Benefits Scheme may be linked together. These legal restrictions are among a set of issues that require resolution before the Integrating Authority model may be fully implemented. Variations in legislation and governance of the protection of personal information across the Australian states introduce difficulties in achieving state participation in national data linkage efforts.

Multiple data custodianship and data sharing

All countries report that there are several national government authorities, agencies or organisations acting as custodians of their national databases. National custodians include governmental departments or agencies responsible for health care or health care insurance; national statistical authorities; cancer registries; birth and death registries; national agencies responsible for health data collection or analysis; national authorities responsible for components of health care such as primary health care or care for veterans; university and scientific institutes; associations of local health authorities; and hospitals.

Denmark provides an example of data custodianship that is not at all atypical. Denmark reports that most health care related national databases are in the custody of the National Board of Health, with the exception of prescription medicines that are in the custody of the Danish Medicines Agency. Population health surveys are in the custody of the National Institute of Public Health, patient experiences surveys are in the custody of the Capital Region for all of Denmark, while the population registry is in the custody of Statistics Denmark.

Some countries report further complexity in their national data infrastructure due to custodianship of national data at a sub-national level. For example, the *United Kingdom* reports custody of databases at the level of the individual countries within it and then, within each of the countries, multiple data custodians. The *United States* reports custodians of national data for particular sub-populations, such as military veterans or enrolees in Medicare and Medicaid insurance programmes. Israel reports that primary care and prescription medicines data are in the custody of four HMOs.

The only exception to multiple custodianship is *Switzerland*, where the Federal Statistical Office is the single custodian of all of the national databases in their country's national health information infrastructure inquired about for this study.

What is important about multiple custodians is that, when they exist, there must then be legal frameworks and information custodian policy frameworks in place that provide for the possibility of the sharing of data. Without this, there is no possibility for any health or health care monitoring or research that requires person-level datasets from more than one custodian. Even when legal frameworks exist, data sharing can involve long and challenging negotiations.

In the United Kingdom, the sharing of identifiable personal health data is permitted among public authorities and the Information Commissioner, who is responsible for the UK Data Protection Act, advises public agencies on data sharing. The Health and Social Care Information Centre (see Chapter 2) will, in 2013, become a repository of data from several data custodians in England for secondary use purposes, including the holding and linking of person-identifiable data where approved and necessary (Department of Health, 2012). This centre will provide services to the Clinical Practice Data-link which is a new English NHS observational data and interventional research service designed to maximise the way de-identified NHS clinical data may be linked to enable research to improve and safeguard public health (Clinical Practice Research Datalink, 2013).

In Australia, there are efforts underway to permit acute care (hospital) data collected and linked at the state level to be amalgamated at the national level, creating the potential for analysis and reporting at a national level and also for data linkage projects with national data in the custody of the Australian Institute for Health and Welfare. The project is challenging because legislation and governance vary across the Australian states. In the United States, federal authorities may enter into agreement with one another to share identifiable data. These agreements must conform to the legislative requirements of each of the participating authorities. The National Centre for Health Statistics negotiated an agreement for the sharing data with the Centre for Medicare and Medicaid Services and the Social Security Administration for the purpose of a data linkage study. The negotiated agreement took two years to complete.

In Canada, the Canadian Institute for Health Information is able to build national identifiable personal health databases by entering into agreements with each of the provincial government authorities for the sharing of identifiable data. CIHI complies with provincial data protection and legal requirements, as may be identified in these agreements.

In Singapore, most national health databases reside in the Ministry of Health. Some databases are mandated by laws, while others are developed from administrative and transactional data, such as claims for government subsidies. The Registry of Births and Deaths in the Ministry of Home Affairs shares birth and death records with the Ministry of Health for statistical purposes.

Italy has 19 territories and two provinces, each with local health authorities that process personal health data for their area. It is very difficult to engage in research with regional data because it is difficult to know how to approach the region with a proposal and what their requirements are for approval. The lack of adequate mechanisms makes it almost an impossible task, even for official institutions, to share data and information across multiple regions.

In Finland, for some national data collections, health authorities and physicians are required by law to collect the data and to provide it to the government. In practice, however, the Finland National Institute for Health and Welfare works actively to engage service providers in this collection effort by presenting them with results of analysis of their data. By showing them interesting trends, service providers become interested in seeing data at the local or regional level. Finland reports that it was difficult to establish disease registries at first because service providers were opposed to data gathering. For example, it took ten years of negotiation to reach agreement with service providers to establish the first medical birth registry 25 years ago.

In *Denmark*, the law permits the sharing of identifiable personal data and the National Board of Health has shared data with Statistics Denmark for the purpose of specific projects requiring data linkages.

Data linkage activities and compliance with legislation

All countries reported entities with the legal authority to conduct record linkages for public health and health services monitoring and research under certain restrictions that relate to legislative requirements for data protection.

Under *Australia's* Privacy Act (1988), national health and medical research guidelines enable the requirement for patient consent to be waived by an authorised ethics committee in cases where the collection of consent is impractical or impossible and where the outcome of the project in terms of the public good outweighs the infringement of patient privacy. In the past, once approval was sought from the relevant data custodian, it was possible for researchers to access identifiable data to undertake their own data linkages for their approved project. In recent years, this practice has become rare. Researchers with an approved research project instead benefit from national or state-level data linkage centres that conduct data linkages on their behalf and provide researchers with access to de-identified data. Researchers applying for approval to undertake a project involving the data holdings of the national Australian Institute of Health and Welfare (AIHW) would be first required to obtain research ethics approval from their own institution, as well as from all of the custodians of the datasets required for the linkage. This could include obtaining research ethics approval at the state level and also from all state-level data custodians whose data may be involved. Under the national principles for data integration, projects involving national identifiable data that are considered to be "high risk", and therefore requiring additional protection of data privacy, would be processed only by an organisation that has been accredited as an integrating authority. Integrating authorities are required to provide a summary of all approved projects on their website. The AIHW, along with the Australian Bureau of Statistics have recently received interim accreditation as integrating authorities. Currently, the AIHW Data Integration Services Centre carries out the linkage of national databases for approved projects. There is also a new national Centre for Data Linkages (CDL) that aims to provide capacity to link data only available at the state level for national or multi-state projects. The AIHW and the CDL, along with the state linkage units, are working together to build a national system where the data holdings at the state and national levels may be linked together for approved projects.

In *Finland*, the National Institute of Health and Welfare (NIHW) and Statistics Finland are both authorised by the Finland Data Protection Authority to conduct data linkages using identification numbers. In practice, the NIHW receives identifiable data from the statistical office and conducts data linkages. National identifying numbers are used in initial processing of the data to edit the data and check the data for errors. When the data is clean, the identity numbers are encrypted and the encrypted numbers are used to perform linkages for approved projects. There was a case, however, where a project involved the linkage of criminal data to health data. For this project, the data protection authority required the linkage to be undertaken by a third party. While exceptional, in Finland it is possible for a request from an external researcher for access to identifiable health data to be granted.

In *Sweden*, the National Board of Health and Welfare conducts data linkages using identification numbers. Analysts within government and external researchers with approved projects are only provided access to de-identified data. Similarly, in *Denmark*, the National Board of Health conducts data linkages. In cases where databases of the National Board of Health would be linked with databases from Statistics Denmark, identifiable data would be provided from the board to Statistics Denmark who would conduct the linkage and de-identify the data. Only de-identified data is provided to researchers within and outside of government.

In the *United Kingdom*, data linkages involving national data are most often undertaken by national authorities. UK law does not rule out, however, the possibility that a non-governmental researcher could receive approval for access to identifiable data and conduct a data linkage. Linkages most often take place using the unique National Health Service number or, in Scotland, the unique Community Health Index number. Probabilistic linkage is used where deterministic linkages fail or when unique numbers are missing. The NHS Information Centre for Health and Social Care reported providing only de-identified data to clients for research (see Chapter 2). The Clinical Practice Research Datalink provides services to academic and other private-sector researchers within the United Kingdom and globally, subject to legal arrangements and approvals (Clinical Practice Research Datalink, 2013). Access is provided to de-identified data.

In *Belgium*, as a result of the legislation specific to the cancer registry, the Privacy Commission has approved the cancer registry to collect identifiable personal health data and to link the data and then to conduct analysis of de-identified data. In general, however, data linkage takes place within the E-health Platform which is a third party authorised by law to access and use identifiable health data and who is trusted to undertake data linkages that are approved by the Privacy Commission. Only de-identified data is provided to governmental and non-governmental researchers for analysis.

Data custodians undertake data linkages in the *United States*. The NCHS conducts data linkages among its own databases with the approval of its Internal Review Board (IRB). There is no unique patient identifying number in the United States; however, it is sometimes possible to conduct linkages using Social Security Numbers. Linkages are typically probabilistic linkages that depend on a set of identifiers in the data (names, dates of birth, marital status, place of birth and race). For a linkage of NCHS survey respondents to health care administrative data held by the Center for Medicare and Medicaid Services (CMS), the linkage was conducted in steps involving three governmental organisations using a deterministic linkage method. Records of respondents in the survey who consented to data linkage were shared with the Social Security Administration; who linked the data to the social security database and corrected any errors in the Social Security Numbers captured on the survey. The corrected data was then sent to the CMS who conducted a deterministic linkage to Medicare and Medicaid records and then removed the Social Security Numbers from the linked file and provided the linked file back to the NCHS. Only de-identified data is ever provided for research and the de-identification process is very strict (see Chapter 6).

In *Canada*, CIHI undertakes data linkages at the national level involving health care administrative data. The main linkage key used is the provincial Health Insurance Number. Health Insurance Numbers are encrypted during data processing at CIHI and deterministic linkages are undertaken using these encrypted numbers and other identifiers such as birth dates and dates of treatment. Typically, de-identified data is provided to internal data analysts or to external third-party researchers. In cases where linkages would require the databases of Statistics Canada, identifiable data has been shared with Statistics Canada who has undertaken the linkage. In some cases, such as for mortality and cancer registry data, linkages are primarily probabilistic due to the unavailability of health insurance numbers (Statistics Canada, 2006). Such data sharing arrangements with Statistics Canada only take place through negotiated agreements and with the approval of the provinces whose data would be involved (Statistics Canada, 2010). Only de-identified data is ever provided for research and the de-identification process is very strict and similar to the US NCHS.

In *Korea*, HIRA undertakes data linkages involving health care administrative data. The principle key for the linkage of patient-level data is the Resident Registration Number. Only de-identified data would be provided to external third-party researchers with an approved project. In this case, all analysis would take place within HIRA's secure facility. Further, requests for access to data by commercial interests, or by academic researchers to prepare a theses or educational materials, would be rejected.

In *Singapore*, different governmental institutions perform data linkages for policy planning and research, including the Ministry of Health. In the ministry, effort has been made to automate data linkages to as high a degree as possible through deterministic matching using the National Registration Identity Card Number (NRIC). The computer algorithm will de-identify the data by replacing the direct identifiers with a patient unique identifier specific for each project. Probabilistic matching techniques are used for data linkages where direct identifiers are not available, i.e. due to sensitivity of records. Only de-identified data is made accessible to researchers (internal or external) and typically under conditions of controlled access (see Chapter 6).

In *Japan* there are no reported legislative barriers to undertaking data linkages and the National Institute of Public Health reports linkage is technically possible involving hospital, pharmaceutical, primary care data and population survey data. The Ministry of Health, Labour and Welfare in Japan, however, reports removing all identifiers from health care databases and rendering record linkage impossible.

In *Germany*, data linkage takes place at the state level, not at the national level, and only when authorised by law. Furthermore, state legislation enabling cancer registries differs regarding which identifying information may be used for record linkage. Names, addresses, dates of birth are available generally, but place of birth is not universally available for probabilistic record linkage. All the German states are able to use the same national pseudonymisation algorithm to render names anonymous. Thus, it is possible to merge de-identified records at the Centre for Cancer Registry Data, and correct for the bias in the registries that would otherwise occur from patient mobility. Only de-identified data is provided to researchers.

Electronic health record systems and compliance with legislation

The most widely reported barrier to building databases from electronic health records reported by 16 of 25 countries responding to this study, is concern about the legal authority to do so. While existing legislations governing the collection and use of personal health data would certainly be applicable for personal health data within electronic health records; some countries have signalled that existing legislations do not always fully respond to questions about the use of data from electronic health records. In *Finland*, for example, the law authorises the development and use of databases from the national electronic health record system; but does not permit analysis of the underlying databank of electronic health records. Such inconsistencies may require legislative reforms. Some countries noted that the consent of patients may be required for statistical or research uses of data from electronic health records. If this consent is not possible to obtain at the point of care, when data is being entering into the record, it will be challenging to obtain it after the fact. For example, in *France*, patients must first provide their consent before their information is entered into the electronic health record system or is viewed by health care providers. There are legal provisions, however, to ensure physician access to patient's electronic records in the event of an emergency where the patient is incapable of consenting.

Privacy continues to be top of mind for all stakeholders in the use of data from electronic health records for secondary use purposes in *Canada*. At the time of the survey, privacy legislation precluded secondary use of EHR data in one province. *Poland* reports legal issues related to access to data which are unresolved despite existence of a new law on medical information. *Slovenia* reports that development of databases from electronic records is limited to data and data use purposes defined in law. *Portugal* reports that the National Commission for Data Protection imposes strict criteria for database creation and the use of data. The Ministry of Law in *Israel* objects to database creation from the EHR system.

United States law protects the privacy of patient data by restricting the manner in which health care providers may use and share data with others. It also requires that those who create databases with patient information have in place administrative, physical and technical security protections. The law also provides governmental authority to enforce compliance with privacy and security requirements. Although there are no legal barriers to the creation or analysis of data from electronic health records, there are legal requirements that may require patient consent to some databases and analysis that would be considered secondary uses of the data. Data custodians and data users are responsible for assuring that they have appropriate permissions before they may access and use the data.

Bibliography

Academy of Medical Sciences (2011), *A New Pathway for the Regulation and Governance of Health Research*, United Kingdom, January.

Australian Government (2008), "For Your Information: Australian Privacy Law and Practice", Australian Law Reform Commission, *Report* No. 108, August.

Barrett, G., J.A. Cassell, J.L. Peacock and M.P. Coleman (2006), "National Survey of British Public's Views on Use of Identifiable Medical Data by the National Cancer Registry", *British Medical Journal*, Vol. 332, No. 7549, pp. 1068-1072.

Clinical Practice Research Datalink (2013), *www.cprd.com/intro.asp*, accessed 19 February 2013.

Davies, C. and R. Collins (2006), "Balancing Potential Risks and Benefits of Using Confidential Data", *British Medical Journal*, Vol. 33, No. 3, pp. 349-351.

Department of Health and NHS Informatics (2012), *Informatics: the Future – an Organisational Summary*, *www.dh.gov.uk/health/2012/07/informatics-future/*, accessed 18 February 2013.

EUBIROD (2010), *WP5 Data Collection: Privacy Impact Assessment Report*, *www.eubirod.eu/documents/downloads/D5_2_Privacy_Impact_Assessment.pdf*.

European Commission (1995), "Directive 95/46/EC", *www.ec.europa.eu/justice_home/fsj/privacy/law/index_en.htm*, accessed 5 October 2012.

European Commission (2012), "COM(2012) Regulation of the European Parliament and of the Council on the Protection of Individuals with Regard to the Processing of Personal Data and on the Free Movement of Such Data (General Data Protection Regulation)", No. 11 final, *www.ec.europa.eu/justice/data-protection/document/review2012/com_2012_11_en.pdf*, accessed 5 October 2012.

Holman, C.D.J. (2001), "The Impracticable Nature of Consent for Research Using Linked Administrative Health Records", *Australia and New Zealand Journal of Public Health*, Vol. 25, pp. 421-422.

International Standards Organisation (2009), "Risk Management Principles and Guidelines, ISO/DIS 31000:2009", Standards Catalogue TC262 Risk Management.

National Institutes of Health (2011), "Institutional Review Boards and the HIPAA Privacy Rule", *www.privacyruleandresearch.nih.gov*, accessed 22 October 2011.

OECD (2009), "OECD Policies for Information Security and Privacy", Free document, OECD Publishing, Paris, *www.oecd.org/sti/ieconomy/49338232.pdf*.

Statistics Canada (2006), *Occupational and Environmental Health Research Projects: A Descriptive Catalogue 1978 to 2005*, No. 82-581XIE, Ottawa.

Statistics Canada (2010), *Privacy Impact Assessment for the Longitudinal Health and Administrative Data Initiative*, Health Statistics Division, Ottawa.

United Nations Economic Commission for Europe (2009), *Principles and Guidelines on Confidentiality Aspects of Data Integration Undertaken for Statistical and Related Research Purposes*, UNECE, Geneva.

United States General Accounting Office (2001), *Record Linkage and Privacy: Issues in Creating New Federal Research and Statistical Information*, No. 01(126SP), Washington, DC.

Vetenskapsrådets (2010), *Rättsliga Förutsättningar för en Databasinfrastruktur för Forskning Vetenskapsrådet* (The Public Access to Information and Secrecy Act – Aspects Relevant for the Construction of Databases), Vetenskapsrådets Rapportserie, Stockholm.

Willison, D.J., L. Schwartz, J. Abelson, C. Charles et al. (2007), "Alternatives to Project-Specific Consent for Access to Personal Information for Health Research: What is the Opinion of the Canadian Public?", *Journal of American Medical Informatics Association*, Vol. 14, No. 6, pp. 706-712.

Chapter 6

Governance of data collection, data linkages and access to data

Eighteen of nineteen countries reported that there are multiple authorities in custody of key national databases for population health and health care monitoring and research. Data custodians in all countries reported significant efforts to protect data. Nonetheless there is variation across data custodians in challenging areas of data security including practices to de-identify data to protect patient privacy so that the data can be used for monitoring and research; and provision of safe mechanisms so that researchers from other government ministries or from academia could access and use data. Some custodians manage risk by refusing data access while others would consider providing access to identifiable patient-level data. Several data custodians noted that fulfilling all the responsibilities associated with data protection is expensive and there are cost pressures. A few countries provide interesting examples of centralising the difficult tasks of linking data, de-identifying data and approving and supervising access to data that have the potential to standardise practices and be more efficient. The sharing of person-level data across borders for international comparisons is rarely reported and there were few examples of data linkages for multi-country comparative studies.

This chapter presents country experiences in the de-identification of data to protect the privacy of individuals; the development of secure facilities for access to data with high re-identification risk; project approval processes for data linkage projects; data security within public authorities holding data and when public authorities provide data to external researchers; and governance of multi-country studies involving personal health data.

Data custodians play a central role in balancing data privacy protection and use of data for monitoring and research as they are responsible for the collection, processing, analysis and dissemination of personal health data. In many countries, data custodians are also responsible for vetting project proposals for the use of data from government and private entities; maintaining a technical capacity to undertake data linkages; maintaining a technical capacity for data de-identification; providing data access modalities to internal and external researchers; and ensuring that through all of their activities the legal requirements for data security and data privacy protection are respected. Several countries noted that fulfilling all of these responsibilities is expensive and that pressure is mounting to trim expenditure. Further, expenses are particularly heavy in countries with decentralised administration of the health system. In these countries, data custodians at sub-national levels are also carrying out these responsibilities. Advancements in techniques to ensure privacy by design and the development of privacy-enhancing technologies may provide avenues to meet both health care data use and privacy protection needs.

Other actors also play important roles in the governance of data collection and use, from legislators who establish governing legal instruments, to privacy regulators who ensure legislations are respected, to, for some countries, delegated bodies who review and approve proposals related to the development and use of personal health data, including independent bodies responsible for the implementation of national electronic health record systems.

De-identification of data

The practice of de-identification of data is widely used across the countries participating in this study; however, there is considerable variation in the interpretation of what constitutes de-identified data that may be legally released from a data custodian to an external researcher. The following are a few examples of different views.

France has invested in methods for data de-identification. This includes a hashing algorithm that converts names to a numerical code that cannot be reversed. These codes are then used to build longitudinal health histories. Given, however, that it is sometimes necessary in a research study to go back and verify content within clinical records, France has developed a reversible hashing algorithm for patient names. Such a reversible code is used, for example, by the Institut National de Veille Sanitaire during the first year of data processing for HIV positive patients, as the patients may need to be contacted by clinicians. After one year, the reversible code is erased and only an irreversible code remains on the file.

In *Finland*, data is considered de-identified when the identity number has been encrypted and names have been removed. Researchers outside of the National Institute of Health and Welfare (NIHW) with approved projects receive data with encrypted identity numbers to conduct their analysis. In *Sweden*, data is de-identified by the National Board of

Health and Welfare by removing national identity numbers, names, addresses and full dates of birth. Files provided to analysts within government and outside of government contain a study number that has been assigned in place of the identity number as well as some personal information on sex, age and home community. In *Denmark*, the National Board of Health data is de-identified by removing names and exact addresses. The national Central Person Register number, however, will remain on the analytical file. This number reveals the sex and birth date of the person.

In *Australia*, the Australian Institute of Health and Welfare (AIHW) considers data to be de-identified when direct identifying variables have been removed, such as names and exact addresses. There are, however, efforts underway to further reduce re-identification risk, where necessary, by introducing additional data processing, such as rolling up response categories for sensitive variables. The de-identification rules used for linked data will depend on the requirements of the custodians of the data supplied to the AIHW and in some cases the outcomes of consultation with the researcher.

In *Korea*, personal information, such as the Resident Registration Numbers and names of people, and information on individual corporations and organisations, such as health institutions, is strictly protected. In cases where researchers are approved to conduct a project involving data linkage, alternate keys are provided that cannot be used to identify individuals or organisations are provided. Further, access to data is only provided in a designated place within the Health Insurance Review Agency (HIRA).

In the *United Kingdom*, the NHS National Services Scotland (NSS) has identified certain fields within personal health data as sensitive (names, health numbers, full birth dates, and addresses). The NSS disclosure review protocol is applied to any personal health data to be disseminated outside of the NSS, which can result in suppression or treatment of variables that may pose a re-identification risk. For approved projects, researchers generally receive from the NSS a file where identifiers have been removed and where the health number has been replaced with a study number. The NHS Information Centre for Health and Social Care reported a similar process (see Chapter 2).

In *Canada*, the Canadian Institute for Health Information (CIHI) accepts encrypted and unencrypted health insurance numbers on administrative health databases that are transferred to CIHI from provinces and territories. When provinces and territories submit encrypted health numbers to CIHI, the encryption algorithm is maintained. When provinces or territories submit unencrypted health numbers, CIHI will encrypt the numbers using an established algorithm. CIHI's privacy disclosure procedures for the provision of de-identified data to third-parties, such as researchers, require the use of project-specific identification numbers instead of encrypted health insurance numbers. Where approved, an external third-party researcher may link databases using project-specific identification numbers.

In the *United States*, the National Centre for Health Statistics considers that data is de-identified when the risk of potentially re-identifying persons within the data has been reduced. This includes removal of identifiers, such as names, exact addresses, full dates and any identifying numbers and also a careful review of possible combinations of remaining sensitive variables within the data file that may indirectly lead to the disclosure of the identity of a person. Individual-level data that has been de-identified to this standard can be made publicly available and can be disseminated over the Internet to the public. For example, the linkage of population survey data to death data has been released as a public-use micro data file. Often, however, the level of detail that is required for an approved research project would create a re-identification risk that is too high for the NCHS to release the data to the researcher. Instead, the NCHS has created a network of secure research data centres that researchers with approved projects must use. Similarly, in *Singapore*, researchers with approved projects may access de-identified data in the Ministry of Health's secured data lab (see below).

Secure facilities for access to data with a high re-identification risk

Custodians of personal health data in the United States, Canada and Singapore have created secure facilities where approved researchers may access de-identified personal health data that is deemed to have a higher than acceptable risk of potentially re-identifying individuals. This step has enabled the custodians to minimise the risk of misuse of the data.

The *United States* National Centre for Health Statistics has created a network of secure Research Data Centres (RDCs) across the United States in partnership with the US Census Bureau. In the RDCs, government and non-government researchers with approved projects access personal data necessary for their project and conduct all of their research. Only aggregated results may exit the facility after they have been reviewed by an NCHS staff member for any risks to data confidentiality. The NCHS has also introduced a new secure remote data access option for researchers, so that it is no longer necessary for all work to take place within the physical locations of the RDCs. Instead, researchers access a secure system called Andre from their own office. Through Andre they may submit programmes to analyse the data and receive the output. The Andre system has an automated process for checking for and preventing misuse of the data. Further, an NCHS staff member checks one-quarter of the data submissions and any detected misuse would terminate the researcher's access to the system.

In *Canada*, Statistics Canada also maintains a network of secure Research Data Centres across the Canadian provinces with similar features to the US RDCs (Statistics Canada, 2011). Researchers with approved projects may only have access to de-identified data with a high re-identification risk within the RDCs. Canada does not yet have a remote data access option, but is beginning to pilot options that may enable this type of access in the future.

In *Australia*, researchers with approval to undertake a project involving personal health data considered to be "high risk" would be able to access the linked de-identified data through a secure data linkage environment called SURE (Secure Unified Research Environment) that is offered through the Australian Population Health Research Network (PHRN). PHRN has received national government funding and is helping to advance data linkage infrastructure at the state and national levels. SURE is a new remote-access computing environment accessed via the internet. Access requires a username, password and authentication token. Key strokes on the local computer are transmitted to the SURE computer. Files cannot be transferred between studies or between the study and the local computing environment. Researchers can look at records on screen to resolve issues with their analysis, but they cannot print the screen or download any data. All outputs of their results are checked for confidentiality.

In *Singapore,* the Ministry of Health has also established a secure data laboratory that has been available for the past year. The ministry was concerned with the risk of re-identification resulting from data involving the ministry's administrative databases. All approved research by government and non-government researchers involving access to de-identified data must take place within the lab. Only aggregated results that have been vetted by a ministry staff member may exit the secure lab.

In the *United Kingdom*, Universities and the Scotland NHS have launched a new initiative, the Scottish Health Informatics Programme (SHIP), that aims to eventually provide researchers with remote access to de-identified data in a secure manner so that it can be accessed at a distance from the data custodian and in a manner where the researchers may use advanced statistical techniques (Scottish Health Informatics Programme, 2011). SHIP also aims to ensure that data is shared across multiple custodians for linkage-based research and will be consulting with the public to define a transparent and publicly acceptable approach to the governance of this research.

Project approval process for data linkages

Across countries where research proposals for data linkages from external researchers may be approved, proposals must specify the data elements that are absolutely needed for their research and must justify the purpose and merits of their project in terms of the public interest.

In *Singapore*, all projects internal to the ministry and those from other governmental and non-governmental researchers involving linkages to the Ministry of Health's databases would have to be approved internally to ensure that linkage and access is legally permissible. Researchers with approved project would access the linked data in the ministry's secure data lab.

In *Korea*, a deliberation committee of the Health Insurance Review and Assessment Service (HIRA) approves data linkage projects on a project-by-project basis in accordance with the requirements of the Privacy Protection Act. Government and non-government researchers external to HIRA, such as non-profit academic researchers or researchers within public-good institutions may apply to the HIRA deliberation committee for access to de-identified personal health data including linked data that HIRA has in its custody.

In *Belgium*, the Privacy Commission approves data linkage projects. Approved projects that are part of the work programme of the Belgian Cancer Registry can have linkages undertaken by the Cancer Registry. Approved projects proposed by government or non-government researchers external to the Cancer Registry would be undertaken by the E-health platform. The platform would then provide de-identified data to the researcher for analysis.

Each registry in *Finland* has one person within it who is qualified to review project proposals for data linkages for scientific merit. If a researcher wishes to have data linked across several registries, the project proposal must be approved by the reviewer of each registry to proceed. All projects receiving approval are then sent to the national Data Protection Authority and the authority has 30 days on which to comment. The same approval process is followed for researchers within government and those outside of government. In *Sweden*, project proposals from within and from outside of government are reviewed and approved by the National Board of Health and Welfare. In *Denmark*, the Danish Data Protection Agency approves proposals for data linkage projects from within and outside of government. Researchers with approved projects then make a request for data linkage to the National Board of Health and Welfare.

In the *United Kingdom*, the UK Data Protection Act provides the legal framework wherein a national approach to decision making about data linkage projects could be developed. The Health and Social Care Act 2008 created the National Information and Governance Board (NIGB). NIGB was a national decision-making body for projects undertaken in the public sector or in the private sector where the consent of the data subjects was not obtained and where the use of the data was not authorised in law. The NIGB Ethics and Confidentiality Committee acted as a national research ethics approval body for all data custodians responsible for health and social care data. Thus, projects initiated by the public or private sector were reviewed for their conformity with the law; and the relative balance between research that is in the public's interest and the respect of privacy principles was weighed. For data files outside of the domain of health and social care, or for regions outside of NIGB jurisdiction (Scotland), the Caldecott Guardian would act as the approval body. Each custodian of personal data is required by law to have a Caldecott Guardian which is a senior official entrusted to protect data privacy and who is responsible for evaluating and approving projects requiring access to and use of personal data. The Health and Social Care Act 2012 transferred the functions delegated to the NIGB Ethics and Confidentiality Committee to the Health Research Authority (HRA) as of 1 April, 2013. The HRA is to protect and promote the interests of patients and the public in health research. It will streamline the current approval system and improve the efficiency and robustness of decisions about research projects (Department of Health, 2011). Changes to the constitution of the National Health Service have been proposed to offer patients a fuller explanation of their rights under existing law and NHS commitments with respect to data. A review of health information governance with an independent panel of experts will make recommendations on the balance between sharing personal information and protecting individuals' confidentiality (Department of Health, 2013).

In *France*, la Commission Nationale de l'Informatique et des Libertés (CNIL) is the French national data protection authority authorised by the *Loi Informatique et Libertés* (Data Protection Act). CNIL is an independent administrative authority that authorises, on a case by case basis, whether projects requiring access to identifiable personal health data will be approved. CNIL has a committee of experts in medicine and research which may advise on the scientific merit of proposed projects. Consideration for approval includes the legality of the request and the legitimacy of the researcher, including whether the researcher is affiliated with a credible organisation and the security measures that will be put into place to protect the data. Further, researchers requesting access to national health insurance data must also demonstrate that they have some authority that permits access to the data, such as an authorising legislation or professional membership. In addition to CNIL approval, non-government researchers must also be approved by the Comité du secret of the National Council for Statistical Information (CNIS).

Australia reports a complex system of project approval steps for researchers within and outside of government. An accredited Integrating Authority (such as the Australian Institute of Health and Welfare or the Australian Bureau of Statistics) will link data for an approved project that includes personal administrative data held by Australian Government agencies as well as state-level authorities. To be approved, however, the researcher has to demonstrate to the accredited Integrating Authority that approval has been secured from all of the data custodians and relevant Human Research Ethics Committees. For example, a linkage of the national cancer database to Pharmaceutical Benefits Scheme (PBS) records would require the approval of all eight cancer registries, state-level approval from one or two authorities, as well as the federal Department of Health and Ageing (the data custodians of the PBS). Human research ethics approval may also be required by each data custodian, particularly in cases where the researcher requires patient consent requirements to be waived. In total, up to 20 separate approvals may be needed. Hospitalisations data must also be requested at the state level for national data linkage projects and obtaining essential approvals would be similarly onerous. An accredited Integrating Authority may return a de-identified linked data file to a researcher for use if the linkage does not involve a "high risk" database; if all of the data custodians involved agree; and if the researcher has the consent of study participants or has received a waiver to patient consent from a Human Research Ethics Committee. Research with "high risk" databases may only occur using a secure on-site data laboratory or within the secure remote data access facility called SURE (see previous section). To access SURE, researchers must also complete the SURE application process, sign an agreement of use and successfully complete SURE user training.

In *Canada*, the Canadian Institute for Health Information will review applications from internal and external researchers in both the public and private sectors for access to personal health data. In all cases, the researcher must apply for access and must justify each of the databases and data elements within the databases that would be required for the project. The researcher must sign a non-disclosure/confidentiality agreement that binds them to data security and confidentiality protection requirements and must commit to a time limit within which the data must be destroyed. CIHI can audit the researchers and researchers are aware of this possibility. Only de-identified data would be provided to the researcher.

In the *United States*, researchers wishing access to de-identified data that carries a re-identification risk must apply to the National Centre for Health Statistics (NCHS) for access to the data. NCHS management, and for some requests its internal review board, will review the research proposal and, if approved, the researcher will be provided access to the data within a secure Research Data Centre or within NCHS headquarters. It is also possible for a researcher to request a customised data linkage and the same process for approval would apply.

Most study participants indicated that commercially motivated research involving requests for access to identifiable data would fail to be determined to be for the public good and be rejected. In *Finland*, requests by commercial interests are ruled out. This is an issue because there is a law requiring pharmaceutical companies to conduct drug safety studies. To comply with that law, these companies would need to analyse personal health data from public registries. There are two solutions available now. The company could be identified as a scientific research centre, but this would be quite rare. Second, the company could hire a university researcher as a third party who could be approved to access data and report only aggregated statistical results back to the company. *Sweden* also does not rule out requests from commercial interests and reports a concern that it is difficult to sometimes ascertain if a research request for access to personal health data from a pharmaceutical company is really in the public's interest or if it is for commercial purposes and should be denied. To address this concern, Sweden is considering introducing new legislation to make clearer the conditions for access to personal data for research and analysis. In the *United Kingdom*, requests for data linkage by commercial interests are not ruled out, however they are more likely to fail to make a case that the request is in the public interest and therefore to not be approved. The Clinical Practice Research Datalink will provide services to researchers in pharmaceutical or medical devices industries, subject to approval and compliance with the law (Clinical Practice Research Datalink, 2013). Written agreements bind researchers to conditions of access to data that include not using data to profile practitioners nor to evaluate advertising campaigns or the effectiveness of sales forces.

The specific case of researchers requesting linkage of their own data cohort

External researchers often request to have a cohort of data they have collected linked to public health databases. A very common occurrence is a request for the linkage of a clinical database or a database of clinical trial participants to subsequent hospitalisations, diseases and death. Such linkages will provide very important information about the effectiveness and safety of treatments and clinical care. At the same time, such linkages pose additional risk to data protection because the researchers involved have a strong ability to re-identify data within a de-identified database.

Virtually all countries that will provide researchers with access to linked data will consider such a request for approval. In all cases, however, the requesting researcher must be able to demonstrate that they had collected the data with the informed consent of the data subjects or had legal authorisation. In *Italy*, however, there are no routine or standardised procedures for a researcher to request a linkage of their own cohort of data to governmental databases and it seems that this type of project is impossible. In *Belgium and France*, the Privacy Commission renders a decision on all project proposals and would hear the proposal.

In *Australia*, the AIHW may agree to conduct a data linkage project involving a researcher's own cohort of data if all data custodians involved have approved the linkage and if a waiver of the need for consent has been provided by all human research ethics committees involved. Further, in Australia, deceased persons are not within the scope of the national Privacy Act (1988) and the AIHW ethics committee has approved that death data may be linked without consent under certain conditions. For similar reasons, the *United States* also reports that death data may be linked to a researcher's cohort without consent.

The *Switzerland* Statistical Office notes that such requests can be costly and that the time required to execute the requests is recovered from the researchers. This practice was also noted by *Denmark*. *Finland* noted that the National Institute for Health and Welfare is trying to keep costs low for external researchers but is under financial pressure. Some countries noted the challenge of charging for data that is a public good, even if the cost of custom data linkages is high. *Australia* reports that it intends to charge user fees for the SURE remote data access facility.

Data security within public authorities

In all of the countries participating in this study, data security and the protection of data confidentiality is given considerable attention. It was common for countries to report that their institution's existence or its ability to continue its programme of work would be placed at risk by any serious breach in data security. The elements of data security identified are accompanied by examples provided by country experts during the telephone interviews. The next section discusses the specific case of data security for de-identified data provided to external researchers.

1. *Require employees to sign a non-disclosure or data confidentiality protection agreement.*

    The Australian Institute of Health and Welfare; the Belgian Cancer Registry; the Canadian Institute for Health Information; and the UK NHS NSS Scotland reported a requirement for new employees to sign a document that they will protect data confidentiality. The United States NCHS and the UK NHS Scotland reported an annual requirement for all employees to sign a document that they will protect data confidentiality.

2. *Provide staff with a written manual or a website describing their responsibilities for data confidentiality protection and security.*

    The US NCHS and the Australian AIHW have a staff manual on data confidentiality protection requirements. Data security and privacy guidelines are communicated to all employees of Korea HIRA using the internal network homepage. At the UK NHS NSS Scotland, standards for data protection and security are described in a document that employees must sign annually.

3. *Institute levels of approved access to data for staff.*

    At the Registerstele Krebsregister Schleswig-Holstein (Institute for Cancer Epidemiology) in Schlewig-Holstein, Germany; the Danish National Board of Health; the Finland National Institute for Health and Welfare (NIHW); the Australian Institute of Health and Welfare (AIHW); and the Canadian Institute for Health Information (CIHI); among others, individuals must be approved for access to data and only can see data relevant for their project requirements or job requirement. Some may have access to identifiable data, some to de-identified data and some have no data access at all. There are finer levels of approved access to data among employees of the Belgian Cancer Registry. Some employees may not see identifiable data; some may see identifiable data but only one record at a time and only to resolve data quality problems; and a small number of employees who work with physicians to receive data transfers and address quality issues may see identifiable data.

4. *Restrict data analysts from access to identifiable data.*

    At the Registerstele Krebsregister Schleswig-Holstein (Institute for Cancer Epidemiology) in Schlewig-Holstein, Germany, data analysts are never given access to personal identifiers and cannot access the computer system used by staff that process data. At the Swedish National Board of Health and Welfare, there is a specific statistical unit, the registry unit, which is permitted access to data containing identifying numbers. This unit cleans and processes the data and conducts data linkages for approved projects and de-identifies the data. Board analysts with permission to access files, see only de-identified data and never have access to the identified data. At the Singapore Ministry of Health, researchers and officers who perform analysis of de-identified linked datasets are restricted from accessing the identifiable constituent databases to minimise inadvertent re-identification and exposure of linked data records.

5. *Track and monitor staff access to data.*

    At the Singapore Ministry of Health, staff analysing linked data must do so from within a secure data lab. The use of the data within the lab is monitored and if there was any inappropriate handling of the data, it would be possible to identify the researchers involved. Employees of the Belgian Cancer Registry with access to identifiable data must have their access logged. At the Swedish National Board of Health and Welfare, a security officer tracks which employees have been granted access to data. The National Board of Health in Denmark monitors who has access to registries and monitors and keeps logged how people with access are using the registry data on a 24/7 basis. The same protection and oversight applies to all national institutions in Denmark. The UK NHS Information Centre regularly reviews access logs to ensure that employees are still using the files that they are approved to access. A similar monitoring has also been introduced at the Swiss Federal Statistical Office.

6. *Provide training for new staff.*

Staffs of the Canadian Institute for Health Information, the Belgian Cancer Registry and the Swedish National Board of Health and Welfare are trained in data security and confidentiality requirements when they are first hired. New employees of the National Board of Health in Denmark and the National Institute of Health and Welfare in Finland are trained in the use of data and data security by experienced colleagues.

7. *Provide refresher training for existing staff.*

The US NCHS employees receive training on data security and confidentiality annually. Further, there are posters put up around the offices reminding staff about data confidentiality protection and security. The Belgian Cancer Registry provides training on global procedures regularly, including data security. The UK NHS Information Centre requires employees to take online training each year in data protection and then to pass a test. Every two months, employees of Korea's HIRA undergo data security and privacy training to ensure strict adherence to guidelines. The Canadian Institute for Health Information requires employees to complete mandatory on-line training annually on data privacy and security and to renew their pledge to protect data confidentiality. Ad hoc mandatory training may be required for some employees throughout the remainder of the year. The UK NHS NSS Scotland has on-line training in data security that is scenario based.

8. *Provide training for external researchers.*

The Finland NIHW provides university-based researchers with a half-day or full-day training course on the NIHW databases, where part of the training is about data protection. The US NCHS requires researchers with approved access to a Research Data Centre to take training on data security and confidentiality annually. All researchers approved to undertake research requiring access to the SURE remote access facility in *Australia* will be required to successfully complete training on data confidentiality and security before accessing SURE.

9. *Require external researchers accessing data to become designated employees of the data custodian in order to place them under the same legal requirements and penalties as a regular staff member.*

In the United States, contractors working for the NCHS who will touch data and external researchers approved to access de-identified data in the NCHS Research Data Centres must become designated employees of the NCHS. As a result, they are under the same legal obligations and penalties as staff of the NCHS to protect the confidentiality of the data they are working with.

10. *Secure buildings and offices.*

The German Institute for Cancer Epidemiology, where analysis of cancer registry data takes place at a national level, has strong physical security including doors that cannot be opened from the outside without a key. There is a clean desk requirement for staff engaged in data entry where no record can be left out at the end of the day. Records to be destroyed are stored in a separate container that cannot be easily accessed and a truck with a shredder comes monthly to security dispose of these materials. The Swedish National Board of Health and Welfare stores data in a building that is locked and secure. At the Finland NIHW, individuals may only share an office with another staff member who has approved access to the same data. Within the Australian AIHW, the Data Integration Services Centre (Data Linkage Centre) is physically separated from the other offices of the AIHW and only authorised personnel may enter the Centre.

11. *Secure transfers of identifiable data.*

In Sweden, data flows into the National Board of Health and Welfare are encrypted and sent in by mail. In Switzerland, the Federal Statistical Office uses secure servers to transfer data, for data storage and for access to data. In Finland, data flows into the National Institute for Health and Welfare (NIHW) take place using a secure electronic transfer. The UK NHS Information Centre uses a secure web transfer system similar to the older FPT protocol for data flows into and out from the Centre and protects the security of the system with a firewall.

12. *Secure computer systems for the storage of identifiable data.*

At the Singapore Ministry of Health, only data custodians and authorised data management staff are allowed access to identifiable personal health databases, meeting internal government standards for data security. The computer system used to process the identifiable data and conduct data linkages is completely separated from the computer system for analysis of de-identified data. The analysis of de-identified data takes place on standalone and isolated computers. In Switzerland, IT security requirements are under a specific federal department (IT) and all federal data is centrally stored and protected. Physical displacement of data is avoided. In Sweden, identifiable databases of the National Board of Health and Welfare are not stored on computers that are connected to a network, which protects the data from unauthorised access. At the Australian AIHW, the Data Integration Services Centre (Data Linkage Centre) has its own computer servers that cannot be accessed by staff outside of the Centre.

13. *Implement whole-of-government regulations or reporting up requirements on data security protection.*

The United States has federal regulations on data security that federal agencies must follow. The US NCHS must report to the government each year on its data security, and on any IT system changes that have occurred. The IT security is accredited every three years by the Centre for Disease Control. All federal agencies in the United States would have a similar oversight and monitoring of their IT security. Korea's HIRA has internal guidelines on the protection of data security and confidentiality including specific guidelines related to data linkage. Under the requirements of the new Personal Information Protection Act, the National Intelligence Service has issued guidelines on data security to government ministries including HIRA. HIRA will report annually to both the internal HIRA auditor and to the National Intelligence Service on its data security. The Belgian Cancer Registry has privacy and information security policies and a data security plan required under the legislation authorising the registry. This plan is updated every three years. Elements of the security plan include how and when access to data is permitted; including levels of access to personal health data. The NHS NSS Scotland data security respects British Standards for Information Management and Data Sharing and NHS Scotland standards. In Singapore, there are guidelines within government for data protection.

14. *Institute third party or external data security audits.*

At the Belgian Cancer Registry, there are security audits by an independent organisation that will attempt to attack the security of the registry. The registry has received a high rating by the independent organisation for the results of its most recent security audit. In Korea, the Ministry of Health and Welfare, Ministry of Public Administration and Security and the National Intelligence Service have the authority to conduct privacy and security audits of HIRA. In Denmark, the Danish Data Protection Agency annually audits the National Board of Health to ensure that the handling of the databases meets legislative requirements. The Danish National Audit Office, which ensures that all national agencies comply with all relevant legislation may also audit the Board, or may rely on the results of the Data Protection Agency audit. In Australia, the data security environment of the Australian Institute of Health and Welfare (AIHW) was audited by a third party as a result of the AIHW's application to become a national integrating authority (national data linkage centre) for high risk linkage projects. Develop protocols in the event of a data security breach.

The United Kingdom NHS NSS Scotland and the NHS Information Centre have reporting systems that are used in the event of a suspected data security breach. In Korea, HIRA has a code to follow in the event of a data security breach.

15. *Institute legal penalties for deliberate breaches of data security.*

Within the US NCHS and Korea's HIRA, penalties for breaches of data security by employees include fines and imprisonment. Legal prosecution is also reported by the Danish National Board of Health as a consequence of a deliberate breach by an employee.

Data security when researchers receive data from public authorities

Data security is highest among data custodians requiring external researchers to access de-identified personal health data within a secure facility that is controlled by the data custodian or a third party. This practice was noted in the United States, Australia, Singapore and Canada. As discussed earlier, many data custodians provide approved researchers with access to de-identified data. Below are several examples of how data security is approached in this situation.

In *Finland*, when a researcher applies to access data, their application must demonstrate how their institution or university respects data protection requirements. Data is provided to the researcher on a compact disk that has been encrypted and the encryption key is provided to the researcher in a separate communication. Only identified and approved individuals who have been named may access the data.

In *Denmark*, the project approval will describe to the researchers the retention period of the file and will bind the researcher to not linking the data to any other databases and to not disclosing the data to a third party. The data protection authority in Denmark is then responsible for follow-up with the researchers to ensure compliance and data security audits take place. Non-compliance is a legal violation and subject to penalties. At the data destruction date, the researcher will be given the option to de-identify the data, if they would like to retain the data for a longer period.

In the *United Kingdom*, the NSS Scotland indicates that the researcher is scrutinised during the approval process. A researcher who is a registered professional risks losing their profession as a result of a deliberate breach and, consequently, would be more likely to be approved. A researcher working within a recognised institution where data protection and data security are known to be high would also be more likely to be approved. Researchers sign their application that binds them to data security; to data confidentiality protection (including following rules for vetting any tables intended for publication); and to not share the data they have received with a third party. The NHS Information Centre for Health and Social Care indicated that there have been cases where linked data was given to a trusted third party for analysis, so that the risk of re-identification could be reduced.

In *Switzerland*, when data files are provided to an external researcher, their contract with the Federal Statistical Office binds them to protect the data and to follow the guidelines they are given. They are warned that they will be required to destroy the data if there is any infringement of these requirements. In practice, researchers want to be able to continue to collaborate with the Statistical Office and will follow the requirements. There is no audit of external researchers but there is tracking of their external publications to ensure that their use of the data is consistent with the agreed-upon purpose of their study.

In *Germany*, academic researchers can access de-identified personal health data for research. The provision of de-identified data for research is part of the laws that authorise cancer registries. While names will never appear on analysis files, some identifiers may be approved to remain on an analysis file, such as date and place of birth, if there is a justification for their inclusion in the research proposal. The decision to retain these identifiers will depend on the potential re-identification risk. Where re-identification risk may be high, solutions can include limiting the geographic variables to a higher level of geography or to retain only the month or year of birth.

Multi-country projects

Multi-country projects pose new challenges for data protection, as the data custodians involved typically have no legal recourse to exert any penalties for misuse of data by a foreign entity. Multi-country projects are difficult for research teams to implement, as the data protection requirements of each participating data custodian must be respected. Nonetheless, multi-country studies can provide a rich source of new information for the benefit of the public's health and the management of health systems and there are good examples of successful work.

The data protection legislations in some European countries make clear that it is possible to share identifiable data with other countries in the European Union. Noting this feature as part of national data protection legislations were *Denmark's* National Board of Health; *France's* Agence des Systèmes d'Information Partagés en santé and the *United Kingdom's* NHS NSS Scotland.

The *United Kingdom* NHS NSS Scotland indicated that under the UK Data Protection Act, it is not acceptable to share de-identified individual data outside of the European Union unless it can be demonstrated that the receiving country has the same standards for data protection as the United Kingdom. Some non-EU countries have been certified as having equivalent standards and, for them, the process is the same as for an EU country. For a country not on the list, the two options for data access are a review of the country's legislation and an application for certification; or the provision of a fully de-identified data set, where there would be a very low risk of re-identification of individuals.

A similar process was reported by *France*. Under French law, the data protection authority (CNIL) may approve a project involving the sharing of personal health data with another EU country, as all EU members have established similar protections for data security and protection of privacy. If a project was to involve a non-EU country, the non-EU country would have to demonstrate that it has legislation that provides similar protection. For example, CNIL approved a project that involved sharing data with a researcher in the United States. Under a safe harbour agreement that was negotiated between the United States and the European Union, a contract was established that confirms that US laws (national and state) provide similar data privacy and security protection to those of EU countries.

Denmark's National Board of Health has contributed de-identified individual data to multi-country studies with other Scandinavian countries and has provided aggregate study results to multi-country studies led by many other countries including France, the United Kingdom and Germany. Similarly, the *Finland* National Institute for Health and Welfare has participated in multi-country studies based on data linkages. The *Belgium* Cancer Registry may contribute de-identified individual-level data to a multi-country study if the Office of Data Protection grants permission.

The *United States* National Centre for Health Statistics can provide a foreign researcher with access to de-identified individual-level data in two ways. In the first, the foreign researcher has equal access to public-use micro data files as does any domestic person. These files have been fully de-identified to result in a very low risk of re-identification of individuals. In the second, foreign researchers may submit a proposal to access data within the NCHS secure research data centres.

Australian researchers have participated in parallel studies where an Australian researcher received approval for the Australian data linkage and returned aggregated analysis to the multi-country study team. It is also possible for a foreign researcher to be approved to analyse *Australian* personal health data if the researcher is based in Australia and follows all of the same approval processes as any Australian national. The Australian Institute of Health and Welfare also recognises the legitimate need to share identifiable data across borders, particularly with New Zealand. There was a previous request to the AIHW from a New Zealand researcher for the linkage of a cohort of New Zealand military personnel to death records in Australia, as many had re-located to Australia and may have died there. The research ethics committee of the AIHW is reluctant to approve this request until they can be certain that legal penalties for any misuse of data by the foreign researcher can be applied.

There is an EU-funded project, EuroREACH, where representatives from participating countries in Europe and outside of Europe with experience in conducting national data linkage studies are working together to develop a website. The website would support researchers within and outside of government in the launch of multi-country health services research based on data linkages. It will draw on best-practice country examples in establishing comprehensive systems of performance measurement in European countries, and in granting research access to patient-level data for the study of health services. It will also report on the person-level databases within countries that could support analysis and research and the steps required to produce population-based linked data sets and use them for multi-national health research projects (EuroREACH, 2011).

Bibliography

Churches, T. (2002), "The Use of Probabilistic Record Linkage, Public Key Cryptography and Trusted Third Parties to Improve the Protection of Personal Privacy and Confidentiality in Disease Registers and Tissue Banks", Symposium on Health Data Linkage Proceedings, Australian Government Department of Health and Ageing, Sydney, pp. 57-61.

Department of Health (2011), "Creation of the Health Research Authority", www.dh.gov.uk/health/2011/12/creation-hra, accessed 19 February 2013.

Department of Health (2013), "Information to Share or Not to Share? Information Governance Review", http://caldicott2.dh.gov.uk/, accessed 19 February 2013.

El Emam, K. (2008), "De-identifying Health Data for Secondary Use: A Framework", CHEO Research Institute, Ottawa.

El Emam, K., E. Jonker and A Fineberg (2011), "The Case for De-Identifying Personal Health Information", Social Science and Research Networks, www.ssrn.com/absract=1744038.

EuroREACH (2011), www.euroreach.net, accessed 25 October 2011.

Fraser, A. (2003) "Privacy and the Secondary use of Data in Health Research in Scotland", Journal of Health Services Research and Policy, Vol. 8, Suppl. 1, pp. 12-16.

Kalra, D., R. Gertz, P. Singleton and H.M. Inskip (2006), "Confidentiality of Personal Health Information Used for Research", British Medical Journal, Vol. 333, No. 7560, pp. 196-198.

Karmel, R., P. Anderson, D. Gibson et al. (2010), "Empirical Aspects of Record Linkage Across Multiple Data Sets Using Statistical Linkage Keys: The Experience of the PIAC Cohort Study", BMC Health Services Research, Vol. 10, p. 41.

Kelman, C.W., A.J. Bass and C.D.J. Holman (2002), "Research Use of Linked Health Data – A Best Practice Protocol", Australian and New Zealand Journal of Public Health, Vol. 26, No. 3, pp. 251-255.

Scottish Health Informatics Programme (2011), www.scot-ship.ac.uk, accessed 25 October 2011.

Statistics Canada (2011), "Research Data Centres", www.statcan.gc.ca/rdc-cdr/index-eng.htm, accessed 25 October 2011.

Chapter 7

Governance of national electronic health record systems data collection

The creation and analysis of national databases from electronic health records to improve the safety and efficiency of health care requires strong governance of the national electronic health record system. Of the 25 countries participating in this part of the study, one-half have a national body that is responsible for EHR infrastructure development and for setting national standards for both the clinical terminology used within the records and the interoperability, or sharing, of records. Five countries have introduced or are planning to introduce legislation requiring health care providers to implement electronic health records that conform to national standards. Seven countries reported a certification process for software vendors to comply with national standards for clinical terminology and interoperability. Eleven countries report incentives or penalties to encourage health care providers to adopt electronic health record systems conforming to national standards; and to use their EHR system and keep records up-to-date. Six countries reported auditing EHR records for the quality of the clinical information. Seven countries reported engaging third parties to centralise one or more of the following tasks: building databases from electronic health records; de-identifying data to protect privacy; and granting access to data.

This chapter explores results of the OECD study of 25 countries regarding the development of national bodies to oversee national EHR implementations; the use of legal requirements to adopt EHRs or adhere to standards; the use of incentives and penalties to encourage quality in the use of EHRs; concerns with data quality and the use of data quality auditing; and the engagement of third parties to assist with building databases, de-identifying data and approving applications for data access.

7. GOVERNANCE OF NATIONAL ELECTRONIC HEALTH RECORD SYSTEMS DATA COLLECTION

The governance of the electronic health record system design and implementation will have a significant impact on whether or not data from electronic health record systems will be eventually useable for national health care quality and health system performance monitoring. Countries that are able to aim toward a single country-wide deployment of one electronic health record system have a clear advantage. Many countries, however, are challenged in this objective because they have a decentralised health care system, where decisions are taken at a sub-national level. Success strategies typically involve setting national standards for the content of the records, such as establishing a minimum set of data, where the content of the record follows terminology standards and the data is structured to be comparable; and setting interoperability standards, so that each electronic record system deployed in the country can speak to another.

This study of 25 countries (see Annex C) explored several dimensions of the governance of the implementation and maintenance of national electronic health record systems and the governance of data use. This included the existence of a national body with primary responsibility for the national EHR infrastructure development and/or a governing body to develop and maintain standards for clinical terminology and for electronic messaging (interoperability). It also explored the existence of any legal frameworks requiring participation in national electronic health record systems; the use of incentives or penalties to encourage compliance; data quality concerns and quality auditing; and the use of third parties for database development, data de-identification, or approval of data access requests.

National bodies with responsibility for the development of National EHR infrastructure

One-half of the study participants have a national body responsible for EHR infrastructure development and who set standards for clinical terminology used within the records and standards for interoperability. Other countries have a national body in place for EHR infrastructure, but limit its role to recommending standards for clinical terminology, or to not discussing such standards. Still others have no national governing body.

In *France*, the Agence des Systèmes d'Information Partagés de Santé (ASIP santé) took responsibility in 2009 for setting all operability standards and agreements with data custodians. It is a multi-disciplinary body with representation from industry, patients, and legal and health professionals. *Austria* established in 2010 a national organisation with responsibility for co-ordinating the implementation of national EHR infrastructure, the ELGA GmbH.

Finland reported that the government, through the National Institute for Health and Welfare (NIHW), is responsible for the national EHR infrastructure. In 2004, the NIHW was involved in the national EHR as an expert. In 2008, the NIHW became responsible for the code server. Since 2011, the NIHW ensures the interoperability of the National EHR and this role is authorised by law. The NIHW consults stakeholder groups. In 2012, the Directorate of Health in *Iceland* became responsible for national EHR development and for setting standards for clinical terminology. The Directorate is also aiming toward national standards for electronic messaging that adhere to international standards. Similarly, the Ministry of Health in *Israel*, took responsibility in 2011 for national EHR system development and for setting clinical terminology standards and defining the national minimum dataset.

The Ministry of Health in *Slovenia* took responsibility in 2008 for setting standards for clinical terminology and interoperability. In *Portugal*, a commission within the Ministry of Health was created in 2011 to set standards for clinical terminology within electronic health records. A separate technical body is responsible for interoperability standards.

In *Spain*, the Ministry of Health, Social Services and Equality, through the Medical Records in the National Health System (HCDSNS) project, took responsibility in 2006 for EHR implementation, including clinical and interoperability standards. The ministry is developing SNOMED-CT derivatives including subsets, extensions, mappings, and translations; subset browsing software; subset editing modules; health record modelling and terminology services studies; and training in interoperability, terminology resources, and clinical documentation standards. The Information Systems Sub-Commission for the national health system discusses alternatives and makes recommendations to the national Interterritorial Council (IC) regarding clinical information standards for EHRs. Its members include stakeholders (autonomous communities), health authorities, and the Ministry of Health. The IC makes decisions on clinical standards and sets priorities.

The responsibility for national EHR implementation is shared in *Sweden* between the National Board of Health and Welfare (NBHW) which sets the clinical terminology standards for electronic health records and the Swedish Association of Local Authorities and Regions (SALAR), which comprises the Center for eHealth in Sweden, and sets national standards for electronic messaging. Governance of EHR infrastructure was initiated in 2000; however the respective roles of these two bodies have evolved over time and continue to evolve. The engagement of stakeholder groups in EHR governance, such as professional groups, is not yet fully established. However, the SALAR and its Center for eHealth is responsible for all health care providers, pharmacies and suppliers while the NBHW ensures national views are represented.

In *Denmark*, the National Board of eHealth (NSI) was established in 2011 to set standards, and to develop strategies and architectures for the whole health sector. It governs eHealth across sectors including databases and registries and runs cross-sectoral projects. It sets clinical terminology and interoperability standards for the national EHR. The *Estonian* E-Health Foundation was established in 2005 and is responsible for implementing clinical terminology and interoperability standards and IT systems and for housing the central system. The foundation publishes standards, educates users and promotes co-operation among stakeholders.

In *Belgium*, the E-Health Platform was established in 2008 and sets standards for clinical terminology and interoperability in conjunction with other organisations. Working groups of the E-Health Platform develop and maintain standards for clinical information and include representatives from PFS Public Health, the National Insurance Institute and other public health related institutions. The working groups on data elements and on semantics receive requests to select particular standards; and undertake projects to analyse and prioritise these requests. The working groups may also adapt proposals to conform better to the standards that are already in place for the country (kmehr format). Working group members include public health institutions, industry, regional networks and, for semantics, representatives from all sectors and experts working in this field. A certification system in Belgium, however, requires adherence to interoperability standards and there is also an incentive policy to improve compliance.

Poland reported that the National Centre for Health Information Systems (CSIOZ) was established in 2009. It is an agency of the Ministry of Health, responsible for implementing two major platforms for eHealth in Poland. This organisation is responsible for developing and setting standards for clinical terminology and interoperability. Clinical terminology standards are the responsibility of the National Normalisation Committee in collaboration with the European Committee for Standardisation (CEN).

In *Slovakia*, the National Health Information Centre (NHIC) took responsibility in 2008 for the development, implementation and operation of the National Health Information System, including the national EHR. Within the NHIC, the Centre for Medical Terminology and Standards is responsible for the preparation, co-ordination and guidance of the implementation of clinical standards. The NHIC is also responsible for interoperability standards. Representatives of universities, medical professional associations, health chambers, IT experts, pharmacists, linguists and others, take part in the work of the Centre for Medical Terminology and Standards.

In *Korea*, the Korea Health and Welfare Information Service is responsible for EHR infrastructure development as part of the Public Health and Medical Institution Informatisation Project. This organisation was established in 2008 and has developed the Korea Standard Terminology of Medicine (KOSTOM) which is now in use in 170 medical institutions and may become the national standard in the future. The Health Insurance and Review Board (HIRA) has developed standards for data coding using insurance claim data. These standards are developed jointly with professional associations, payers, government and medical service providers. The Public Health and Medical Institution Informatisation Project was authorised by law.

EHealth Suisse, or the Swiss Co-ordination Office for eHealth Confederation Cantons, is responsible for co-ordinating the work of four working groups on standards and architecture; pilots and implementation; and education in *Switzerland* and was established in 2008. Different organisations develop and maintain clinical information standards and they are unified within a working group on standards. In *Singapore*, MOH Holdings Pte. Ltd. was established in 2008 to provide the governance, change management, enterprise architecture and the clinical and interoperability standards for the national EHR system.

The *United Kingdom* reported that the NHS Connecting for Health was established in 2005 to be responsible for national EHR infrastructure in England, including delivering programs and managing services, and clinical terminology and interoperability standards. The Information Standards Board appraises and approves standards for clinical information. Its members include clinical, managerial and technical experts. In *Scotland*, there is no independent body established for the development of EHR infrastructure and it is managed by the Scottish Government eHealth Division. The eHealth Division recommends clinical terminology and interoperability standards and other organisations engage in the development and maintenance of these standards. The organisations consult with stakeholders.

The *Netherlands* reported that after the legal closure of the initiative to develop a national EHR in 2011, the Association of Health Care Providers for Health Care Information Sharing has, of its own volition, made a new start with the goal of establishing electronic health records that can be exchanged within regions. This association includes general practitioners, pharmacists, primary care organisations providing after-hours care, and hospitals. There is neither government involvement nor a role for government in the initiative. The Association consults with patient organisations and health care insurers in the plans for the EHR system. Three other national organisations also play a role. The National IT Institute for Health Care (NICTIZ) is a private organisation that develops national standards for electronic communications in health care. The Quality of Care Institute stimulates the development of clinical guidelines. The societies of medical specialists and general practitioners are responsible for the development of clinical guidelines and advise on the content of EHRs.

In *Canada*, the Canada Health Infoway was established in 2001 to develop a national vision and to guide the development of electronic health records in Canada (EHR blueprint). Infoway jointly invests with the provinces and territories to implement health information systems. It supports and sustains communications and technology standards that enable health information systems to share patient health information accurately and securely. Infoway works with the clinical community to foster and support the adoption and use of health information technologies by clinicians. The Canadian Institute for Health Information works with jurisdictions to encourage adoption of national standards for database content including, primary health care data content standards, and the adoption of International Residential Assessment Instrument (InterRAI) standards for mental health, long-term care, home care and rehabilitative care. Standards are available to provinces and territories and are adopted on a voluntary basis. Stakeholders engaged in Canadian EHR development include EHR vendors, health care organisations, jurisdictions, health care providers, professional associations, governments and other organisations interested in implementing standards-based EHR solutions.

The *United States* reports that there is no separate private or public entity for national EHR infrastructure. The Department of Health and Human Services adopts national standards and regulates the certification of EHR products. By statute, there is a politically appointed National Co-ordinator for Health Information Technology who heads the Office of the National Co-ordinator for Health Information Technology (ONC) and who reports directly to the Secretary of Health and Human Services. ONC was established in accordance with this statute in 2009 and is responsible for co-ordinating development of the nation's EHR infrastructure, including developing and administering regulations necessary for the Secretary to adopt standards. The ONC recommends voluntary consensus standards to the extent possible, including internationally recognised standards, such as HL7 and SNOMED-CT. Where there are no voluntary consensus standards available, the ONC works with private-sector standards development organisations and standards bodies to promote the development of standards to fill these gaps. The governance of the exchange infrastructure (interoperability) is currently being developed.

In *Germany*, Gematik is an organisation of health care providers and representatives of the statutory health insurance system that is responsible for establishing a national telematics infrastructure for health care. Gematik is expected to provide some guidance on the implementation of interoperable documentation systems. There is no organisation in Germany to set clinical terminology or interoperability standards at the national level.

In *Indonesia*, the Centre for Data and Information is responsible for developing and implementing standards related to health statistics as well as the development of information systems and databases and, since 2007, has been responsible for national EHR infrastructure development. It is not yet responsible for setting EHR terminology or interoperability standards. The Directorate General of the Health Care Effort is also involved in setting standards for clinical information.

There is no national organisation in *Mexico* that is responsible for EHR infrastructure or to set standards for clinical terminology or interoperability. In Mexico, the Direccion General de Informacion en Salud (DGIS) is responsible for the integration of health information for statistical purposes and develops and maintains standards for clinical information. There are also no national organisations in *Japan* responsible for EHR infrastructure development or standards development.

Legal requirements to adopt electronic health records and adhere to standards

A challenge for all countries is to ensure that health authorities and health care providers implement the requirements of the national electronic health record system. Some countries have introduced, or are planning to introduce, laws or regulations that require health care providers to adopt and use electronic health record systems that conform to national requirements for clinical terminology and interoperability. This is a strong stimulus toward full participation of health care providers in the national EHR system.

In Belgium, Denmark, Germany, Indonesia, Japan, Korea, Mexico, the Netherlands, Portugal, Slovenia, Singapore, Spain, Sweden, and the United Kingdom, there are no laws or regulations that require health care providers to adopt electronic health records, nor to adhere to particular standards.

French law stipulates that once a patient has an electronic health record, health care professionals must refer to it and complete it. This law, which came into effect in 2004, also binds health care providers to using SNOMED 3.5 vf standards for clinical terminology and to adopt CDA HL7/CDA R2 interoperability standards.

In *Finland and Estonia*, there are legal requirements for health care providers to adopt electronic health records and to ensure conformance with clinical terminology and interoperability (HL7) standards. Finnish legal requirements took effect in 2006 and those in Estonia took effect in 2009. In *Israel*, a Ministry of Health regulation requires health care providers to adopt electronic health records.

Slovakia is developing a law that will govern the National EHR. It is in the negotiation phase and the requirements of the law have not yet been set, however it is expected to require adoption of international standards including HL7 for interoperability. It may take effect by 2014. Similarly, there is a law in development in *Poland* that will require health care providers to adopt electronic record systems and to conform to clinical terminology standards and interoperability standards (HL7). It is expected to take effect in 2014.

A law is under development in *Switzerland*. The proposed law ensures that only certified communities of health care providers can have access to shared electronic health records. The law is not expected to require the use of electronic health records. Electronic transmission of data is only mandatory for reimbursement purposes. *Austria* is also progressing toward the introduction of legal requirements for health care providers to adopt electronic health records and plans for the requirements to enter effect by 2013.

While there is no national law requiring adoption of electronic health records nationally, some *Canadian* jurisdictions have passed laws requiring pharmacy vendors to adopt pan-Canadian HL7 drug standards as part of their drug information systems.

In *Iceland*, there are no laws or regulations requiring the adoption electronic health records, however, a Health Records Act states that health records should be electronic whenever possible.

Encouraging data quality within electronic health records

Most countries who have already implemented all or part of their national EHR are concerned with the quality of the data within the records. Noted obstacles to quality include the complexity of the EHR system, which may make it difficult to use; the complexity of the structured data elements and terminology standards, that may be a barrier to their use or to their correct use; and remaining reluctance or scepticism among health care providers to use the system or to appreciate the benefits of using the system.

Strategies to address these issues include financial incentives to implement and use records and efforts to work with vendors to increase the user-friendliness of the system (Table D.18). Very few countries, however, are auditing the clinical content of electronic records for quality yet. Audit processes for electronic billing information are more common. Processes to evaluate the usability of data from electronic health records for statistical purposes are more widely reported. For the most part, these efforts occur, hand in hand, with database creation and analysis of electronic health records.

Most countries have also explored incentives or penalties to encourage the adoption of the national EHR. Penalties include barriers to participation in the national EHR for providers with a non-conforming EHR system; and financial penalties for failure to meet commitments to EHR implementation and use requirements. Incentives include payment support to ease the transition to the national EHR solution; certification for EHR vendors whose solutions meet national requirements; and increased payments to providers implementing and using EHR solutions that meet national requirements.

Nine countries reported having instituted certification processes to ensure that the electronic health record systems available to heath care providers conform to national standards. Most require the systems to meet national standards for clinical terminology.

Eleven countries have also introduced incentives, penalties or both incentives and penalties for health care providers to adopt electronic health record systems from a certified vendor and/or to adopt EHR systems that conform to standards and use structured data (Table D.18). Seven countries have also introduced incentives or penalties to ensure that health care providers keep their electronic health records up to date.

The *United States* has a certification program for vendors of electronic health record systems pursuant to a statutory mandate that requires the adoption of standards. Legislation provides for several years of incentive payments for the adoption and meaningful use of certified electronic health record systems by physicians, including optometrists and podiatrists, and hospitals serving patients enrolled in public health insurance programs (elderly, low-income or disabled persons). Selected non-physicians who can prescribe medicines also can qualify for incentive payments if they provide services to low-income persons. Payment penalties will apply to these providers by 2015 if they cannot meet requirements for "meaningful use" of EHR technology, with the exception of providers who provide care to low-income persons under federal and state insurance programs. The capture and use of structured data is a requirement for meeting meaningful use criteria.

Belgium reported an incentive for physicians, nurses and physiotherapists to adopt a certified EHR system of EUR 840 per year. There is also an incentive of EUR 12 000 per year for hospitals to adopt national EHR standards. Belgium's Federal Public Health Service conducts audits of hospitals for the quality of their electronic records related to reimbursement.

Portugal has a certification process for vendors of electronic health record systems that requires vendors to adopt standards and use structured data. For electronic prescribing, hospitals and primary care centres are required to install systems from certified vendors only. Assessment of provider performance depends on provision of information from electronic record systems, which acts as an incentive for providers to register with the national system and to use the required structured coding.

In *Estonia,* permission from the E-health Foundation is a prerequisite to submitting information to the central EHR system. This permission will only be granted if national standards have been followed. As a result, there is a strong incentive for software vendors and health care providers to adopt EHR systems that conform to national requirements.

Similarly, *Finland* does not have a certification process for EHR vendors; however, the national EHR is restricted to only those systems that conform to national standards. After 2014, the only possible system for health providers will be the national EHR.

France requires vendors to provide electronic health record system solutions that are compatible with the national EHR, including requirements to comply with the standards of the national EHR. In *Switzerland*, the law currently in progress will require communities of health professionals to be certified in order to access the cross-community (interoperable) EHR.

In the *United Kingdom,* Scotland has a certification process for IT systems for primary care physicians, where some aspects of the system must be accredited through the SEF process (Scottish Enhanced Functionality). In Scotland, primary care physicians are required to use a national electronic record system for payments and hospitals are required to use the national system to produce standardised mortality rates and quality indicators. England has a certification process for vendors that requires adoption of a set of relevant standards. England withholds payment for services for primary care providers and hospitals that do not use an EHR system from a certified vendor, that do not adopt required standards or do not use the EHR system and keep records up-to-date.

Canada reported having pre-implementation certification by Canada Health Infoway in certain technology classes (ambulatory care, electronic medical records, consumer health applications, diagnostic imaging, drug information systems, and client, provider and immunisation registries). Some jurisdictions have lists of certified vendors of, for example, electronic medical records for primary care physician offices. Some jurisdictions also require vendors to meet standards for structured data elements in their procurement processes. Canada also offers incentives in the form of payments from Canada Health Infoway to deploy electronic medical record systems (primary care) and to integrate electronic medical record systems and hospital information systems.

Slovakia reported planning to introduce a certification process for vendors of electronic health records that includes adoption of standards, as well as incentives or penalties to adopt electronic health records from a certified vendor. These will be prepared after the adoption of the law through other regulations and directives.

Sweden reported requiring vendors of electronic record systems to be certified as conforming to European standards (CE certification).

There is no certification process for EHR vendors in *Mexico*; however, there is an evaluation that is required of all new EHR procurements for public institutions. A similar approach is taken in *Indonesia*.

Austria has put into place incentives for physicians, hospitals and pharmacies to adopt electronic health records by sponsoring implementation costs. These same groups face penalties for any misuse of data or discrimination against patients not participating in the electronic health record. *Japan* has an incentive for hospitals to adopt standards and use structured data in their electronic health record system through small add-on reimbursement payments.

Spain provided funding at the European Union and national level (AVANZA I and II) and through the Ministry of Health (Cohesion funds) that could be used by regions for investment in the development of electronic health record systems conforming to national standards. Further, in some communities in Spain, privately managed hospitals and health care centres that participate in public health care must assume the same obligation as public health care networks to adopt and keep up-to-date an EHR system conforming to national requirements.

Germany does not have incentives or penalties for the adoption of EHR systems or systems with particular standards in general. It does, however, have standards for billing information and certified systems must be used for billing in the ambulatory sector.

While no incentives or penalties are in place yet, *Israel* is planning to introduce penalties for health care organisations that do not conform to requirements of the national EHR system.

Data quality concerns and auditing

Many countries (16) have expressed concerns with the data quality within electronic records. Only six countries, however, are auditing the clinical content of electronic health records to verify and maintain data quality (Table D.18). Auditing processes for electronic billing information are more common.

The *Estonian* E-health Foundation audits electronic health records of physicians, hospitals and other health care providers for quality. Technical rules have been used to electronically detect data quality problems within electronic records submitted to the central system. Estonia reports that more controls, including adoption of additional rules, are needed to achieve better quality.

Iceland reports that the Directorate of Health conducts quality audits of the content of the minimum datasets used in primary health care and hospital admissions. Iceland reports concerns that data are frequently not coded in a timely manner. Further, internal data quality audits within each health care institution are often lacking.

Belgium's Federal Service for Public Health audits electronic health records in hospitals for quality in conjunction with audits of reimbursements. Belgium is concerned with under coverage and poor quality or unusable data elements within electronic health records.

Spain reports that health records are audited for quality in all health services. Audits are conducted by the Spanish Medical Inspection Body; and by internal committees within hospitals and health care provider areas. The Ministry of Health e-health governance team (HCDSNS) audits the content of the minimum dataset (CMDIC). Spain is concerned that the coverage of EHR applications and the use of the EHR by providers is irregular; that the use of standards remains limited; that support for the development of terminology standards is lacking; and that their remain patients in transition, where both paper and electronic records are being maintained.

Electronic records are also audited for quality in Portugal across all health services. The Central Administration of the Health System (ACSS) and the Directorate General for Health (DGS) conduct the audits. Data quality concerns in Portugal include the completeness and validity of the data, as well as some concerns with the potential for gaming or fraud to increase service payments.

In the *United Kingdom*, England reports quality audits of electronic health records undertaken by the UK Audit Commission as well as sometimes by the Royal Colleges. England is concerned with both the quality and completeness of electronic health records and notes that patient access to their records has highlighted the existence of potential inaccuracies. Scotland is concerned that most electronic health records are unchecked and that the quality of the records is up to the individual user's attitude and ability.

The *United States* reported that it does not audit provider's data quality per se. Providers using either paper or electronic records, however, are subject to audit of these records to assure the quality and safety of the services provided as well as the accuracy of claims for insurance reimbursement. Outcome incentives were chosen in lieu of a compliance-audit model.

Communities of health care providers in *Switzerland* are expected to undertake audits of their electronic records. Switzerland is concerned about records containing incorrect data or data that has not been kept up-to-date. There is also a worry about missing or invalid information within the records.

Poland reported that it does not audit electronic health records for quality, however, it does have control mechanisms for data associated with insurance claims, including the use of DRGs and automatic quality verification. Poland has concerns with up-coding related to DRG reimbursement, but it is very difficult to prevent these practices. Similarly, *Slovenia* reported that data is often entered into the EHR system for reimbursement purposes and can be skewed as a result.

Mexico expresses concerns with the quality of data in electronic health records and the potential impact of data quality problems on national statistics, public health decisions and other policy decisions, medical mistakes and medical services planning errors.

Finland has some concerns with coding accuracy. For the overall content, concerns with the quality of electronic records are similar to those for paper records. *Denmark* expresses a concern with the burden on clinical communities of EHR documentation that may lead to poor data quality and a misuse of physician's time.

Canada reports concerns with data quality emanating from the existence of legacy systems in hospital and primary care settings that have fallen behind in terms of recommended standards. *Singapore* expressed concern that the quality of data within electronic health records varies across institutions.

As is the case for other states in the early stages of implementation, it is too soon for *France* to determine if there are data quality concerns. Security audits are being conducted by ANSSI (Agence Nationale de la Sécurité des Systèmes d'Information) and data security and protection of data confidentiality audits are also being conducted by CNIL (National commission on information technologies and liberties). General inspectors of public social services may also audit the quality and overall efficiency of the EHR, but data quality audits are not performed for now.

The *Netherlands* is concerned that the national EHR does not yet exist and also with its eventual development. The quality of the data that will be collected through the proposed system, in terms of the creation of national databases, may be compromised by limited participation of patients, due to the possibility of an opt-in system; and a regional approach that would further limit national use of patient data. There are also concerns about the protection of patient privacy and security of stored data. The *Netherlands* reported that the EHR that can be used to share records across health care settings (interoperable) was built with a tool called EDPscan to help general practice physicians to ensure the quality of their electronic records. This tool could be used to scan medical files for completeness, structure, actuality and general quality. EDPscan for GPs is the responsibility of the Netherlands Institute for Health Services Research Scientific Institute of Quality for Health Care and the Dutch college of GPs.

There are no quality audits of electronic health records in *Germany*; however, physicians must meet standards for quality management. There are no valid data in Germany to assess the quality of electronic health records, as systematic monitoring is difficult due to data privacy concerns.

Engagement of third parties

Given the complexity of building national databases from electronic health records, a possible strategy for countries is the engagement of specialist third parties, separated from governments, insurers and health care providers, to assume responsibility of one or more difficult dimensions (Table D.19). Three areas were explored in this questionnaire, the potential use of third parties to build databases from electronic health records, to de-identify data to render the data anonymous and therefore more protective of patient privacy; or to render decisions from the potentially numerous applications for access to databases built from electronic health records for research projects and monitoring.

A small number of countries indicated that they are pursuing the engagement of third parties, the *United Kingdom, Korea, Indonesia, France, Canada, Estonia* and *Belgium*.

The National Commission on Information Technologies and Liberties (CNIL) in *France* already acts as a central decision-making body for the approval of research projects requiring access to personal health data for research and would fulfil this role for access to databases from electronic health records. *Belgium* has already established a third party that is engaged in the de-identification of data derived from electronic health records and the Belgian Privacy Commission approves or declines requests for access to databases built from electronic health records. *Estonia* has created an additional ethical committee to approve or decline requests for access to databases built from electronic health records.

In the *United Kingdom*, England reported encouraging a market of information providers that could, as third parties, assist with de-identification of databases and requests for access to data. England has already established a third party for the approval of projects requiring access to databases developed from electronic health records.

The Health Insurance Review and Assessment Service (HIRA) in *Korea* collects patient-level insurance claims data through electronic data interchange and builds databases that are analysed to monitor health care quality. The HIRA develops databases, de-identifies the data and approves or rejects access to data.

In *Canada*, the Canadian Institute for Health Information's role is to co-ordinate national health information and it expects to play a continued role in the creation of databases from electronic health records in the future. Further, some jurisdictions have created research data centres which can act as third parties for the development and analysis of provincial and territorial databases from electronic health records.

In the *United States*, third parties exist that are or are planning to create databases from electronic health records, however, these parties (such as professional associations and public-interest organisations concerned with improving health care quality and safety and advancing clinical science) have not been established by government. The establishment of a third party to de-identify data and to approve or decline requests for access to databases from electronic health records is an approach that the ONC may consider as an element of the governance of the exchange of health information and the National Health Information Network (NwHIN).

Indonesia reports that a third party has been engaged to develop the health data warehouse from electronic health records and related business intelligence tools.

Chapter 8

Progress and challenges in use of personal health data

There is optimism among most study respondents that national health information infrastructure is growing stronger and more capable of supporting health and health care monitoring and research. The technical capacity to undertake data linkage studies is growing and there is optimism about the potential for data from electronic health record systems to be used for health care quality monitoring. Respondents from six countries, however, indicated that it has become harder to use personal health data to monitor health and health care quality over the past five years. Respondents from five countries indicated that it is unlikely or impossible that any data from electronic health record systems will be used for national health care quality monitoring over the next five years. A particular worry across countries today is that legislative reforms that are on the horizon, or that may be stimulated due to the implementation of electronic health record systems, may turn back the clock on the progress that has been made in enabling data linkages and providing access to linked data for research. A second worry is that the quality of data within electronic health records presents a barrier to the creation of national databases. Resource limitations, and not meeting expectations of timeliness, are worries among bodies that approve project proposals and among bodies that conduct data linkages on behalf of others.

This chapter presents overall views of the participants to the OECD study of the secondary use of personal health data followed by views about the future use of data from EHR systems from participants to the OECD study on electronic health record system development.

In general, the outlook for the future is positive in terms of the opinions of the experts and researchers interviewed in this study toward their country's technical ability to undertake data linkages to monitor and report on the health of their people and the quality of their health care. Many countries were also positive about future capability of extracting data from electronic health record systems for health care quality monitoring and research. There is nearly universal agreement that data infrastructures are growing stronger and more capable of supporting this type of work. Many were also of the view that some of the growing pains associated with working with data protection authorities to arrive at ways of working effectively together were passing and that the process for seeking approval and safely and appropriately undertaking data linkage studies was getting clearer on both sides. Nonetheless, many countries still face significant challenges.

Countries where it is becoming easier to use personal health data to monitor health and health care quality

All participants to this study (see Annexes A and B) were able to express their opinion about whether it has become easier or harder to use personal health data to monitor health and health care quality over the past five years. Respondents in *Australia, Denmark, France, Malta, Norway, Poland, Portugal, Singapore and the United States* felt it was becoming easier.

In *Australia*, privacy law reforms were among the recommendations from the 2008 Australian Law Reform Commission report, *For Your Information: Australian Privacy Law and Practice* (Australia, 2008). The report recommended a range of changes to improve Australia's privacy framework and acknowledged the value of research involving data on human subjects including health, education, justice and other domains. The report also acknowledged that it is relevant to engage in data linkage to support this research. As a result of this report, there have been recommendations that would make it easier to engage in health-related data linkage studies but the first of these are only just being implemented. The Australian Government recently established a set of principles that cover the integration (linkage) of national data for statistical and research purposes. Changes in the health policy environment may increase the demand for data and linkages in the future. For example, through data linkage it should be possible to identify the population that is using mental health care services and work is underway to develop this indicator. Australia is slowly moving toward improving the indicator set which may lead to greater use of data linkage in the future.

Strengths of the *Danish* information infrastructure for data linkage include its policy applications. Data linkage studies contribute to evidence-based decisions across a range of important policies from human resource planning for the number of doctors and medical specialists that will need to be educated today to meet the health care needs of the population in the future; to how best to roll out population-based screening for cancer; to where to focus efforts to control rising health expenditures and the degree to which changes in tax rates could play a role in improving the fiscal balance. Data linkages have helped to demonstrate the effectiveness of breast-cancer screening in real-world populations and to understand the effectiveness of drug and alcohol treatment approaches. Through data linkage, *Denmark* is able to evaluate options for consolidation of hospital services in terms of their impact on the population served.

Processes for working with external researchers have been simplified in *Denmark*. For many years it has been possible for researchers to receive data from the National Board of Health, but it was not until 2007 that a unit was established within the NBH to handle the delivery of data to researchers. Four years ago, it became possible for scientists to request a running approval from the Data Protection Authority for data linkage. With this type of approval, they may have the same linkage repeated over several years and need not reapply to the DPA each time a linkage would be needed for the same project. An example would be a linkage to death certificates every year for several years for an on-going clinical cohort study.

France has had processes in place for many years to de-identify data for research and statistical purposes. The techniques used in France provide a high level of security for the data and the application of these techniques has been more widespread in France than is the case in other countries. France is working toward ensuring that data is processed in a systematic and consistent manner to permit it to be used for statistics and research to improve the health of the population. Electronic medical records are just being introduced in France and it will take years to achieve coverage of the population and to develop the information systems necessary to manage the data. Individual electronic records for pharmaceuticals are in the planning stage. Over the past five years it has become easier to conduct data linkage projects in France as the process for project approval becomes better established and understood. On the other hand, the databases and the data linkage techniques necessary to analyse them are becoming more complex. Further, France is grappling with the problem of the use of different unique identifiers between health insurance and hospital and electronic medical records. Solving the problem will involve both technical strategies and decisions about information governance. The reform of the EU directive on the protection of information privacy still requires study; however, it is unlikely to have a substantial impact on the current practices of the data protection authority (CNIL).

In 2011, there was a public health scandal in France as a result of the use of a prescription medicine Mediator that was directed toward diabetic care and was also prescribed for weight loss. The drug had been widely prescribed and then was later determined to have increased the risk of serious cardiovascular problems and to have resulted in deaths. The scandal heightened awareness in France of the need to use databases about the health of people to monitor the health consequences of prescription medicines and to move toward resolving the problem of the lack of a unique identifier, and the associated issues about information governance, that are limiting this work at present. The Institut des Données de Santé (IDS) facilitates the use of health data for public health by bringing together the different parties that constitute the health care system in France. In December 2011, a decree was published that facilitates access to national primary care data (SNIIRAM) for both public health organisations and research centres working in the field of public health.

In *Poland*, there are commitments to protect the privacy of personal information within the constitution, as well as legislation that protects privacy in the processing of personal data. In practice, it is not possible for data custodians to share data containing unique person identifying numbers, nor to use these numbers for any data linkage projects. It is, however, possible to conduct probabilistic linkage based on other identifying information. Other limitations to data linkage projects in Poland relate to concerns with the quality, timeliness, coherence and comparability of the data. Data quality concerns include redundancy in data collection and incoherent standards for data collection and dissemination; the inability to collect information where and when it is needed; the on-going use of paper-based registries; IT systems that have not kept up with organisational changes; difficulties managing data due to incompatible IT systems across organisations; and the lack of inclusion of data users in the design of IT systems.

There is optimism in Poland, however, that it is getting easier to use personal health data to monitor health care quality. There is a pilot project to link the cancer registry to data on breast cancer screening. There is also work in progress to develop a national electronic health record system "eHealth Poland" from 2011 to 2015. The project's goals include to create IT conditions that would enable a long-term perspective to support health care policy decisions; to develop a sustainable IT system that would permit consistent data collection over time; to decrease information gaps preventing an optimal health care model; and to have a system of data collection, transformation and use that would permit data exchange; reduce redundancy in data collection; support the secondary uses of data and information for statistical purposes; and decrease the administrative burden of data collection and data collection costs.

The *United States* is behind other OECD countries in terms of infrastructure for health data linkage. It does not have a unique patient identifier for health care encounters; there are so many different data custodians; there are multiple and complex laws regarding the use of personal health data; and the United States has been slow to implement EHRs. One person was of the view that the United States is not meeting its responsibility for the public's health and that the population was unaware of the risks to their health that have resulted. For example, when an individual is in a health emergency, their care is similar to a battlefield response because their caregivers know nothing about them, including the medications they may be taking. Emergency response could be much safer with the secure sharing of medical records. There is a need to build awareness of the health consequences of not having a national health identifying number. For example, even among members of Kaiser Permanente, which has a high adhesion, people move in and out of the plan and their health records are incomplete. Medicaid recipients also move in and out of this plan. If there was a rolling back of eligibility for Medicare and Medicaid, there would be less information in the future. It is very difficult to understand health outcomes and health care quality as a result; and this problem is the worst among the most vulnerable people, because that is where long-term adhesion to particular insurance plans is the lowest.

Two of the important barriers to a UPI in the United States are the public's trust in the use of their personal information in general, and the public's trust in government's use of personal information. Another challenge is the separation of state rights from federal rights, so that the federal government may not necessarily dictate what the states must do. Further, Congress, who allocates resources for federal agencies, is not always aware of the benefits to government of information from data linkages. This awareness is starting to rise with, for example, the opportunity to analyse survey data linked to Medicare and Medicaid records to identify the utilisation of care and the cost of care for vulnerable

Figure 8.1. **Over the past five years, has it become easier or harder to use personal health data to monitor health and health care quality?**

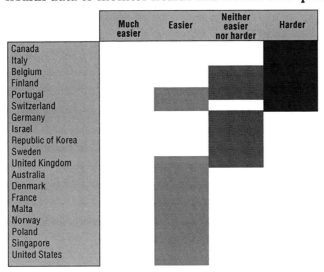

Note: In some countries there were differences of opinion and all responses are reported. No opinion was expressed by Japan.
Source: OECD HCQI Questionnaire on Secondary Use of Health Data and Follow-up Telephone Interviews, 2011/12.

populations so that federal spending on these programmes can be allocated more efficiently.

In the United States, linkage is improving from a technical viewpoint. Computers are getting faster and there have been improvements in linkage methodologies that have made linkage projects easier to do. The analytical file from the linkage of population survey data to Medicare and Medicaid records at the NCHS is proving to be a challenging file to analyse. Methodological challenges result because the number of observations is affected by both the number eligible to link and the number eligible for government programmes and there is a project-by-project necessity to re-weight the data to correct for bias. An on-line tutorial is being developed to help researchers to use the data.

As a result of the Affordable Care Act, there will be greater need to provide evidence of the impact of the Act. There are great expectations that data linkages will help to inform health policy, particularly in the area of effectiveness of care. If linkage studies in the next few years can show benefits to policy, data linkage will take off. There is a governmental push for EHR systems. With many commercial software developers, there is a need to promote uniformity so that interoperability will be possible. On the horizon is also the use of genetic information from bio-banking in long-term epidemiological research. It may take 20 years or more of exposure to tobacco smoke, dust, and air pollution to develop diseases. It therefore will take long-term linkage studies with genetic information, information on environment exposures, and information on health and health behaviours to know what factors are responsible for disease and to develop good policy responses. Future studies may involve a greater use of devices such as accelerometers to measure physical exertion or other devices to measure air quality and noise.

In *Singapore*, the data linkage projects that have taken place have had an impact on policy. At first, there were small sub-national studies and national efforts focussed on standards for data and data coding to improve the quality of person-level health databases. Once the quality of the databases was high, the door was then open for high-quality data linkages to monitor the performance of the health system. For example, stroke care quality is not just about care at the time of the acute event, it is about seeing how patients are doing six months later. Similarly, linkages have permitted evaluation of the effectiveness of breast cancer screening. Through linkages there is better sight on blind spots at the national level that helps with a better assessment of how the health system is performing. For example, it is possible to monitor whether persons suffering from heart attacks were known to suffer from hypertension and diabetes and whether these conditions were being well managed in primary care.

It has taken time to develop a process for application and review of research proposals in Singapore that conforms to the legislative framework; and to arrive at the establishment of a secure data lab. It is on-going work to be respectful of privacy and to find the right balance between data protection and access. This is because new types of projects keep coming up that have never been considered before, including, for example, new projects where researchers may want cross-sectoral linkages. As new models of care develop, it will be important that there remains data available to follow a patient's care path. In Singapore, a new Personal Data Protection Act came into effect in January 2013 to provide governance of the collection, use and disclosure of personal data. There is also a roll-out of a national EHR and there is a question of whether or not this could require additional legislation that would complement the Personal Data Protection Act. There is potential to create confusion with too many pieces of legislation related to data protection. Singapore has acquired a national license for SNOMED-CT and is in the midst of incorporating the terminology into the national EHR and institutional EMR systems. It will be important to ensure that coding is appropriate, so that the data quality is high and research results are valid. As more data becomes available in Singapore it may be necessary to consider a single body for conducting data linkages. The advantage would be economies of scale and standardisation of linkage methods. Running data protection offices within each data custodian is expensive. A disadvantage could result from this approach, however, if it failed to service research needs in a timely fashion.

Countries where it is neither easier nor harder today than five years ago to use personal health data to monitor health and health care quality

A second group felt that it was neither harder nor easier to use personal health data to monitor health and health care quality today than five years ago (*United Kingdom, Sweden, Israel, Korea, and Germany*). Views about the United Kingdom ranged from easier to neither harder nor easier.

Korea notes that its strength comes from a unique identifying number that is used throughout the health care system; a national system of health insurance that provides health care data for all patients; and a very strong technical infrastructure, where data is captured and stored electronically. The identifying number in Korea provides additional information to strengthen data linkages including full date of birth and place of birth. The conduct of data linkage has provided great benefits to Korea. Through analysis of health care claims, Korea is able to report on the quality of services provided by physicians, clinics, hospitals and long-term care. The Health Insurance Review Agency (HIRA) is also able to report on the cost of services and, with both quality and cost information, provide evidence for policy decisions. About ten years ago there was little discussion of protection of data privacy in Korea. With the new legislation and increased awareness, the balance between respect for patient privacy and the need for health research is sounder today.

It has never been easy to undertake data linkage studies in *Germany*. While scientists have always been aware of the benefits of data linkage studies, there is a rising awareness among authorities of the benefits to policy. The mammography screening study that was mandated by law is a good example of this rising awareness. Moreover, in 2011, legal provisions that allow data from a "morbidity-oriented risk adjustment scheme" of the statutory health insurance system were introduced that allow this data to be used for health services research and to advance the statutory health insurance system. Another point of progress are the recently awarded scientific grants from German Cancer Aid, a non-governmental organisation that awards scientific grants for research projects with cancer registry data, some of which involve record linkage with other data sources. The awards signify recognition of the scientific value of data linkages. Germany is doing well in the field of cancer registration in an international context. Since 2006, Germany has cancer registration for the complete population of 80 million people. The quality of data linkages based on pseudonyms and a limited number of other identifiers available from German cancer registries remains questioned by some. Certainly the probabilistic linkages are costly. It remains unclear whether or not the changes that would be required to enable deterministic linkages in Germany would be supported by the population.

In *Sweden*, the coverage of the health care quality registers is better now than five years ago and it has not become harder or easier to undertake data linkage studies. The project to assess the impact of guidelines on processes of care and on patient health was requested by government and the results have been taken seriously. Because there are public quality reports for hospitals by name, the conduct of the assessment alone has lead to quicker adoption of care guidelines in hospitals. There is increasing interest in the benefits of cross-sectoral studies in Sweden with data on social care and education to better understand the needs and the health outcomes of particular groups in the population and any differences in health care quality for different groups.

The government of Sweden is considering new legislation regarding access to data and data linkages. The new legislation is to address the issue of commercial interests wanting to access personal health data. In particular, insurance companies are interested in using personal data to decide on when to approve or deny coverage. While this is an important issue, the concern is that the new legislation may have a negative impact on research that is in the public interest.

In *Israel*, there remain some impediments that limit analysis of personal health data for health care quality monitoring. While Israel has an ID number that is used throughout the health care system, some of Israel's databases important for health care quality monitoring have encrypted the ID number and others have not done so. Without sharing among custodians of either the encryption methodology, or the unencrypted numbers, it is not possible to link these databases for statistical or research purposes. A further challenge is that health care quality monitoring requiring the linkage of primary care and hospitalisation data is possible within the HMOs within Israel, but is not undertaken at the national level. In general, HMOs do not share identifiable data outside of their organisation. Legal permission is necessary to receive any identifiable information in Israel and researchers external to government face this constraint.

In the *United Kingdom*, there is greater interest in and political support for data linkage studies now than five years ago. There is recognition that these studies can meet needs for greater transparency about the quality of patient care and can improve health research and evaluation of outcomes of clinical trials. There is a new maternity strategy in Wales that has recognised there is not enough information on birth outcomes and infant health and pilot studies to evaluate whether data linkage could be used instead of primary data collection are leading to regular linkage programmes. In the future, the linking of lab data and medical images will become possible and, in Scotland, a national database for the storing of radiology images is already in place.

Compared to five years ago, the establishment of the legislative framework and the creation of the National Information and Government Board (NIGB) as a governing body helped to clarify for all researchers what is required to undertake a study and to provide a good mechanism to submit applications for consideration and approval. The new Health and Social Care Information Centre and the NWIS in Wales are now providing services to facilitate data linkages and linkages will likely be used more in the future as they are much less expensive than primary data collection. Concern was expressed about the pressure on existing resources as the research community becomes more aware of data linkage services.

From the perspective of researchers in the United Kingdom, it may seem that the approval process is long. It can take up to six months for a decision from NIGB and the Scotland NSS indicates that the average time from submission of an application to a decision is three months, with all applications finalised before six months. Resource constraints limit the Scotland NSS from being able to speed up the process. There have been a few instances of data loss in the United Kingdom that have raised public concerns about and interest in information governance, and have made data security and confidentially rules tighter and processes for applicants wishing to access databases more difficult. Recent reforms in England, such as the launch of the Clinical Practice Research Datalink and the establishment of the Health Research Authority, support researchers in navigating the approval process and improve efficiency in research approval decision making.

Countries where it is becoming harder to use personal health data to monitor health and health care quality

A third group felt that it was becoming harder to use personal health data to monitor health and health care quality (*Canada, Italy, Belgium, Finland, Portugal and Switzerland*). Views were divided in Switzerland between easier and harder; views in Portugal ranged from easier to harder; and views about Belgium and Finland ranged from neither easier nor harder to harder.

In *Canada*, data sharing among public authorities is becoming increasingly complex as new legislations are introduced at both the provincial and federal levels. Within Ontario, one of the first provinces to introduce legislation specific to the protection of health data privacy, the legislation has helped to clarify consent requirements and to end ambiguity about which law governed the work process. The introduction of electronic health records will pose new challenges.

The benefits of data linkage studies to public policy and patient care have been clearly demonstrated at the provincial level. The Institute for Clinical and Evaluative Sciences at the University of Toronto has published thousands of peer-reviewed scientific articles. Through data linkage at a population level, information is produced that informs about the effects of treatments in real-world populations with multiple morbidities which can differ from results of controlled trials. There is evidence that research results have influenced policy and a good relationship with the Ontario Ministry of Health that appreciates that the study results help policy makers understand what can be done to improve the health care system. Further, there is rising interest among provincial policy makers in data to inform about the continuity of care and such information is made possible through data linkages.

There is growing interest in data linkages at the national level and a growing appreciation that data linkage adds information value to databases that is over and above their value as silos. The province of Ontario also reports a growing interest at the provincial and national levels in comparing across provinces and that discussion is underway on how to move forward using comparable data based on data linkage studies, and liberating data as has not been experienced previously. There is also growing interest in cross-sectoral data linkages to, for example, understanding how health effects educational outcomes of young people or to understand when a province should place driving restrictions on elderly people with Alzheimer disease. The province of Manitoba is leading the way for others in demonstrating the utility and importance of cross-sectoral linkages in Canada.

Canada notes that there is an emphasis on knowledge translation to government from research work so that research results contribute to evidence-based decisions. The inverse knowledge translation, where governments help to clarify for researchers the legal requirements related to the use of personal health data, needs the same attention. Within Canada, often people are saying the same thing but using different language and therefore not communicating clearly. There would be a benefit in developing clear definitions that are portable across provinces and in standardising the interpretation of laws.

Strengths of the *Italian* infrastructure include a large academic community and a long history of health and biological studies; established data flows for a spectrum of health services; universal health coverage which provides complete coverage of all patients in public data files; a unique identifying number that facilitates linkages; and an organisation of care where each person is assigned to a physician which makes it much easier to study their care path. A number of new databases are being developed by the Health Ministry including cancer screening, emergency services and mental health services that offer the potential to improve population health monitoring at the national level.

One of the challenges for Italy is the fragmented nature of the administration of the health system. There is no adequate mechanism to share data across territories and provinces in Italy and sharing is nearly impossible, even for official institutions. Researchers seeking funding from granting agencies for projects where individual-level data would be needed from regions face great uncertainty about whether the project they have planned could be approved. This is because the criteria used by the regions to evaluate proposals are not known. The approval process is not transparent for those without a government partner and many researchers seek funding or collaboration with public authorities in order to have confidence that their project could be approved. For example, the National Outcomes Project is linking hospital and death records to develop more accurate indicators of deaths following treatment. The National Agency for Regional Services (AGENAS) is assisting and coverage is improving, but still the linkage is occurring in only a few regions. While some regions have technical problems, many are unsure if they can legally share de-identified data for a national project. Further, the project is at risk from increasingly strict interpretations of privacy legislation that would only allow local authorities to link data for direct patient care. While regions have been authorised to conduct research and analysis with registry data, there is a growing concern that the Privacy Guarantor may revoke this approval. This concern has put a chill on health research in Italy, as regions are becoming reluctant to participate in research studies. A concerning development is the emergence of views in Italy that there should be an irreversible split between patient identifiers and the information about patient health and health care. Should these voices influence authorities, any data linkage of individual-level data would become impossible for both regional and national governments.

Overall it is more difficult to conduct linkages in Italy today than it was five years ago. A consequence is that policy decisions are lacking a strong evidence base. For example, media reports on cases of medical errors alarm the public, but there is no national data on the extent of medical errors and whether the situation is improving or deteriorating. Policy focus is on expenditure control, and budget cuts may risk undermining health care quality or disease prevention. For example, the Abruzzo region, whose capital experienced a recent earthquake, has a large deficit and has experienced a sharp reduction in budget for health expenditures, including hospital closures and restrictions on pharmaceutical prescribing. This same region has published no report on the public health outcomes of this budget cut and lacks autonomous capacity to use its health information for public health monitoring.

Italy would benefit from clear guidelines from public authorities on the process to seek approval for a health research project and best practices in the processing of personal health information including data linkage. Greater transparency in procedures where information is shared with the public is needed, such as a check list available on a website. There is no office at the national level to fulfil this role. Further, if approval processes to link and analyse health data could be standardised among the regions, so that there was one process for approval in Italy, it would be a great improvement. Guidance from the European Union and the OECD could make clearer organisational approaches to providing access to personal health data; and the advantages for and the rights of the population in conducting analysis based on linked data. This could better inform local, regional and national authorities in Italy.

Belgium reports doing well compared with some of the challenges faced by other cancer registries. The registry has been able to satisfy the requirements of the Privacy Commission, while at the same time, preserving the quality of the registry. The new E-Health Platform provides a helpful service at no cost to the registry. The time required to attend to all of the required procedures and to prepare applications for the Privacy Commission, however, creates an administrative burden that is costly in terms of human resources. The Privacy Commission takes about three months from the receipt of a submission to render a decision. Sometimes, however, questions are returned and another three months will be needed. Further, whenever an external researcher proposes a linkage involving the cancer registry, the Privacy Commission holds the registry responsible. The cancer registry must work with the researcher to prepare the application and then have the proposal vetted by its internal review board for scientific merit and must declare to the Privacy Commission that they would be willing to provide the data.

Belgium has received a huge benefit to public health of having a registry and being able to produce indicators of health care quality. Analysis of the registry has influenced policy decisions and published results have contributed to scientific research. A further benefit of linkages is that they avoid the need to ask too much of physicians providing data to the registry. Helping to reduce the burden on physicians is important; particularly as new disease registries emerge. Lastly, linkage and analysis of linked data provide new views of the quality of the data and reveal problems that otherwise would remain uncorrected.

Finland has invested in high-quality registers, has strong data protection legislation, and has a national identity number to facilitate linkages. Data linkages have had an impact on policy decisions in Finland. The PERFECT study on outcomes of hospital treatment in the year following the hospitalisation indicated that low birth-weight infants have higher mortality in non-university hospitals and a law was passed that all low birth-weight infants should be cared for in university hospitals. There have also been audits of lower-performing hospitals as a result of PERFECT study results. In *Finland*, there are plans underway to expand the current monitoring of the quality of hospital care to primary care, long-term care and social services.

Compared with five years ago, there is more bureaucracy around the preparation of record-linkage study proposals for approval by the Research Ethics Board (REB) and the time required to prepare the applications is not insignificant. The PERFECT project team is presenting a proposal to the REB almost every month, as any project that requires new data to be linked necessitates a new application to the REB.

Finland is challenged to keep its strength in data linkage studies. The legislation that enables the registries will need to be updated. The current legislation, from the late 1980s, enabled registries to grow and develop over time. For example, the legislation refers to data about health care activities, without narrowly specifying those activities. As a result, as new forms of care have emerged, such as outpatient care, the registries have evolved. The concern in Finland is that harmonising with EU legislation may restrict the content of the legislation when it is revised. Other concerns are related to staff and resource cutbacks that may limit the NIHW. Thus far, the NIHW has been able to find ways to keep costs down for external researchers by entering into research collaborations at no cost, and only recovering the cost of staff time for very time consuming requests.

Compared with some European countries, *Switzerland* may be viewed as behind in terms of its infrastructure for data linkage. However, Switzerland is privileged to have a full population cohort study that does not exist in many other countries. In Switzerland, there is increased sensitivity of populations to the protection of privacy and this is reflected in more restrictive guidelines that have made data linkages more difficult today than five years ago. Further, a law is being developed to create a national cancer registry. This law is likely to clarify patient consent requirements and may set the course for linkages in Switzerland with stronger patient identifiers. Nonetheless, there is concern that long-standing studies, such as the Swiss National Cohort, could be negatively affected if a determination was made that any of the limited set of identifiers the cohort team uses now for probabilistic linkages are no longer legal.

Switzerland is moving away from a questionnaire-based population census to a registry-based census. The data on the register will be updated annually and thus will provide much more up-to-date information on the population than the census did. The address register will also have Social Security Numbers (SSN). SSN are available on health insurance and mortality data. If it were ever possible in Switzerland to use an encrypted SSN to conduct deterministic data linkages, then there would be an important improvement in data quality and external researchers would be confident of linkages executed within government. The Switzerland FSO is considering amending the ordinance to its authorising legislation to include collection of the SSN. This is as a result of a legal opinion of the Swiss Federal Data Protection and Information Commissioner's Office that the satisfaction of this condition would enable the FSO to use the SSN in data linkages. The Cancer Registry does not have SSN, however, and probabilistic linkages would continue to be necessary.

Data linkages create efficiencies and reduce the burden on health care providers. The FSO would like to extend current data linkage efforts from a focus on in-patient treatments to a focus on out-patient treatments in hospitals and day-surgery centres. This extension would increase the ability to monitor health care quality and would add valuable information that will likely increase interest in data linkage. Real statistical programmes are also more than just collections of data. The data needs to be made analysis ready with good information about the data and its quality; and the data elements included need to be of good quality and ready for use. The preparation of analysis-ready data is also part of the planning for the future of the health data programme.

Outlook on the use of data from electronic health record systems

Country participants to the OECD study (see Annex C) were divided on the extent to which it is likely that data from national electronic health record systems will be used within the next five years for national health care quality monitoring (Table 8.1). *Finland, Indonesia, Israel, Singapore, Sweden and the United Kingdom* consider it very likely that electronic health records will contribute to national monitoring over the near term. A further ten countries, *Belgium, Canada, Estonia, France, Iceland, Japan, Korea, Poland, Portugal, and Slovakia* consider this outcome to be likely. There is uncertainty in *Denmark, Slovenia, Spain and the United States*, and five countries consider this eventually to be unlikely or out of scope, *Austria, Germany, Mexico, Netherlands and Switzerland*.

Countries that view monitoring within the next five years as very likely

The national electronic health record system in *Finland* is well in operation and database creation and reporting is already incorporated within short term plans. Nonetheless, the implementation of electronic health records remains challenging as there has been on-going restructuring of the health care system. Health care providers are reluctant to invest their time and resources in updating their electronic record systems, if there is a risk that their hospital district, for example, will be reorganised in a few years time. Also, the new national EHR system is complicated and there are concerns with its usability. Further, the legal framework for health data protection and privacy in Finland is now out of date and does not cover new innovations in health care. The update of this legislation may pose challenges or changes to current practices in the secondary use of data from electronic health records. Finally, health care organisations have implemented electronic record systems from different vendors and the interoperability of all of these systems still needs further work.

The national electronic health record system is fully implemented in *Sweden* and, for many years, electronic health record data has been widely used for selected purposes and in restricted settings. However, problems with comparability and interoperability across jurisdictional settings still exist, including difficulties sharing data between social care and health care sectors. Legal requirements and restrictions on primary and secondary uses of electronic health records for specific purposes are important, as are values of openness

Table 8.1. **How likely is it that data from electronic health records will be used for national health care quality monitoring within the next five years?**

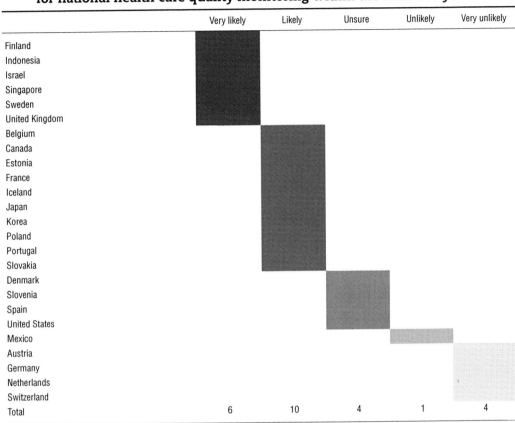

	Very likely	Likely	Unsure	Unlikely	Very unlikely
Finland	■				
Indonesia	■				
Israel	■				
Singapore	■				
Sweden	■				
United Kingdom	■				
Belgium		■			
Canada		■			
Estonia		■			
France		■			
Iceland		■			
Japan		■			
Korea		■			
Poland		■			
Portugal		■			
Slovakia		■			
Denmark			■		
Slovenia			■		
Spain			■		
United States			■		
Mexico				■	
Austria					■
Germany					■
Netherlands					■
Switzerland					■
Total	6	10	4	1	4

Source: OECD HCQI Questionnaire on Secondary Use of Health Data: Electronic Health Records, 2012.

and transparency. Interest in openness and transparency in government will be an important driver of the development of aggregated quality measures in health care in Sweden; especially given health care services are mainly publicly funded.

The *United Kingdom* reports very strong business drivers supporting this development through the Quality and Outcomes Framework in England. Scotland has made progress to ensure that data captured locally can feed the national information system. There remains some opposition to the development of national electronic health records from clinical groups and there are financial pressures. Patient groups, however, are supportive of the development of the EHR. There are also fair questions to be addressed about the secondary use of data from electronic health records and the need for data security, particularly safeguards against re-identification of records accessed for secondary uses.

Israel indicates that it is very likely that regular national monitoring of health care quality will take place using electronic medical records within the next five years. The implementation of the national EMR is on-going, as is the use of these records for health care quality monitoring. *Israel* is starting to monitor health care quality indicators based on electronic medical records in January 2013. New legislation was recently approved which enables the Ministry of Health to draw health information from EMRs into a national database.

The second phase of the National EHR project in *Singapore* includes secondary data analytics and aims to establish the framework and policies to support secondary data use.

There remain technical challenges to the implementation of the national EHR, as patient information within electronic medical records, and the EMR systems themselves, differ across institutions. The national EHR was primarily implemented for patient care, and the policies for secondary data use have not yet been established.

Indonesia already has a national policy to implement EHR and the system is currently under development, so it is very likely that, within the next five years, data from the EHR will be used for regular monitoring of national health care quality.

Countries that view monitoring in the next five years as likely

Estonia considers it likely that data from the electronic health record system will be used for regular national monitoring of health care quality within the next five years. Gaps in the data related to the submission of discharge summaries (epicrisis) are anticipated to be resolved within this period. Nonetheless, barriers to EHR implementation remain in Estonia, including the adequacy of financial and technical resources and resistance among some health care providers. While not an issue currently, the detection of data quality limitations may pose challenges for the analysis of data from the EHR system.

In *France,* the national EHR is being implemented, however the system still needs to be generalised to support the generation of statistics for health care quality monitoring at the national level. The main barrier to the EHR implementation relates to reluctance among health care providers. Some are unwilling to change from a paper-based or older system and others complain that contribution to the EHR is an additional administrative task that they should be paid to undertake. Each authorisation to use health data from electronic health records will be approved by the Commission on Information Technology and Liberties (CNIL). To be approved, each project will need to comply with all requirements for data security and data confidentiality protections.

In *Poland* it is likely that electronic health records that are currently contributing to the development of a large database maintained by the National Health Fund will be used to monitor health care quality at a national level over the next five years. In terms of the national electronic health record system, there remain challenges to be addressed that are mainly derived from resistance by health professionals and, partly, also some resistance among the public.

Belgium indicates that it is likely that data from electronic health records will contribute to national monitoring of some aspects of health care quality over the next five years. There will be, however, a minimum of three years needed for providers to use the system and to develop trust in the system. The use of data to monitor health care quality for specific sub-sectors of health is likely within the five year window. The creation of a "chain of trust" among health care providers is essential to the implementation of the national electronic health record system. The main barriers to the secondary use of data from electronic health records for health care quality monitoring include the potential for a lack of production of useable clinical information; the lack of structured data; and the need for specific legal provisions to allow for electronic health records to be processed for health care quality monitoring (or a specific authorisation from the Privacy Commission). In the initial deployment of the national electronic health record, making mandatory the use of electronic health records for health care quality monitoring could be detrimental to building the chain of trust and thus, these uses, should be introduced over time.

Slovakia expects that it is likely that data from electronic health records will be used for regular national monitoring of health care quality over the next five years. There is political will and public support for the effort. There remain challenges to the implementation of the national electronic health record system, including resistance among health care providers, technical barriers, and legal and jurisdictional considerations.

Administrative health data is widely used in *Canada* for secondary analysis; however, secondary analysis of data from electronic health records is not yet wide spread. Both will be used for national health care quality monitoring over the next five years, with EHR data increasing in importance with time. Canada Health Infoway and the Canadian Institute for Health Information are working with various levels of government to plan and implement a vision for moving the Secondary Use of Health Data Agenda forward. Canada Health Infoway committed to a risk management approach to EHR implementation in 2005. EHR implementation projects are evaluated for risks with both a high probability of occurrence and a high impact on success. Mitigation strategies are then put in place. Risks may relate to the timeliness of project completion or involve even a failure to integrate point of service systems into the EHR and to deliver a viable and interoperable EHR solution. Change management also presents challenges, including slow adoption of clinical terminology and interoperability standards by vendors of legacy EHR systems and a reluctance of provinces and territories to change or replace legacy systems.

Barriers to the secondary use of data from electronic health records in Canada include: building the necessary technical infrastructure to support it; data privacy concerns; resistance among some members of the general physician community; financial resources to broaden the scope of the national plan to include secondary data use; some jurisdictional barriers to the adoption of standards and the replacement of legacy systems that don't meet current standards; the lack of a definition of health system use (or secondary use) of data from electronic health records; shortages of human resources with the correct skill set to undertake the work; the legacy of information silos where specific programs own the data and are reluctant to share data or to provide access to data for research; and that health system use (secondary use) is not recognised as a priority.

In *Japan*, the government's IT strategy includes the use of data from electronic health records for national health care quality monitoring and, as a result, it is likely that data from EHRs will be used for this purpose within the next five years. There remain, however, legal barriers in Japan to both the implementation of national electronic health records and to the secondary use of these records for health care quality monitoring that will need to be addressed.

In *Korea*, it is likely that data from electronic records will contribute to health care quality monitoring over the next five years. There remain, however, challenges to the implementation of electronic health records including inadequate financial resources among medical institutions to invest in electronic health records and inadequate financial incentives to encourage investments. There is also resistance among health care providers including negative options on sharing medical records, and negative feeling following the introduction of a fee-for-service payment system which reduced medical service fees. There is inadequate capability among health service providers to invest in patient information security. There is also no legal basis for collecting electronic health record data in Korea and inadequate legislation for the protection of health information privacy.

In *Iceland*, efforts are underway to improve the quality of electronic documentation within the EHR at a national level. Further, a project has been launched to evaluate the feasibility and cost of implementing the EHR at a national level (beyond the regional systems in place currently). There remain barriers to this implementation, including financial barriers and resistance among some health care providers.

Portugal also considers it likely that regular national monitoring of health care quality will take place using electronic health records within the next five years. The implementation of the national EHR is on-going, as is the use of these records for health care quality monitoring. There are, however, challenges to the full national implementation of the EHR, including financial, technical, jurisdictional and legal impediments, as well as some resistance among health care providers. None of these challenges, however, are considered to be a strong barrier to progress. There are also concerns with the quality and availability of data within the national EHR system and with ensuring data privacy and confidentiality that can pose barriers to the secondary use of the data.

Countries that are unsure monitoring will occur within the next five years

In the *United States*, the sustained support and significant interest in quality measurement using data from electronic health records is expected to result in the ability to measure high-priority quality indicators at the national level within the next five years. The United States is not implementing national electronic health records per se. Instead, it has chosen a distributed strategy, where providers are encouraged and incentivised to implement and use an interoperable EHR, and where patients use electronic personal health records. By facilitating secure, standards-based data exchange infrastructure, the United States aims to offer citizens all of the benefits of electronic health records without the need to develop and maintain a single national electronic health record system for a population exceeding 300 million.

The United States HITECH Act of 2010 and its payment incentives for meaningful use have dramatically accelerated the transition from paper to electronic records among hospitals and physicians. The payment incentives require quality measurement as part of meaningful use criteria. Building forward from substantial prior development and early experience with meaningful use criteria, public and private sector stakeholders support EHR-based quality measurement. The United States is currently working on defining the data required from electronic health records to support health care quality indicators that are crucial to driving quality improvement and that correspond with emerging payment models rewarding value of care, rather than volume of procedures. The definition of this data could lead to an expansion or refinement of the content that is minimally expected in patient summary records.

Denmark has already invested in the primary reporting of clinical and administrative data to an established system of national databases and data repositories. It is unlikely that an investment would be made again in developing databases from electronic health records unless there is a strong business case to do so. In terms of the development of EHR infrastructure, the main challenges still faced in Denmark are financial and legal.

Slovenia indicates that there are risks to the further development and use of the EHR for data quality monitoring, but there is certainly potential that this objective could be reached. The national EHR strategy is not clear and is not being executed on time. There are jurisdictional and legal concerns and technical barriers to overcome. Health care providers are experiencing financial barriers to adoption and some lack the time or motivation to engage.

The current economic situation in *Spain* makes it difficult to plan for the future development of the EHR system. Currently, limited resources for teams and software tools are a barrier to EHR implementation. Changes in policy priorities to address the economic crisis may result in additional financial constraints. The economic situation is not, however, expected to impede progress on regulatory action. The use of data from electronic health record systems for health care quality monitoring is constrained by the absence of legislation or regulation that address the technical requirements for the secondary use of clinical information. Further, no secondary uses of data are supported by the national EHR system design. Databases would be administered by each health care authority (region).

Countries that view monitoring within the next five years as unlikely

In *Mexico*, the national electronic health record project is in an initial phase of development and priorities are focussed on clinical information more than on quality of care information. It is therefore unlikely that Mexico will be able to use data from electronic health records for national monitoring of health care quality within the next five years. Further, Mexico's national EHR project is experiencing financial challenges, as there is not a federal budget for the effort but rather the effort depends on the participating institutions, which have differing levels of resourcing for EHR development. There is also a lack of technical infrastructure and information technology know-how across the different areas of the country.

Countries that view monitoring within the next five years as very unlikely

The *Netherlands* reported that it is very unlikely that electronic health records will be used to monitor national health care quality over the next five years. The organisation has to be established; the ICT infrastructure needs to be developed; jurisdictional and legal barriers need to be addressed; decisions about patients opting-in or opting-out have to be taken; the opt-in or opt-out process must be completed; the possibility of using data from electronic health records has to be incorporated into the strategy; and the approval for using electronic health record data for data quality monitoring needs to be obtained. A new start to the development of a national electronic health record system has only recently been made. It may be that the resistance to a national EHR will be softening because government is no longer leading the initiative, nor playing a role in it. Instead, health care providers are leading the initiative and the participation of health providers is voluntary. This approach may be more promising.

In *Germany*, it is possible now for data from medical records kept by health care providers and data kept by the statutory health insurance system to be analysed for a specific approved project, as long as specific procedures for data retrieval and de-identification are followed. Electronic health records, however, may not be a good choice as a data source for health care quality monitoring, as they may never cover a large enough portion of relevant health care processes in Germany.

In *Switzerland*, it will take some years to establish an EHR system with enough structured data to be used for standardised analysis. Further, the secondary use of data from the EHR system is not addressed as part of the new national law to enable it.

Implementation of the national EHR remains challenging, due to the absence of financial incentives, unclear financing, the absence of a national law to enable the EHR; and doubts among health care providers about the benefits of exchanging records.

Austria reports that the use of data from electronic health records for national monitoring of health care quality is not in scope. The implementation of the EHR system remains challenged by financial barriers and, to some extent, by resistance to it among health care providers.

Chapter 9

Strengthening health information infrastructure: Next steps

The next five years appear promising, in terms of both the number of countries that plan to implement national electronic health record systems and the number of countries that consider it likely that the data from these systems will be used for some aspects of health care quality monitoring. They also appear promising for the further use of existing personal health databases and for the linkage of multiple sources of data to generate new evidence to improve population health, health care quality and the performance of the health system. Nonetheless, there are considerable and troubling differences across OECD countries in the extent to which existing health data may be used for public benefit. A role for the OECD in the coming years is to continue to support countries in reaching the goal of strengthening health information infrastructure so that privacy-respectful uses of data for health, health care quality and health system performance monitoring and research become widespread, regular activities. This requires monitoring national progress and assisting countries in overcoming obstacles to privacy-respectful data use.

This chapter summarises the results of the 2011/12 OECD studies of the development and use of personal health data and the development and use of data from electronic health record systems, and makes recommendations for international actions.

These OECD studies indicate that national data infrastructure is improving across countries and the technical capacity to analyse and report from personal health information data assets is greater today than it was five years ago. Case studies included in this report demonstrate how many countries are linking and analysing personal health data to report on the quality and cost-effectiveness of treatments; to address underuse, overuse and misuse of therapies; to reduce variation in care practices; to assess and revise clinical care guidelines; and to manage health expenditures.

In some countries, there is potential to continue and to expand data linkage studies into the future due to having reached a shared understanding with their privacy officials of the requirements to respect principles of data privacy. This includes standardised processes for project approval, access to data and data security. There is also potential for data from electronic health record systems to be used for health care quality monitoring over the next five years. This is due to both the number of countries that plan to implement national electronic health record systems and the number of countries that consider it likely that data from these systems will be used for some aspects of health care quality monitoring.

There are considerable and troubling differences across OECD countries, however, in the extent to which personal health data may be collected, linked and analysed and the extent to which such data are currently contributing to monitoring population health and the quality of health care. OECD privacy guidelines provide a unifying framework for the development of national data protection legislation. However, cross-country differences in the application of privacy principles are significant and can be attributed to differences in risk management in the balancing of individual rights to privacy and collective rights to safe and effective health care and to a high performing health system. Many countries report legislative barriers to the use of personal health data, including enabling data linkages and developing databases from electronic health records.

Some of the countries with weaker information infrastructure have decentralised the administration of health systems and have not reached a consensus within the country of how the levels of government could work together. Data from decentralised systems needs to be brought together to support national information infrastructure and capacity for data use at the level of the country. A principle challenge is the lack of clarity about the interpretation of legislations concerning the protection of data privacy at the national and sub-national levels. This includes the legality of data sharing among public authorities and providing access to data for research.

The resources required to comply with legislative requirements to enable data use is a secondary problem, as is the cost of developing the technical capacity to undertake the work. Countries have provided evidence of the considerable effort they put in to protect data security and to safeguard personal health data from loss or deliberately malicious acts. Efforts were clearly demonstrated in this study related to project approval processes; internal data security; de-identification of data to protect privacy; and security measures for external researchers. Efforts to balance protection of data privacy and access to data for research are also clearly evident. Resource limitations, and not meeting expectations of timeliness, are worries among bodies that approve project proposals and among bodies that conduct data linkages on behalf of others. New forms of whole-of-government approaches to project proposal review and data linkage services are very interesting developments. Not only do these help to standardise requirements and practices for both the government and external researchers, they have the potential to be more efficient.

A particular worry across countries today is that legislative reforms that are on the horizon, or that may be stimulated due to the implementation of electronic health record systems, may turn back the clock on the progress that has been made in enabling access to and use of personal health data for research. A second worry is that a transition to reliance on data from electronic health record systems has the potential to set back the quality of national databases, by creating holes in the health care pathway or lowering the quality of the data elements, such as the coding of diagnosis. A widely reported barrier to the use of data from electronic health record systems is concerns with the quality of the data, including both a lack of coded data and poorly coded data.

This study has revealed a set of factors that have enabled countries to make progress toward the implementation of a national electronic health record system that meets the characteristics of a well-functioning statistical system. The first, and the most important factor, is the governance of the electronic health record system design and implementation. There are clear advantages for countries aiming toward a single country-wide deployment of one electronic health record system. There are also advantages where there are national standards for the content of the records, such as a minimum set of data where the content follows terminology standards; and national interoperability standards. One-half of study participants have a national body responsible for EHR infrastructure development and who set standards for clinical terminology used within the records and standards for interoperability.

Less than half of countries participating in this study have succeeded in implementing a system where all electronic health records have key data elements using a clinical terminology standard, such as for diagnosis, current medications and laboratory test results. Many countries are contending with the use of multiple standards for the same data element. Where data is unstructured, and where statistical analysis is desired, the use of human coders or sophisticated technologies would be needed to create structured data. A widely reported barrier to the use of data from electronic health record systems is concerns with the quality of the data, including both a lack of coded data and poorly coded data.

One half of countries report that data from electronic health records are currently contributing to regular public health monitoring. Fewer report regularly conducting research with this data or using this data to monitor patient safety or health system performance. In countries with one or very few custodians of databases from electronic health records, it may be easier to enable data use by centralising responsibility for database creation, data de-identification and review of applications for access to the data for monitoring and research. In countries with a large number of custodians of databases from electronic health records, there are likely to be challenges from within country variation in data privacy protection legislations and practices; and custodian willingness to share data.

The most widely reported challenge to building databases from electronic health records is the current legal framework enabling the creation of the EHR and protecting patients' data privacy. In some countries there are known legislative obstacles to the use of data, while in others, obstacles are suspected. Some countries also report concerns with a lack of resources or technical capacity to support database creation and to de-identify the data. A few also noted that a greater number of analysts with the skill sets necessary to analyse the data are needed.

International action

A role for the OECD in the coming years is to continue to support countries in reaching the goal of strengthening health information infrastructure so that privacy-respectful uses of data for health, health care quality and health system performance monitoring and research become widespread, regular activities. Further, the OECD can contribute to assuring that national health information infrastructures become better capable of supporting multi-country monitoring and multi-country research.

On-going monitoring of the development of health information infrastructure would help to promote shared learning about advancements and challenges in the development and use of health data; promote international comparability of data and data linkages; and uncover new opportunities for the development of internationally comparable indicators of the quality of care. It will be important for the OECD to monitor the deployment and use of electronic health record systems as part of current plans for the ongoing monitoring of national information infrastructure. Of particular interest will be the adoption of international consensus standards for clinical terminology. Such standards will be very meaningful toward the eventual development of internationally comparable indicators from electronic health records. The OECD could also contribute toward advancing the development of such standards, where there are existing gaps.

Another important step will be to support countries in reducing unnecessary obstacles to data use that can arise from differences in legislations regarding the protection of health information privacy and/or differences in the interpretation of what is necessary and helpful to assure that patients' privacy rights are respected in the conduct of health monitoring and research.

The results of this study were brought to the attention of experts in the field of privacy regulation through a joint consultation with health experts in May 2012. Participants to the joint consultation concluded that where international action of the OECD could be helpful is in the development of a risk classification of data and data uses, to help to identify cases of higher risk to patient's information privacy, and to associate the classification with recommended data privacy protection practices that will enable even very sensitive data to be used for research and monitoring that is in the public's interest. There is also value in developing a common vocabulary so that experts in health, data privacy regulation and information technology can better speak with each other to reach a common understanding of the problem and the solutions.

Working together is particularly important now as there are legislative reforms on the horizon in many countries, including proposed reforms to the 1995 Data Protection Directive to be translated into legislation within EU member states. International actions to help to reduce unnecessary heterogeneity in privacy protections will support all countries in developing privacy-respectful statistical and research uses of data and will promote the advancement of internationally comparative indicators and evidence to improve health, health care quality and health system performance.

Strengthening Health Information Infrastructure for Health Care
Quality Governance
Good Practices, New Opportunities and Data Privacy Protection
Challenges
© OECD 2013

ANNEX A

Questionnaire on secondary use of health data

Members of the OECD Health Care Quality Expert Group participated in a questionnaire to explore the potential, the barriers and the best practices to link existing data to inform about health and health care quality. The questionnaire sought information about the general environment in countries for the secondary use of personal health data, as well as specific case studies involving the use of personal health data. The questionnaire also asked for the names of contact persons that could be invited to a follow-up telephone interview to learn more about the general environment for secondary use of personal health data and the specific case studies.

The questionnaire was developed by the OECD and was reviewed by six members of the HCQI Expert Group, one external expert, and seven members of the OECD Secretariat. Table A.1 provides a list of country representatives that co-ordinated their country's response to the questionnaire. Responses were received from August 31, 2011 through to March, 2012.

Table A.1. **Countries that responded to the 2011-12 HCQI questionnaire on secondary use of health data**

Country	Contact persons for the completion of the questionnaire
Australia	Greg Coombs, Assistant Secretary, Economic and Statistical Analysis Branch, Department of Health and Ageing
Belgium	Chr. Decoster, Director General FPS Health, Federal Public Service Health; L. Van Eycken, Director, Cancer Registry
Canada	Kira Leeb, Director, Health System Performance, Canadian Institute for Health Information
Denmark	Niels Herman, National Board of Health
Finland	Päivi Hämäläinen, Director of Department, THL National Institute for Health and Welfare
France	Marie-Camille Lenormand, International Policy Officer, Ministry of Health
Germany	Irene Keinhorst, Senior Advisor, Federal Ministry of Health; Christa Scheidt-Nave, Head of Division, Department of Epidemiology and Health Monitoring, Robert Koch Institute
Israel	Ziona Haklai, Head of Department of Health Information, Ministry of Health
Japan	Etsuji Okamoto, Senior Researcher, National Institute of Public Health
Malta	Sandro Distefano, Consultant in Public Health Medicine, Department of Health Information & Research, Health Division
Norway	Hanne Narbuvold, Director, Norwegian Directorate of Health
Poland	Ewa Dudzik-Urbaniak, Senior Specialist, National Centre for Quality Assessment in Health Care
Portugal	Paulo Boto, Consultant, Department of Quality in Health, Directorate General of Health
Korea	Sun Min Kim, Commissioner of Healthcare Quality, Health Insurance Review and Assessment Service
Singapore	Eng Kok Lim, Deputy Director, Healthcare Performance Group, Ministry of Health
Sweden	Max Köster, Senior Researcher, The National Board of Health and Welfare; Ms. Marie Lawrence, the National Board of Health and Welfare
Switzerland	Jacques Huguenin, Head of Health Care Statistics, Swiss Federal Statistical Office

Table A.1. **Countries that responded to the 2011-12 HCQI questionnaire on secondary use of health data** *(cont.)*

Country	Contact persons for the completion of the questionnaire
United Kingdom	Alexandra Lazaro, Assistant Statistician, Department of Health; Anthea Springbett, Programme Principal, NHS NSS Information Services Division; Gavin Shivers, Health Statistics and Analysis Unit, Welsh Government
United States	Edward Sondik, Director, National Center for Health Statistics

ANNEX B

Telephone interviews on secondary use of health data

The OECD conducted a series of telephone interviews with individuals identified within the country questionnaire responses as persons to contact to either discuss the country's current capacity to undertake health studies requiring the analysis and linkage of personal health data for public health and health services research or to discuss a specific project. In some cases, the same individual provided information on both the general environment and a specific project.

Table B.1. **Countries that responded to the 2011-12 HCQI telephone interview on secondary use of health data**

Country	Participants in a telephone interview
Australia	Phil Anderson, Head, Data Linkage Unit, Australian Institute of Health and Welfare
Belgium	L. Van Eycken, Director, Cancer Registry Pascal Meeus, National Institute for Health and Disease Insurance Xavier Van Aubel, National Institute for Health and Disease Insurance
Canada	Anne-Marie Phillips, Chief Privacy Officer, Canadian Institute for Health Information Cheryl Gula, Manager, Health Reports, Canadian Institute for Health Information Josh Fagbemi, Project Leader, Canadian Institute for Health Information Pamela Slaughter, Chief Privacy Officer, Institute for Clinical and Evaluative Sciences, University of Toronto
Denmark	Anne-Marie Andersen, National Board of Health
Finland	Mika Gissler, Research Professor, THL National Institute for Health and Welfare Unto Häkkinen, Research Professor, THL National Institute for Health and Welfare
France	Jeanne Bossi, Secrétaire Générale, Agence des systèmes d'information partagé en santé
Germany	Alexander Katalinic, Director, Institute of Clinical Epidemiology/Institute of Cancer Epidemiology, University of Luebeck
Italy	Fabrizio Carinci, Consultant AGENAS and Technical Co-ordinator, EUBIROD Project, University of Perugia Concetta Tania Di Iorio, Serectrix snc
Japan	Natsuko Fujii, International Affairs Division, Ministry of Health, Labour and Welfare
Korea	Sun Min Kim, Commissioner of Healthcare Quality, Health Insurance Review and Assessment Service Yong Tai Ryu, Manager, Research Division, Health Insurance Review
Singapore	Eng Kok Lim, Deputy Director, Healthcare Performance Group, Ministry of Health and Dr. Lee, Ministry of Health
Sweden	Björn Nilsson, Researcher, The National Board of Health and Welfare
Switzerland	Jacques Huguenin, Head of Health Care Statistics, Swiss Federal Statistical Office Adrian Spörri-Fahrni, Swiss National Cohort Manager, Bern University, Institute for Social and Preventative Medicine
United Kingdom	Xanthe Hannah, Section Head, NHS Information Centre for Health and Social Care Janet Murray, Public Health Consultant and Caldecott Guardian, NHS Scotland Gwyneth Thomas, Statistician, Welsh Government Julie Messer, Principal Researcher, Health, Office for National Statistics, Wales Trudy Corsellis, Assistant Director of Planning & Performance, Torbay Care Trust
United States	Eve Powell-Griner, Confidentiality Officer, National Center for Health Statistics Jennifer Parker, Chief, Special Projects Branch, National Center for Health Statistics Donna Miller, Special Projects Branch, National Center for Health Statistics Mark Hornbrook, Chief Scientist, Kaiser Permanente

ANNEX C

Questionnaire on electronic health record systems and the secondary use of health data

Members of the OECD Health Care Quality Indicators (HCQI) Expert Group participated in a questionnaire to explore best practices in the design of electronic health record systems to support secondary uses to inform about health care quality. This questionnaire sought information about progress in the planning, design, implementation and governance of electronic health record systems that could contribute to the extraction of high quality data from these systems.

The questionnaire was developed by the OECD and was reviewed by six members of the HCQI Expert Group and by members of the OECD Secretariat. Table C.1 provides a list of country representatives that co-ordinated their country's response to the questionnaire. Responses were received from March 2012 through to August, 2012.

Table C.1. **Countries that responded to the 2012 HCQI questionnaire on electronic health record systems and the secondary use of health data**

Country	Contact persons for the completion of the questionnaire
Austria	Silvia Türk, Head of Quality Management and Health Systems Research, Federal Ministry of Health
Belgium	Luc Nicolas, Expert, ICT for Health, Public Federal Service Public Health
Canada	Nathalie Robertson, Manager, Strategic Initiatives, Canadian Institute for Health Information
Denmark	Kenneth Ahrensberg and Mr. Ivan Lund Pedersen, National Board of E-health
Estonia	Pille Kink, Head, E-health Department, Ministry of Social Affairs
Finland	Päivi Hämäläinen, Director of Department, National Institute for Health and Welfare
France	Marie-Camille Lenormand, Chargée de mission, Ministère du Travail, de l'Emploi et de la Santé
Germany	Irene Kienhorst, Federal Ministry of Health
Iceland	Gudrun Audur Hardardottir, Project Manager, Directorate of Health
Indonesia	Jane Soepardi, Head of the Centre for Data and Information, Secretariat General, Ministry of Health
Israel	Nachman Ash, Deputy Director General for Health Informatics, Ministry of Health
Japan	Etsuji Okamoto, Senior Researcher, national Institute of Public Health
Korea	Sun Min Kim, Commissioner of Healthcare Quality, Health Insurance Review and Assessment Service
Mexico	Ing. José Manuel Castañeda, Electronic Health Services Director, Health Ministry, Office of Health Information
Netherlands	Michael van den Berg and Ronald Gijsen, National Institute of Public Health and the Environment
Poland	Kazimierz Fraczkowski, Expert for IT e-Health, National Centre for Health Information Systems
Portugal	Paulo Alexandro Boto, Consultant, Department of Quality in Health, Directorate General of Health
Singapore	Eng Kok Lim, Deputy Director, Clinical Benchmarking, Clinical Quality Improvement Division, Ministry of Health
Slovak Republic	National Health Information Centre
Slovenia	Matic Meglic, Head of the Healthcare Informatics Centre, National Institute of Public Health
Spain	Arturo Romero Gutierrez, Project Director, Digital health Record for the National Health System (HCDSNS), Ministry of Health, Social Services and Equity

Table C.1. **Countries that responded to the 2012 HCQI questionnaire on electronic health record systems and the secondary use of health data** (cont.)

Country	Contact persons for the completion of the questionnaire
Sweden	Kristina Bränd Persson, Head of Unit, Terminology, classifications and Informatics, National Board of Health and Welfare, Sweden
Switzerland	Adrian Schmid, Head of eHealth Suisse, Swiss Co-ordination Office for eHealth
United Kingdom	Jeremy Thorp, Programme Delivery Director, NHS Information Reporting Services Programme, NHS Connecting for Health
United States of America	Rachel Nelson, Senior Advisor, Office of the National co-ordinator for Health Information Technology

ANNEX D

Supplementary tables

Table D.1. **Data available at a national level**

	Hospital in-patient data	Primary care data	Cancer registry data	Prescription medicines data	Mortality data	Formal long-term care data	Patient experiences survey data	Mental hospital in-patient data	Population health survey data	Population census or registry data
Australia	Yes	Yes	Yes	Yes	Yes	Yes	Yes	Yes	Yes	Yes
Belgium	Yes	Yes	Yes	Yes	Yes	Yes	n.r.	Yes	Yes	Yes
Canada	Yes	No	Yes	No	Yes	Yes	No	Yes	Yes	Yes
Denmark	Yes	Yes	Yes	Yes	Yes	No	Yes	Yes	Yes	Yes
Finland	Yes	Yes	Yes	Yes	Yes	Yes	Yes	Yes	Yes	Yes
France	Yes	Yes	Yes	Yes	Yes	Yes	Yes	Yes	Yes	Yes
Germany	Yes	Yes	Yes	Yes	Yes	Yes	No	No	Yes	Yes
Israel	Yes	Yes	Yes	No	Yes	Yes	Yes	Yes	Yes	Yes
Japan	Yes	Yes	No	Yes	Yes	Yes	n.r.	n.r.	Yes	Yes
Korea	Yes	Yes	Yes	Yes	Yes	Yes	Yes	Yes	Yes	Yes
Malta	Yes	Yes	Yes	No	Yes	Yes	No	Yes	Yes	Yes
Norway	Yes	Yes	Yes	Yes	Yes	Yes	Yes	Yes	Yes	Yes
Poland	Yes	Yes	Yes	Yes	Yes	Yes	Yes	Yes	Yes	Yes
Portugal	Yes	Yes	Yes	Yes	Yes	n.r.	n.r.	Yes	Yes	Yes
Singapore	Yes	Yes	Yes	No	Yes	Yes	No	Yes	Yes	Yes
Sweden	Yes	No	Yes	Yes	Yes	No	Yes	Yes	Yes	Yes
Switzerland	Yes	No	No	No	Yes	Yes	No	Yes	Yes	Yes
United Kingdom	Yes	Yes	Yes	Yes	Yes	Yes	Yes	Yes	Yes	Yes
United States	Yes	Yes	Yes	Yes	Yes	Yes	Yes	Yes	Yes	Yes
Total Yes	19	16	17	14	19	16	11	17	19	19

Note: The data custodian should be a national authority and data should be included even when it does not cover 100% of the nation. n.r.: no response.
Source: OECD HCQI Questionnaire on Secondary Use of Health Data, 2011/12.

Table D.2. **National data used to regularly report on health care quality**

	Hospital in-patient data	Primary care data	Cancer registry data	Prescription medicines data	Mortality data	Formal long-term care data	Patient experiences survey data	Mental hospital in-patient data	Population health survey data	Population census or registry data
Australia	Yes	Yes	Yes	Yes	Yes	Yes	Yes	Yes	Yes	No
Belgium	Yes	Yes	Yes	Yes	Yes	Yes	n.a.	Yes	Yes	ns
Canada	Yes	n.a.	Yes	n.a.	Yes	Yes	n.a.	Yes	Yes	Yes
Denmark	Yes	Yes	Yes	No	No	n.a.	Yes	Yes	No	Yes
Finland	Yes	n.a.	Yes	Yes	Yes	No	No	Yes	No	n.a.
France	n.r.	Yes	Yes	Yes	Yes	n.r.	No	n.r.	Yes	Yes
Germany	Yes	Yes	Yes	Yes	Yes	Yes	n.a.	n.a.	Yes	Yes
Israel	Yes	Yes	Yes	No	Yes	Yes	Yes	Yes	Yes	Yes
Japan	n.r.	n.r.	n.r.	n.r.	n.r.	n.r.	n.r.	n.r.	n.r.	N.r.
Korea	Yes	Yes	Yes	Yes	Yes	Yes	Yes	Yes	No	No
Malta	Yes	No	Yes	n.a.	Yes	No	n.a.	Yes	Yes	No
Norway	Yes	Yes	Yes	Yes	Yes	Yes	Yes	Yes	Yes	Yes
Poland	Yes	Yes	Yes	No	Yes	No	Yes	Yes	No	No
Portugal	Yes	Yes	No	Yes	No	n.r.	n.r.	No	Yes	n.r.
Singapore	Yes	n.a.	Yes	n.a.	Yes	Yes	n.a.	n.a.	Yes	Yes
Sweden	Yes	n.a.	Yes	Yes	Yes	n.a.	Yes	Yes	Yes	No
Switzerland	Yes	n.a.	n.a.	n.a.	Yes	Yes	n.a.	Yes	No	Yes
United Kingdom	Yes	Yes[1]	Yes	Yes	Yes	Yes	Yes[1]	Yes	Yes	Yes
United States	Yes	Yes	Yes	Yes	Yes	Yes	Yes	Yes	Yes	Yes
Total Yes	17	12	16	11	16	11	9	14	13	10

Note: The data custodian should be a national authority and data should be included even when it does not cover 100% of the nation. n.a.: not applicable; n.r.: no response.
1. England only.
Source: OECD HCQI Questionnaire on Secondary Use of Health Data, 2011/12.

ANNEX D

Table D.3. **National data containing records for patients (persons)**

	Hospital in-patient data	Primary care data	Cancer registry data	Prescription medicines data	Mortality data	Formal long-term care data	Patient experiences survey data	Mental hospital in-patient data	Population health survey data	Population census or registry data
Australia	Yes	Yes	Yes	Yes	Yes	Yes	Yes	Yes	Yes	Yes
Belgium	No	Yes	Yes	Yes	Yes	Yes	n.r.	No	No	n.r.
Canada	Yes	n.a.	Yes	n.a.	Yes	Yes	n.a.	Yes	Yes	Yes
Denmark	Yes	Yes	Yes	Yes	Yes	n.a.	No	Yes	No	Yes
Finland	Yes	Yes	Yes	Yes	Yes	Yes	Yes	Yes	Yes	Yes
France	ns	Yes	Yes	Yes	Yes	ns	No	Ns	Yes	Yes
Germany	Yes	Yes	Yes	No	Yes	Yes	n.a.	n.a.	Yes	Yes
Israel	Yes	No	Yes	No	Yes	Yes	Yes	Yes	Yes	Yes
Japan	n.r.	n.r.	n.r.	n.r.	n.r.	n.r.	n.r.	n.r.	n.r.	n.r.
Korea	Yes	Yes	Yes	Yes	Yes	Yes	Yes	Yes	Yes	Yes
Norway	Yes	Yes	Yes	Yes	Yes	Yes	No	Yes	Yes	Yes
Poland	Yes	Yes	Yes	Yes	Yes	No	No	Yes	Yes	Yes
Portugal	Yes	Yes	No	Yes	No	n.r.	n.r.	Yes	Yes	n.r.
Malta	Yes	Yes	Yes	n.a.	Yes	Yes	n.a.	Yes	Yes	Yes
Singapore	Yes	No	Yes	n.a.	Yes	Yes	No	Yes	Yes	Yes
Sweden	Yes	n.a.	Yes	Yes	Yes	n.a.	Yes	Yes	Yes	Yes
Switzerland	Yes	n.a.	n.a.	n.a.	Yes	Yes	n.a.	Yes	Yes	Yes
United Kingdom	Yes	Yes	Yes	Yes[1]	Yes	Yes	Yes	Yes	Yes	Yes
United States	Yes	Yes	Yes	Yes	Yes	Yes	Yes	d.k.	Yes	Yes
Total Yes	16	13	16	12	17	13	7	14	16	16

Note: The data custodian should be a national authority and data should be included even when it does not cover 100% of the nation. d.k.: don't know; n.a.: not applicable; n.r.: no response.
1. Scotland only.
Source: OECD HCQI Questionnaire on Secondary Use of Health Data, September and October 2011.

Table D.4. **National data contains a unique patient identifying number that could be used for record linkage**

	Hospital in-patient data	Primary care data	Cancer registry data	Prescription medicines data	Mortality data	Formal long-term care data	Patient experiences survey data	Mental hospital in-patient data	Population health survey data	Population census or registry data
Australia	No	Yes	No	Yes	No	No	No	No	No	No
Belgium	Yes	Yes	Yes	Yes	Yes	No	n.r.	No	Yes	n.r.
Canada	Yes	n.a.	Yes	n.a.	Yes	Yes	n.a.	Yes	Yes	No
Denmark	Yes	Yes	Yes	Yes	Yes	n.a.	No	Yes	No	Yes
Finland	Yes	Yes	Yes	Yes	Yes	Yes	No	Yes	No	Yes
France	ns	Yes	No	Yes	Yes	n.r.	No	n.r.	Yes	Yes
Germany	No	Yes	Yes	No	No	No	n.a.	n.a.	Yes	No
Israel	Yes	No	Yes	No	Yes	Yes	No	Yes	Yes	Yes
Japan	Yes	Yes	n.a.	Yes	Yes	Yes	n.r.	n.r.	Yes	Yes
Korea	Yes	Yes	Yes	Yes	Yes	Yes	No	Yes	Yes	Yes
Malta	Yes	Yes	Yes	n.a.	Yes	Yes	n.a.	Yes	No	Yes
Norway	Yes	Yes	Yes	Yes	Yes	Yes	No	Yes	Yes	Yes
Poland	No	No	Yes	Yes	Yes	Yes	No	No	No	No
Portugal	Yes	Yes	No	Yes	No	n.r.	n.r.	Yes	No	n.r.
Singapore	Yes	No	Yes	n.a.	Yes	Yes	n.a.	Yes	Yes	Yes
Sweden	Yes	n.a.	Yes	Yes	Yes	n.a.	No	Yes	Yes	Yes
Switzerland	Yes	n.a.	n.a.	n.a.	No	Yes	n.a.	Yes	No	No
United Kingdom	Yes	Yes[1]	Yes	Yes[2]	Yes	Yes[1]	Yes[1]	Yes	Yes[1]	Yes
United States	No	No	No	No	No	No	No	No	No	No
Total Yes	14	12	13	12	14	11	1	12	11	11

Note: The data custodian should be a national authority and data should be included even when it does not cover 100% of the nation. d.k.: don't know ; n.a.: not applicable; n.r.: no response.
1. England only.
2. Scotland only.
Source: OECD HCQI Questionnaire on Secondary Use of Health Data, September and October 2011.

Table D.5. **National data contains identifying variables such as name, sex, birth date, and address that could be used for record linkage**

	Hospital in-patient data	Primary care data	Cancer registry data	Prescription medicines data	Mortality data	Formal long-term care data	Patient experiences survey data	Mental hospital in-patient data	Population health survey data	Population census or registry data
Australia	No	Yes	Yes	Yes	Yes	Yes	Yes	Yes	Yes	Yes
Belgium	Yes	Yes	Yes	Yes	Yes	Yes	n.r.	No	No	n.r.
Canada	Yes	n.a.	Yes	n.a.	Yes	Yes	n.a.	Yes	Yes	Yes
Denmark	Yes	Yes	Yes	Yes	Yes	n.a.	No	Yes	No	Yes
Finland	Yes	Yes	Yes	Yes	Yes	Yes	No	Yes	No	Yes
France	n.r.	Yes	Yes	Yes	Yes	n.r.	No	n.r.	Yes	Yes
Germany	No	No	No	No	No	No	n.a.	n.a.	No	No
Israel	No	No	Yes	No	Yes	Yes	No	Yes	Yes	Yes
Japan	n.r.	n.r.	Yes	n.r.	n.r.	n.r.	n.r.	n.r.	n.r.	n.r.
Korea	Yes	Yes	Yes	Yes	Yes	Yes	No	Yes	Yes	Yes
Malta	Yes	Yes	Yes	n.a.	Yes	Yes	n.a.	Yes	No	Yes
Norway	Yes	Yes	Yes	Yes	Yes	Yes	No	Yes	Yes	Yes
Poland	Yes	Yes	Yes	Yes	Yes	No	No	Yes	Yes	Yes
Portugal	Yes	Yes	No	Yes	No	n.r.	n.r.	Yes	No	n.r.
Singapore	Yes	No	Yes	n.a.	Yes	Yes	n.a.	Yes	Yes	Yes
Sweden	Yes	n.a.	Yes	Yes	Yes	n.a.	No	Yes	Yes	Yes
Switzerland	Yes	n.a.	n.a.	n.a.	Yes	Yes	n.a.	Yes	No	Yes
United Kingdom	Yes	Yes[1]	Yes	Yes[2]	Yes	Yes	Yes[1]	Yes	Yes	Yes
United States	Yes	Yes	Yes	Yes	Yes	Yes	Yes	Yes	Yes	Yes
Total Yes	14	12	16	12	16	12	3	15	11	15

Note: The data custodian should be a national authority and data should be included even when it does not cover 100% of the nation. Identifying variables can include name, address, postal code, date of birth. d.k.: don't know; n.a.: not applicable; n.r.: no response.
1. England only.
2. Scotland only.
Source: OECD HCQI Questionnaire on Secondary Use of Health Data, 2011/12.

Table D.6. Sub-national infrastructure for data linkage – regional or state-level record-linkage projects by type of data involved

	Hospital in-patient data	Primary care data	Cancer registry data	Prescription medicines data	Mortality data	Formal long-term care data	Patient experiences survey data	Mental hospital in-patient data	Population health survey data	Population census or registry data
Australia	Yes	No	Yes	Yes	Yes	No	Yes	Yes	Yes	No
Belgium	Yes	n.r.	n.r.	No	No	No	n.r.	No	d.k.	n.r.
Canada	Yes	Yes	Yes	Yes	Yes	Yes	Yes	Yes	Yes	Yes
Denmark	n.a.	n.a.	n.a.	n.a.	n.a.	n.a.	n.a.	n.a.	n.a.	n.a.
Finland	n.a.	n.a.	n.a.	n.a.	n.a.	n.a.	n.a.	n.a.	n.a.	n.a.
France	ns	ns	Yes	ns	ns	ns	ns	ns	ns	ns
Germany	No	No	Yes	No	Yes	No	No	No	Yes	No
Israel	No	No	No	No	Yes	No	No	No	No	No
Japan	n.r.	n.r.	Yes	n.r.	No	n.r.	n.r.	n.r.	n.r.	n.r.
Korea	n.a.	n.a.	n.a.	n.a.	n.a.	n.a.	n.a.	n.a.	n.a.	n.a.
Malta	n.a.	n.a.	n.a.	n.a.	n.a.	n.a.	n.a.	n.a.	n.a.	n.a.
Norway	n.a.	n.a.	n.a.	n.a.	n.a.	n.a.	n.a.	n.a.	n.a.	n.a.
Poland	No	No	No	No	No	No	No	No	No	No
Portugal	No	No	Yes	No	No	n.r.	n.r.	No	No	n.r.
Singapore	n.a.	n.a.	n.a.	n.a.	n.a.	n.a.	n.a.	n.a.	n.a.	n.a.
Sweden	Yes	Yes	Yes	Yes	Yes	Yes	Yes	Yes	Yes	Yes
Switzerland	n.r.	n.r.	n.r.	n.r.	n.r.	n.r.	n.r.	n.r.	n.r.	n.r.
United Kingdom	Yes[1]	n.r.	n.r.	Yes[1]	n.r.	n.r.	n.r.	n.r.	n.r.	n.r.
United States	d.k.	d.k.	Yes	d.k.	d.k.	d.k.	d.k.	d.k.	d.k.	d.k.
Total Yes	5	2	8	4	5	2	3	3	4	2

Note: d.k.: don't know; n.a.: not applicable; n.r.: no response.
1. Scotland only.
Source: OECD HCQI Questionnaire on Secondary Use of Health Data, September and October 2011.

Table D.7. **Sub-national infrastructure for data linkage – networks of health care organisations record linkage projects by type of data involved**

	Hospital in-patient data	Primary care data	Cancer registry data	Prescription medicines data	Mortality data	Formal long-term care data	Patient experiences survey data	Mental hospital in-patient data	Population health survey data	Population census or registry data
Australia	n.r.	n.r.	n.r.	n.r.	n.r.	n.r.	n.r.	n.r.	n.r.	n.r.
Belgium	Yes	No	n.r.	No	No	No	n.r.	No	No	n.r.
Canada	Yes	Yes	Yes	d.k.	Yes	Yes	d.k.	Yes	Yes	Yes
Denmark	n.a.	n.a.	n.a.	n.a.	n.a.	n.a.	n.a.	n.a.	n.a.	n.a.
France	No	No	No	No	No	No	No	No	No	No
Finland	n.a.	n.a.	n.a.	n.a.	n.a.	n.a.	n.a.	n.a.	n.a.	n.a.
Germany	Yes	Yes	Yes	Yes	No	Yes	No	No	No	No
Israel	Yes	Yes	No	Yes	Yes	Yes	Yes	Yes	Yes	Yes
Japan	n.r.	n.r.	n.r.	n.r.	n.r.	n.r.	n.r.	n.r.	n.r.	n.r.
Korea	n.r.	n.r.	n.r.	n.r.	n.r.	n.r.	n.r.	n.r.	n.r.	n.r.
Malta	n.r.	n.r.	n.r.	n.r.	n.r.	n.r.	n.r.	n.r.	n.r.	n.r.
Norway	No	No	No	No	No	No	No	No	No	No
Poland	No	No	No	No	No	No	No	No	No	No
Portugal	Yes	Yes	Yes	Yes	No	n.r.	n.r.	No	No	n.r.
Singapore	Yes	No	No	No	No	Yes	No	No	No	No
Sweden	No	No	No	No	No	No	No	No	No	No
Switzerland	No	No	No	No	No	No	No	No	No	No
United Kingdom	No	No	No	No	No	No	No	No	No	No
United States	Yes	Yes	Yes	Yes	Yes	Yes	Yes	Yes	Yes	Yes
Total Yes	7	5	4	4	3	5	2	2	3	3

Note: d.k.: don't know; n.a.: not applicable; n.r.: no response.
Source: OECD HCQI Questionnaire on Secondary Use of Health Data, 2011/12.

Table D.8. **National data is used to undertake record linkage projects**

	Hospital in-patient data	Primary care data	Cancer registry data	Prescription medicines data	Mortality data	Formal long-term care data	Patient experiences survey data	Mental hospital in-patient data	Population health survey data	Population census or registry data
Australia	No	Yes	Yes	Yes	Yes	Yes	No	No	No	Yes
Belgium	Yes	Yes	Yes	Yes	Yes	Yes	n.r.	No	Yes	n.r.
Canada	Yes	n.a.	Yes	n.a.	Yes	Yes	n.a.	Yes	Yes	Yes
Denmark	Yes	Yes	Yes	Yes	Yes	n.a.	No	Yes	No	Yes
Finland	Yes	n.a.	Yes	Yes	Yes	Yes	No	Yes	No	Yes
France	n.r.	Yes	No	Yes	Yes	n.r.	No	n.r.	Yes	No
Germany	No	No	No	No	No	No	n.a.	n.a.	No	No
Israel	Yes	No	Yes	No	Yes	Yes	No	Yes	Yes	Yes
Japan	Yes	Yes	n.a.	Yes	n.r.	No	n.r.	n.r.	Yes	Yes
Korea	Yes	Yes	Yes	Yes	Yes	Yes	No	Yes	No	No
Malta	Yes	No	Yes	n.a.	Yes	No	n.a.	No	No	No
Norway	Yes	Yes	Yes	Yes	Yes	Yes	No	No	Yes	Yes
Poland	No	No	No	No	No	No	No	No	No	No
Portugal	No	Yes	No	Yes	No	n.r.	n.r.	No	No	N.r.
Singapore	Yes	n.a.	Yes	n.a.	Yes	Yes	n.a.	No	Yes	No
Sweden	Yes	n.a.	Yes	Yes	Yes	n.a.	No	Yes	Yes	Yes
Switzerland	Yes	n.a.	n.a.	n.a.	Yes	Yes	n.a.	Yes	No	Yes
United Kingdom	Yes	Yes[1]	Yes	Yes[2]	Yes	Yes[2]	No	Yes	Yes[2]	Yes
United States	Yes	Yes	Yes	Yes	Yes	Yes	Yes	d.k.	Yes	Yes
Total Yes	14	10	13	12	15	11	1	8	10	11

Note: The data custodian should be a national authority and data should be included even when it does not cover 100% of the nation. d.k.: don't know; n.a.: not applicable; n.r.: no response.
1. England only.
2. Scotland only.
Source: OECD HCQI Questionnaire on Secondary Use of Health Data, 2011/12.

Table D.9. **National data is used to undertake record linkage projects on a regular basis**

	Hospital in-patient data	Primary care data	Cancer registry data	Prescription medicines data	Mortality data	Formal long-term care data	Patient experiences survey data	Mental hospital in-patient data	Population health survey data	Population census or registry data
Australia	No	Yes	Yes	Yes	Yes	No	No	No	No	Yes
Belgium	Yes	Yes	Yes	Yes	Yes	Yes	n.r.	No	No	n.r.
Canada	Yes	n.a.	ns	n.a.	Yes	n.r.	n.a.	n.r.	Yes	Yes
Denmark	Yes	Yes	Yes	Yes	Yes	n.a.	No	Yes	No	Yes
Finland	Yes	n.a.	Yes	Yes	Yes	Yes	No	Yes	No	Yes
France	ns	Yes	No	Yes	Yes	ns	No	ns	Yes	Yes
Germany	No	No	No	No	No	No	n.a.	n.a.	No	No
Israel	Yes	No	Yes	No	Yes	Yes	No	Yes	Yes	Yes
Japan	No	No	n.a.	No	n.r.	n.r.	n.r.	n.r.	n.r.	n.r.
Korea	Yes	Yes	Yes	Yes	Yes	Yes	No	Yes	No	No
Malta	Yes	No	Yes	n.a.	Yes	No	n.a.	No	No	No
Norway	No	No	Yes	No	Yes	No	No	No	Yes	Yes
Poland	No	No	No	No	No	No	No	No	No	No
Portugal	No	Yes	n.r.	Yes	n.r.	n.r.	n.r.	No	n.r.	n.r.
Singapore	Yes	n.a.	No	n.a.	Yes	No	n.a.	No	No	No
Sweden	Yes	n.a.	Yes	Yes	Yes	n.a.	No	Yes	Yes	Yes
Switzerland	Yes	n.a.	n.a.	n.a.	Yes	Yes	n.a.	Yes	No	Yes
United Kingdom	Yes	Yes[1]	Yes	Yes[2]	Yes	No	No	Yes	Yes[2]	Yes
United States	Yes	Yes	Yes	Yes	Yes	Yes	Yes	d.k.	Yes	Yes
Total Yes	12	8	11	10	15	6	1	7	7	11

Note: A regular basis indicates that there is usually a project underway. d.k.: don't know; n.a.: not applicable; n.r.: no response.
1. England only.
2. Scotland only.
Source: OECD HCQI Questionnaire on Secondary Use of Health Data, September and October 2011.

Table D.10. **National record linkage projects are used for regular health care quality monitoring**

	Hospital in-patient data	Primary care data	Cancer registry data	Prescription medicines data	Mortality data	Formal long-term care data	Patient experiences survey data	Mental hospital in-patient data	Population health survey data	Population census or registry data
Australia	No	No	No	No	Yes	No	No	No	No	No
Belgium	Yes	Yes	Yes	Yes	Yes	n.r.	n.r.	No	No	n.r.
Canada	Yes	n.a.	n.r.	n.a.	n.r.	n.r.	n.a.	n.r.	n.r.	n.r.
Denmark	Yes	Yes	Yes	Yes	Yes	n.a.	No	Yes	No	Yes
France	n.r.	No	No	No	No	n.r.	No	n.r.	No	No
Finland	Yes	n.a.	Yes	Yes	Yes	Yes	No	Yes	No	Yes
Germany	No	No	No	No	No	No	n.a.	n.a.	No	No
Israel	Yes	No	Yes	No	Yes	Yes	No	Yes	No	Yes
Japan	No	No	n.a.	No	n.r.	n.r.	n.r.	n.r.	n.r.	n.r.
Korea	Yes	Yes	Yes	Yes	Yes	Yes	No	Yes	No	No
Malta	Yes	No	Yes	n.a.	Yes	No	n.a.	No	No	No
Norway	Yes	No	Yes	No	Yes	No	No	No	Yes	Yes
Poland	No	No	No	No	No	No	No	No	No	No
Portugal	No	Yes	n.r.	Yes	n.r.	n.r.	n.r.	No	n.r.	n.r.
Singapore	Yes	n.a.	Yes	No	Yes	Yes	No	No	Yes	No
Sweden	Yes	n.a.	Yes	Yes	Yes	n.a.	No	Yes	Yes	n.r.
Switzerland	No	n.a.	n.a.	n.a.	No	No	n.a.	No	No	No
United Kingdom	Yes	No	Yes	No	Yes	No	No	No	No	No
United States	Yes	No	Yes	Yes	Yes	No	Yes	No	Yes	Yes
Total Yes	12	4	11	7	12	4	1	5	4	4

Note: d.k.: don't know; n.a.: not applicable; n.r.: no response.
Source: OECD HCQI Questionnaire on Secondary Use of Health Data, 2011/12.

Table D.11. **Use of electronic medical and patient records by physicians and hospitals**

	Primary care physician offices			Medical specialist physician offices			Hospitals				
	Capture patient diagnosis and treatment electronically	Proportion with electronic data capture	Share some information about patients electronically	Capture patient diagnosis and treatment electronically	Proportion with electronic data capture	Share some information about patients electronically	Capture data on in-patient diagnosis and treatment electronically	Proportion with electronic data capture	Capture emergency room patient diagnosis and treatment electronically	Proportion with electronic data capture	Share some information about patients electronically
Austria	Yes	> 80%	Yes	Yes	> 90%	Yes	Yes	100%	Yes	n.a.	Yes
Belgium	Yes	70%	Yes	Yes	80%	Yes	Yes	75%	Yes	n.a.	Yes
Canada	Yes	41.3%*	Yes	Yes	36.2%*	Yes	Yes	n.a.	Yes	n.a.	Yes
Denmark	Yes	51%	Yes	Yes	10%	Yes	Yes	100%	Yes	100%	Yes
Estonia	Yes	98%	Yes	Yes	50%	Yes	Yes	100%	Yes	n.a.	Yes
Finland	Yes	100%	Yes	Yes	100%	Yes	Yes	100%	Yes	100%	Yes
France	Yes	n.a.	Yes	Yes	n.a.	Yes	Yes	n.a.	Yes	n.a.	Yes
Germany	Yes	> 80%	Yes	Yes	> 80%	Yes	Yes	> 90%	Yes	n.a.	Yes
Iceland	Yes	100%	Yes	Yes	> 60%	Yes	Yes	100%	Yes	100%	Yes
Indonesia	Yes	≈ 20%	Yes	Yes	n.a.	n.a.	Yes	n.a.	Yes	n.a.	Yes
Israel	Yes	100%	Yes	Yes	≈ 95%	Yes	Yes	100%	Yes	80%	Yes
Japan	Yes	15.2%**	Yes	Yes	15.2%**	Yes	Yes	14.2%	Yes	n.a.	Yes
Korea	Yes	63.5%	No	Yes	52-66%***	Yes	Yes	52-66%***	Yes	52-66%***	Yes
Mexico	Yes	≈ 15%	Yes	Yes	n.a.	No	Yes	≈ 30%	Yes	n.a.	Yes
Netherlands	Yes	100%	Yes	Yes	100%	Yes	Yes	100%	Yes	100%	Yes
Poland	Yes	≈ 15%	Yes	Yes	≈ 10%	Yes	Yes	≈ 5%	Yes	n.a.	No
Portugal	Yes	90%	Yes	Yes	50%	Yes	Yes	70%	Yes	95%	Yes
Singapore	Yes	14%	No	Yes	60%	Yes	Yes	80%	Yes	80%	Yes
Slovak Republic	Yes	n.a.	n.a.	Yes	n.a.	n.a.	Yes	n.a.	Yes	n.a.	No
Slovenia	Yes	90%	Yes	Yes	90%	Yes	Yes	90%	Yes	90%	Yes
Spain	Yes	90%	Yes	Yes	≈ 25%	Yes	Yes	≈ 70%	Yes	≈ 45%	Yes
Sweden	Yes	100%	Yes	Yes	100%	Yes	Yes	100%	Yes	100%	Yes
Switzerland	Yes	20%	Yes	Yes	n.a.	Yes	Yes	90%	Yes	n.a.	Yes
United Kingdom	Yes	≈ 100%	Yes	Yes	20%[1]	Yes	Yes	100%	Yes	100%	Yes
United States	Yes	57%**	Yes	Yes	57%**	Yes	Yes	18.9%	Yes	n.a.	Yes
Total Yes	25		22	25		22	25		25		23

Note: n.a.: not applicable.
1. England only.
* Percentage of physicians (not physician offices).
** Percentage of physician offices (both GPs and specialists).
*** 66% of tertiary/general hospitals and 53% of hospitals are using EMRs.
Source: OECD HCQI Questionnaire on Secondary Use of Health Data: Electronic Health Records, 2012.

Table D.12. **National plan or policy and the inclusion of secondary data use**

	National plan or national policy to implement EHRs	National Plan or national policy includes one or more secondary uses of data	Secondary data uses included in national plan or policy to implement EHRs					
			Public health monitoring	Health system performance monitoring	Patient safety monitoring	Facilitating and contributing to clinical trials	Supporting physician queries about care given to groups of patients	Research to improve patient care, health system performance or population health
Austria	Yes	Yes	No	No	No	No	Yes	No
Belgium	Yes	Yes	Yes	Yes	Yes	No	Yes	Yes
Canada	Yes	No	No	No	No	No	No	No
Denmark	Yes	Yes	No	No	No	No	Yes	No
Estonia*	Yes	Yes	Yes	Yes	No	Yes	Yes	Yes
Finland	Yes	Yes	Yes	Yes	Yes	Yes	Yes	No
France	Yes	Yes	Yes	Yes	Yes	Yes	Yes	Yes
Germany	No	n.a.	n.a.	n.a.	n.a.	n.a.	n.a.	n.a.
Iceland	Yes	Yes	Yes	Yes	No	No	No	No
Indonesia	Yes	Yes	Yes	Yes	Yes	Yes	Yes	Yes
Israel	Yes	No	No	No	No	No	No	No
Japan	Yes	Yes	No	No	No	No	No	Yes
Korea	Yes	Yes	Yes	Yes	Yes	Yes	Yes	Yes
Mexico	Yes	Yes	Yes	Yes	Yes	Yes	Yes	Yes
Netherlands	No	n.a.	n.a.	n.a.	n.a.	n.a.	n.a.	n.a.
Poland	Yes	Yes	Yes	Yes	Yes	Yes	Yes	Yes
Portugal	Yes	Yes	Yes	Yes	Yes	No	No	Yes
Singapore	Yes	Yes	Yes	Yes	Yes	Yes	Yes	Yes
Slovak Republic	Yes	Yes	Yes	Yes	Yes	Yes	Yes	Yes
Slovenia	Yes	Yes	Yes	Yes	No	No	No	No
Spain	Yes	No	No	No	No	No	No	No
Sweden	No	n.a.	n.a.	n.a.	n.a.	n.a.	n.a.	n.a.
Switzerland	Yes	No	No	No	No	No	No	No
United Kingdom	Yes	Yes	Yes	Yes	Yes	No	Yes	Yes
United States	Yes	Yes	Yes	Yes	Yes	Yes	Yes	Yes
Total Yes	22	18	15	15	12	10	14	13

Note: * System is implemented. n.a.: not applicable.
Source: OECD HCQI Questionnaire on Secondary Use of Health Data: Electronic Health Records, 2012.

ANNEX D

Table D.13. **Links to plans or policies to develop national EHR systems**

	Links to national plans or policies	Country notes
Austria	Unknown	
Belgium	www.ehealth.fgov.be/fr/basic_service; www.reseausantewallon.be; www.health.belgium.be/filestore/19069387/1%20Serveur%20terminologie%20general%20strategy%20ehealth.pdf	Although there is not yet a global consensus document covering all aspects of the EHR implementation, there is a plan based on four main pillars: 1) Development of basic essential services, authentication and national standards (e-health platform); 2) Development of quality interoperable health records through an official certification process in each profession (e-health platform with other public health institutions); 3) Development of regional health networks (shared electronic health records) under the responsibility of health care providers and institutions; and 4) Development of a semantic interoperability layer (PFS Public Health, INAMI and E-health platform). The links refer to these pillars.
Canada	www.infoway-inforoute.ca; www2.infoway-inforoute.ca/Documents/ar/Annual_Report_2010-2011_en.pdf;%20www2.infoway-inforoute.ca/Documents/Infoway_Sum.Corp.Plan.2012-2013_EN.pdf; www2.infoway-inforoute.ca/Documents/Vision_2015_Advancing_Canadas_next_generation_of_healthcare[1].pdf (full report); www2.infoway-inforoute.ca/Documents/Vision_Summary_EN.pdf (summary of the report); www.infoway-inforoute.ca/lang-en/component/content/article/115-knowledgeway/657-ehrs-blueprint-v2	Health care is a provincial and territorial responsibility in Canada and each of these jurisdictions is responsible for their EHR system. The national government supports EHR implementation through Canada Health Infoway Inc. whose responsibility it is to develop the architecture and interoperability standards. Canada Health Infoway has provided funds to jurisdictions for the purchase and implementation of elements of the EHR. Initial focus was on labs, digital information and drug systems. More recent focus has been on electronic medical records in general physician offices. The link is to the blueprint for an EHR system in Canada. It is not mandatory but jurisdictions are encouraged to use it and have generally been using it as a starting point for their EHR implementation.
Denmark	www.nsi.d.k.	
Estonia	Unknown	
Finland	Unknown	The national EHR plans are written into legislation and into the program of the current government.
France	www.esante.gouv.fr; www.esante.gouv.fr/dmp_presse/presse/dossier_01.pdf	
Iceland	Unknown	The national policy is to implement an interoperable and sharable EHR.
Indonesia	www.buk.depkes.go.id	
Israel	www.health.gov.il/hozer/mk11_2011.pdf	Another policy paper about primary care information systems will be published soon.
Japan	www.kantei.go.jp/jp/singi/it2/100511honbun.pdf	Pursuant to the IT Act of 2001, a strategic plan for national IT was developed. Health Care was a top consideration in this plan, as well as in the plans for the introduction of a universal personal ID number. The most recent version of the plan, published in May 2010, proposed 1) A personal EHR nicknamed "My Hospital Everywhere" to be introduced by 2013; 2) Seamless record sharing among health care providers to facilitate inter-provider critical pathways; 3) Effective use of the national claims database to improve quality and efficiency; and 4) Development of a multi-hospital EHR database "Japan sentinel project" to ensure drug safety. The link is to documents available only in Japanese.
Korea	Unknown	The implementation of a national EHR project was part of a 2005 National Health Information Infrastructure Plan under the provisions of the Framework Act on Health and Medical Services. The EHR project, however, was not allocated budget in 2009. Dimensions of the plan are underway including 1) Informatisation of public health and medical institutions; 2) Development of a national health information infrastructure master plan; 3) Proliferation and management of information standards and enactment of necessary legislation; 4) Development of a national health information system; and 5) Development and implementation of a pilot project for a national e-health service.

Table D.13. **Links to plans or policies to develop national EHR systems** *(cont.)*

	Links to national plans or policies	Country notes
Mexico	www.dgis.salud.gob.mx/snece/	In December 2008, an interoperability roadmap for electronic health records was elaborated by the Health Ministry with the help of an external consultancy. The roadmap is updated yearly and includes the following stages: 1) 2007-10, collaborative establishment of political and technical definitions; 2) 2010-17, progressive integration and implementation; 3) 2013-19, consolidation; and 2014-20, integration with global electronic services scenarios.
Poland	www.ikp.gov.pl/; www.csioz.gov.pl	Actions to develop e-Health in Poland are authorised by an act of parliament of April 18, 2011 regarding system information in health care (see first link). The second link is to a document describing the national project to develop the Electronic Platform for Collection, Analysis and Sharing of Digital Medical Records.
Portugal	www.portaldasaude.pt/portal/conteudos/a+saude+em+portugal/informatizacao/PDSenglishm.htm	This link is to a description of the Portuguese Health Record which enables provider sharing of clinical information.
Singapore	http://69.59.162.218/HIMSS2012/Venetian%20Sands%20Expo%20Center/2.22.12_Wed/Marcello%204502/Wed_0945/95-21_Sarah_Muttitt_Marcello%204502/95Muttitt.pdf	Link provides a presentation on the national electronic health record development and plans.
Slovakia	www.ezdravotnictvo.sk	Link is to a complete set of strategic documents for the implementation of e-Health including goals, feasibility studies, and implementation program.
Slovenia	www.mz.gov.si/fileadmin/mz.gov.si/pageuploads/mz_dokumenti/delovna_podrocja/zdravstveno_varstvo/kodele/ezdravje_ang.pdf	
Spain	www.msssi.gob.es/en/profesionales/hcdsns/home.htm	
Switzerland	www.e-health-suisse.ch/index.html?lang=en	
United Kingdom	www.dh.gov.uk/en/Publicationsandstatistics/Publications/PublicationsPolicyAndGuidance/DH_4008227; www.dh.gov.uk/en/Publicationsandstatistics/Publications/PublicationsPolicyAndGuidance/DH_086073; www.scotland.gov.uk/Resource/Doc/357616/0120849.pdf	The first two links are to plans for England. This strategy is expected to be superseded by a new information strategy. The third link is to the Scottish NHS eHealth Strategy.
United States	www.healthit.gov/sites/default/files/utility/final-federal-health-it-strategic-plan-0911.pdf	Link to the US Federal Health Information Technology Strategic Plan.

Source: OECD HCQI Questionnaire on Secondary Use of Health Data: Electronic Health Records, 2012.

Table D.14. Implementation of a national electronic health record system

	Implemented or starting to implement a national electronic health record system	National electronic health record system features sharing information among providers treating the same patient including....							
		Physician offices	Physician offices and hospitals	Current medications – sharing among physician offices	Current medications – sharing among physician offices and hospitals	Laboratory test results – sharing among physician offices	Laboratory test results – sharing among physician offices and hospitals	Medical imaging results – sharing among physician offices	Medical imaging results – sharing among physician offices and hospitals
Austria	Yes	No	Yes	Yes	Yes	Yes	Yes	Yes	Yes
Belgium	Yes	Yes	Yes	Yes	Yes	Yes	Yes	Yes	Yes
Canada	Yes	Yes	Yes	Yes	Yes	Yes	Yes	Yes	Yes
Denmark	Yes	Yes	Yes	Yes	Yes	Yes	Yes	Yes	Yes
Estonia	Yes	Yes	Yes	Yes	Yes	No	No	Yes	Yes
Finland	Yes	Yes	Yes	Yes	Yes	Yes	Yes	Yes	Yes
France	Yes	Yes	Yes	Yes	Yes	Yes	Yes	Yes	Yes
Germany	No	n.a.	n.a.	n.a.	n.a.	n.a.	n.a.	n.a.	n.a.
Iceland	No	n.a.	n.a.	n.a.	n.a.	n.a.	n.a.	n.a.	n.a.
Indonesia	Yes	Yes	Yes	Yes	Yes	Yes	Yes	Yes	Yes
Israel	Yes	Yes	Yes	Yes	Yes	Yes	Yes	Yes	Yes
Japan	Yes	Yes	Yes	Yes	Yes	Yes	Yes	No	No
Korea	Yes	Yes	n.r.	Yes	n.r.	n.r.	n.r.	Yes	n.r.
Mexico	Yes	Yes	Yes	Yes	Yes	Yes	Yes	Yes	Yes
Netherlands	No	n.a.	n.a.	n.a.	n.a.	n.a.	n.a.	N.a.	n.a.
Poland	Yes	Yes	Yes	Yes	Yes	Yes	Yes	Yes	Yes
Portugal	Yes	Yes	Yes	Yes	Yes	Yes	Yes	Yes	Yes
Singapore	Yes	Yes	Yes	Yes	Yes	Yes	Yes	Yes	Yes
Slovak Republic	Yes	Yes	Yes	Yes	Yes	Yes	Yes	Yes	Yes
Slovenia	No	n.a.	n.a.	n.a.	n.a.	n.a.	n.a.	n.a.	n.a.
Spain	Yes	Yes	Yes	Yes	Yes	Yes	Yes	Yes	Yes
Sweden	Yes	Yes	Yes	Yes	Yes	Yes	Yes	No	No
Switzerland	Yes	Yes	Yes	Yes	Yes	Yes	Yes	Yes	Yes
United Kingdom	Yes	No	Yes[1]	Yes[2]	Yes	No	No	No	No
United States	No	n.a.	n.a.	n.a.	n.a.	n.a.	n.a.	n.a.	n.a.
Total Yes	20	18	19	20	19	17	17	17	16

Note: n.a.: not applicable.
1. England only.
2. Scotland only.
Source: OECD HCQI Questionnaire on Secondary Use of Health Data: Electronic Health Records, 2012.

Table D.15. Minimum data set defined as part of the National EHR system

	Minimum data sets for the exchange of electronic health records include...										
	A minimum dataset has been defined	Patient unique identifiers	Health care provider unique identifiers	Patient demographic information	Patient socio-economic data	Patient current medications	Patient clinically relevant diagnostic concerns	Patient clinically relevant procedures	Patient clinically relevant physical characteristics	Patient clinically relevant behaviours	Patient clinically relevant psycho-social or cultural issues
Austria	No	n.a.	n.a.	n.a.	n.a.	n.a.	n.a.	n.a.	n.a.	n.a.	n.a.
Belgium	Yes	Yes	Yes	Yes	No	Yes	Yes	No	No	Yes	Yes
Canada	Yes	Yes	Yes	Yes	Yes	Yes	Yes	Yes	Yes	Yes	Yes
Denmark	Yes	Yes	Yes	Yes	Some	Yes	Yes	Yes	Yes	Yes	No
Estonia	Yes	Yes	Yes	Yes	No	Yes	Yes	Yes	No	No	No
Finland	Yes	Yes	Yes	Yes	No	Yes	Yes	Yes	Yes[2]	No	No
France	No	n.a.	n.a.	n.a.	n.a.	n.a.	n.a.	n.a.	n.a.	n.a.	n.a.
Germany	No	n.a.	n.a.	n.a.	n.a.	n.a.	n.a.	n.a.	n.a.	n.a.	n.a.
Iceland	No	n.a.	n.a.	n.a.	n.a.	n.a.	n.a.	n.a.	n.a.	n.a.	n.a.
Indonesia	Yes	Yes	Yes	Yes	Yes	Yes	Yes	Yes	Yes	Yes	Yes
Israel	Yes	Yes	Yes	Yes	No	Yes	Yes	Yes	No	No	No
Japan	No	n.a.	n.a.	n.a.	n.a.	n.a.	n.a.	n.a.	n.a.	n.a.	n.a.
Korea	Yes	Yes	Yes	Yes	Yes	Yes	Yes	Yes	Yes	Yes	No
Mexico	Yes	Yes	Yes	Yes	Yes	No	Yes	Yes	No	Yes	No
Netherlands	n.a.	n.a.	n.a.	n.a.	n.a.	n.a.	n.a.	n.a.	n.a.	n.a.	n.a.
Poland	Yes*	Yes	Yes	Yes	No	Yes	Yes	Yes	Yes	Yes	No
Portugal	Yes	Yes	Yes	Yes	No	Yes	Yes	Yes	Yes	Yes	No
Singapore	Yes	Yes	Yes	Yes	Yes	Yes	Yes	Yes	No	No	No
Slovak Republic	Yes*	Yes	Yes	Yes	Yes	Yes	Yes	Yes	Yes	Yes	No
Slovenia	No	n.a.	n.a.	n.a.	n.a.	n.a.	n.a.	n.a.	n.a.	n.a.	n.a.
Spain	Yes	Yes	Yes	Yes	No	Yes	Yes	Yes	No	Yes	No
Sweden	Yes	Yes	Yes	Yes	No	Yes	Yes	Yes	No	No	No
Switzerland	Yes	Yes	Yes	Yes	No	Yes	Yes	Yes	No	No	No
United Kingdom	Yes	Yes	Yes[1]	Yes[1]	No	Yes	Yes	No	No	No	No
United States	Yes	Yes	Yes	Yes	No	Yes	Yes	Yes	Yes	No	No
Total Yes	18	18	18	18	6	17	18	16	9	10	3

Note: * In development. n.a.: not applicable.
1. Scotland only.
2. Children only.
Source: OECD HCQI Questionnaire on Secondary Use of Health Data: Electronic Health Records, 2012.

Table D.16. **Data elements within electronic health records are structured**

Data elements are entered as structured elements using a controlled vocabulary (terminology standard)...
is True for all records, True for most records, True for some records or is False

	Socio-economic information	Medications	Diagnosis	Laboratory tests	Medical imaging results	Surgical procedures	Physical characteristics	Behaviours	Psychosocial or cultural issues
Austria	T	T	T	T	T	n.a.	n.a.	n.a.	n.a.
Belgium	Tm	Tm	Ts	Tm	Tm	Ts	Ts	Ts	Ts
Canada	Tm	Ts	Ts	Tm	Ts	F	Ts	F	F
Denmark	Ts	T	T	T	T	T	Ts	Ts	Ts
Estonia	T	T	T	T	T	T	T	T	F
Finland	Ts	Tm	T	T	T	Tm	Ts	n.a.	n.a.
France	T	T	T	T	T	T	T	T	T
Germany	n.a.	n.a.	n.a.	n.a.	n.a.	n.a.	n.a.	n.a.	n.a.
Iceland	Tm	T	T	Tm	Tm	Tm	F	Ts	Ts
Indonesia	T	T	T	T	T	T	T	T	T
Israel	Ts	Tm	Tm	T	Ts	Tm	Ts	Ts	Ts
Japan	u	u	u	u	u	u	u	u	U
Korea	T	T	T	T	T	T	T	T	n.a.
Mexico	T	T	T	Tm	Tm	T	Ts	Ts	Ts
Netherlands	n.a.	n.a.	n.a.	n.a.	n.a.	n.a.	n.a.	n.a.	n.a.
Poland	Ts	Ts	T	Ts	F	T	n.a.	n.a.	F
Portugal	F	Tm	Tm	Tm	Ts	Ts	Ts	Ts	F
Singapore	T	T	T	T	F	F	n.a.	n.a.	n.a.
Slovak Republic	T	T	T	T	T	T	T	T	T
Slovenia	Ts	Tm	Tm	Tm	Ts	Tm	Ts	Ts	Ts
Spain	n.r.	Ts	Ts	Ts	Ts	F	Ts	Ts	Ts
Sweden	F	Tm	Tm	Tm	F	Ts	Ts	Ts	F
Switzerland	n.a.	n.a.	n.a.	n.a.	n.a.	n.a.	n.a.	n.a.	n.a.
United Kingdom	Ts	Tm	Tm	Tm	Tm[1]/Ts[2]	Tm	Ts	F[1]/Ts[2]	F[1]/Ts[2]
United States	Ts	T	T	Tm	Ts	Tm	Ts	Ts	n.a.
Total true	8	11	13	10	8	8	5	5	3

Note: F: false, n.a.: not applicable, n.r.: not reported, T: true for all, Tm: true for most, Ts: true for some, u: undetermined.
1. England only.
2. Scotland only.
Source: OECD HCQI Questionnaire on Secondary Use of Health Data: Electronic Health Records, 2012.

Table D.17. **Terminology standards for structured data elements**

	Socio-economic information	Medications	Diagnosis	Laboratory tests	Medical imaging results	Surgical procedures	Physical characteristics	Behaviours	Psychosocial or cultural issues
Austria	IHE, HL7	ATC	ICD-10	LOINC	DIACOM/WADO				
Belgium	ISO	ATC	SNOMED-CT	LOINC	DICOM	SNOMED-CT	SNOMED-CT	SNOMED-CT	
Canada	HL7v3	Drug identification number (DIN), ATC	ICD-10 vCanada and vCII, DSM-4, SNOMED-CT	LOINC	DICOM, SNOMED-CT	Canadian classification of health interventions (CCI), SNOMED-CT		SNOMED-CT	
Denmark		ATC	ICD-10, ICPC	IUPAC	ICD10	NOMESCO, NCSP			
Estonia	National standards	ATC	ICD-10	LOINC	DICOM	NCSP	National standards	National standards	National standards
Finland		ATC	ICD-10 and ICPC2 mapped	Finloinc – mapped to LOINC	DICOM and Finland national coding		Finloinc		
France	PCS-ESE (occupation)	CIS, CIP	ICD-10	LOINC vf 1.3	HL7v3/DICOM	SNOMED 3.5 vf	UCUM	SNOMED 3.5 vf	SNOMED 3.5 vf
Germany		National coding system	ICD-10 (GM for ambulatory care)			OPS			
Iceland		ATC	ICD-10 and ICPC-2	SNOMED-CT (pathogens) LOINC	DICOM	NCSP/NCSP-IS			
Indonesia	WHO	WHO	ICD-10, ICPC	Local system	Local system	ICD-9 CM		WHO	
Israel	Local system	Israeli drug catalogue (YARPA)	ICD9-CM	Local system	Local system	ICD-9 CM, CPT			
Japan		Japan national drug codes	Japan diagnostic codes			Japan procedure codes	Japan codes (only for health screening data)		
Korea		Korea drug codes – mapped to ATC	Korean Standard Terminology of Medicine (KOSTOM)	Health insurance fee codes	Health insurance fee codes	KOSTOM- mapped to ICD-9 CM	KOSTOM		
Mexico	INEGI	National medication codes	ICD-10 v Spanish	LOINC	DICOM	ICD-9 CM(Spanish)			
Netherlands									
Poland		Central Drug Vocabulary, OSOZ, BLOZ	ICD-10		DICOM	ICD-9	BMI		
Portugal		ATC	ICD-9 CM, ICD-10	LOINC	DICOM	ICD-9 CM	EPSOS	EPSOS	
Singapore		Singapore drug dictionary	ICD-9&10, SNOMED-CT						
Slovak Republic	SNOMED, ICD-10, Alliance NNN, 13606, archetypes	ATC, EDQM	ICD-10	LOINC	DICOM		BMI	ICD-10	ICD-10
Slovenia		ATC	ICD-10 CM	LOINC		Local codes			
Spain		National code, SNOMED-CT	ICD-9 CM, ICD-10, SNOMED-CT	LOINC, SNOMED-CT	Local codes (SERAM and SEMNIM catalogue)	ICD-9 CM, ICD 10, SNOMED CT			
Sweden									
Switzerland									
United Kingdom (England)		SNOMED-CT Drug extension	ICD-10	HL7	DICOM	OPCS4			

Table D.17. **Terminology standards for structured data elements** (cont.)

	Socio-economic information	Medications	Diagnosis	Laboratory tests	Medical imaging results	Surgical procedures	Physical characteristics	Behaviours	Psychosocial or cultural issues
United Kingdom (Scotland)	Local codes (READ v2, SMR, OSIAF)	DM+d, Local coding system	ICD-10, Local codes (READ)	Local codes (READ-pathology bound list)		Local codes (READ v2), OPCS		ICD-10, Local codes (READ)	ICD-10, Local codes (READ)
United States		RxNorm, NCPDP Script 10.6-electronic prescriptions	ICD-10-CM (for the encounter), SNOMED-CT (for problems)	LOINC 2.38	DICOM PS3	ICD-10-PCS/ HCPCS, CPT-4	LOINC 2.38 (for question), UCUM (for units of measure)	Smoking was defined in US regulation	

Source: OECD HCQI Questionnaire on Secondary Use of Health Data: Electronic Health Records, 2012.

Table D.18. **Encouraging quality of electronic health records**

	Vendors of EHR Systems		Incentives or penalties			Quality	
	Certification process	Certification requires vendors to adopt terminology standards	To install an EHR system from a certified vendor	To adopt standards (use structured data)	To use the EHR system to ensure patient records are kept up-to-date	Quality audits of EHR records	Concerns with the quality of data within EHR
Austria	No	n.a.	Yes	No	Yes	No	No
Belgium	Yes	Yes	Yes	Yes	No	Yes	Yes
Canada	Yes	No	Yes	Yes	No	No	Yes
Denmark	n.r.	n.r.	No	No	No	No	Yes
Estonia	No	n.a.	Yes	Yes	Yes	Yes	Yes
Finland	No	n.a.	Yes	Yes	Yes	No	Yes
France	Yes	Yes	No	No	No	No	d.k.
Germany	Partly	Partly	No	No	No	No	n.r.
Iceland	No	No	No	No	No	Yes	Yes
Indonesia	No	No	No	No	No	No	n.r.
Israel	No	n.a.	No	No	No	No	Yes
Japan	No	n.a.	No	Yes	No	No	No
Korea	No	n.a.	No	No	No	No	n.r.
Mexico	Yes	Yes	No	No	No	No	Yes
Netherlands	No	n.a.	No	No	No	No	Yes
Poland	No	n.a.	No	No	No	No	Yes
Portugal	Yes	Yes	Yes	Yes	Yes	Yes	Yes
Singapore	No	n.a.	No	No	No	n.r.	Yes
Slovak Republic	Yes	Yes	Yes	Yes	Yes	No	n.r.
Slovenia	No	n.a.	No	No	No	No	Yes
Spain	No	n.a.	Yes	Yes	No	Yes	Yes
Sweden	Yes	No	No	No	No	No	n.r.
Switzerland	No	n.a.	Yes	Yes	No	No	Yes
United Kingdom	Yes	Yes	Yes[1]	Yes	Yes	Yes[1]	Yes
United States	Yes	Yes	Yes	Yes	Yes	No	n.r.
Total (Yes)	9	7	11	11	7	6	16

Note: d.k.: don't know; n.a.: not applicable; n.r.: no response.
1. England only.
Source: OECD HCQI Questionnaire on Secondary Use of Health Data: Electronic Health Records, 2012.

Table D.19. **Building databases from EHR records for monitoring and analysis**

	Databases		Challenges to building databases from EHR records					Third parties established to...		
	Building databases	Number of custodians of databases from EHR records	Legal barriers to the creation or analysis of databases	Lack of resources or technical capacity to create databases	Concerns with the quality of EHR records	Lack of resources or technical capacity to de-identify data	Other challenges	Create databases from EHR records	De-identify databases	Approve requests for data access
Austria	No	n.a.	No	No	No	No	n.r.	No	No	No
Belgium	Yes	> 20	Yes	No	Yes	No	n.r.	No	Yes	Yes
Canada	Yes	n.r.	Yes	Yes	Yes	Yes	n.r.	Yes	No	No
Denmark	No	n.a.	No	No	No	No	No	No	No	No
Estonia	Not yet	n.r.	No	Yes	Yes	No	n.r.	No	No	Yes
Finland	Yes	1	Yes	Yes	No	No	n.r.	No	No	No
France	Not yet	1	Yes	n.r.	n.r.	n.r.	n.r.	No	No	Yes
Germany	Not directly	n.a.	Yes	n.a.	n.a.	n.a.	n.r.	No	No	No
Iceland	Yes	2-5	No	No	Yes	Yes	No	No	No	No
Indonesia	Not yet	n.a.	n.a.	n.a.	n.a.	n.a.	n.a.	Yes	n.a.	n.a.
Israel	No	n.a.	Yes	No	No	No	n.r.	No	No	No
Japan	No	n.a.	Yes	No	No	No	Yes	No	No	No
Korea	Yes	2-5	Yes	No	Yes	No	No	Yes	Yes	No
Mexico	No	n.a.	n.r.	n.r.	n.r.	n.r.	n.r.	No	No	No
Netherlands	No	n.a.	Yes	Yes	No	No	Yes	No	No	No
Poland	Yes	2-5	Yes	Yes	Yes	No	n.r.	No	No	No
Portugal	Yes	2-5	Yes	No	Yes	No	n.r.	No	No	No
Singapore	No	n.a.	Yes	No	Yes	Yes	Yes	n.r.	n.r.	n.r.
Slovak Republic	Not yet	1	No	No	No	No	No	No	No	No
Slovenia	Yes	2-5	Yes	Yes	Yes	Yes	n.r.	No	No	No
Spain	Yes	> 20	No	No	Yes	Yes	Yes	No	No	No
Sweden	Yes	> 20	Yes	Yes	Yes	No	n.r.	No	No	No
Switzerland	No	n.a.	Yes	Yes	Yes	Yes	No	No	No	No
United Kingdom	Yes	> 20	Yes[2]	No	Yes	Yes[2]	Yes	No	Yes[1]	Yes[1]
United States	Yes	> 20	No	Yes	Yes	No	No	n.r.	n.r.	n.r.
Total (Yes)	12		16	9	14	7	5	3	3	4

Note: d.k.: don't know; n.a.: not applicable; n.r.: no response.
1. England only.
2. Scotland only.
Source: OECD HCQI Questionnaire on Secondary Use of Health Data: Electronic Health Records, 2012.

ANNEX D

Table D.20. **Data usability evaluation and current secondary uses**

	Databases from EHRs	Regular use of electronic health records for secondary analysis						EHR vendors database creation tools	
	Process to evaluate the usability of EHR data	Public health monitoring	Health system performance monitoring	Patient safety monitoring	Facilitating and contributing to clinical trials	Supporting physician treatment decisions	Research	Create software enabling clients to create and analyse EHR databases	Any public sector controls on these databases to protect patient privacy
Austria	No	No	No	No	No	No	No	n.r.	n.r.
Belgium	Yes	Yes	No	Yes	No	Yes	Yes	No	n.a.
Canada	No	No	No	No	No	No	No	Yes	Yes
Denmark	No	No	No	No	No	No	No	No	n.a.
Estonia	Yes	Yes	No	No	No	No	No	No	n.a.
Finland	Yes	Yes	Partly	Yes	No	Yes	Partly	Yes	Yes
France	No	Yes	Yes	Yes	Yes	Yes	Yes	No	n.a.
Germany	No	No	No	No	No	No	No	Yes	Yes
Iceland	Yes	Yes	No	No	No	No	Yes	No	n.a.
Indonesia	Yes	Yes	Yes	Yes	Yes	Yes	Yes	Yes	No
Israel	No	No	No	No	No	No	No	Yes	Yes
Japan	No	Yes	No	No	No	No	Yes	No	n.a.
Korea	Yes	Yes	No	Yes	No	No	Yes	Yes	Yes
Mexico	No	No	No	No	No	No	No	Yes	Yes
Netherlands	No	No	No	No	No	No	No	No	n.a.
Poland	No	Yes	Yes	No	No	Yes	Yes	Yes	n.r.
Portugal	No	Yes	Yes	Yes	No	No	Yes	Yes	Yes
Singapore	Yes	No	No	No	No	No	No	No	n.a.
Slovak Republic	Yes	Not yet	Not yet	Not yet	Not yet	Not yet	Not yet	n.r.	n.r.
Slovenia	No	Yes	Yes	Yes	No	No	Yes	Yes	Yes
Spain	No	No	No	No	No	No	No	Yes	Yes
Sweden	No	Yes	Yes	Yes	Yes	Yes	Yes	No	n.a.
Switzerland	Yes	No	No	No	No	No	No	No	n.a.
United Kingdom	Yes	Yes	Yes	Yes[1]	Yes	Yes	Yes	Yes	Yes
United States	Yes	No	No	No	No	No	No	Yes	Yes
Total (Yes)	11	13	7	9	4	7	11	13	11

Note: d.k.: don't know; n.a.: not applicable; n.r.: no response.
1. Scotland only.
Source: OECD HCQI Questionnaire on Secondary Use of Health Data: Electronic Health Records, 2012.

ANNEX E

Additional information on participating countries current use of electronic medical and electronic patient records by health care providers

Many countries provided details about the current use of electronic medical and patient record systems. This information complements the results presented in Chapter 4 of this report.

In the *United Kingdom*, England and Scotland have established facilities for the exchange of electronic records within primary care practices; and also among primary care offices when a patient changes to a new practice. Specific transactions are also shared between primary and secondary care in England including orders, results, referrals, discharges and appointment bookings. A patient summary record is also available nationally to authorised users. Scotland reports that all primary care providers exchange patient data on demographics, referrals, lab results, and medications using a common gateway (SCI) that can be accessed by secondary care providers and can be used to transfer patient records. In Scotland, patient emergency care summaries are extracted nightly from primary care practices and can be accessed by hospitals providing emergency and acute care. A more detailed electronic medical record is shared among clinicians, which is targeted to supporting the care of patients with chronic health conditions.

In Scotland, all medical specialists work within hospitals and are able to access and share lab results and medical images and are able to view medications prescribed in primary care. Some hospitals enable medical specialists to update patient records electronically and to update medication information. England reports that all hospitals are able share information electronically including ordering and reporting, letters, clinical notes and medical images. Scotland reports that hospitals access the same gateway for demographics, referrals, lab results, medications and record transfers as do primary care physicians, providing a single view of a patient record. Medical specialists, who are resident in hospitals in England, benefit from these services.

Poland reported that primary care physicians and medical specialists in some private health care networks of clinics and hospitals are sharing patient medical data regarding physician visits and laboratory results. A consortium of hospitals in Lower Silesia is sharing radiation results electronically. As of 2014, it will be mandatory for all health care providers in Poland to use electronic medical records.

In *Denmark*, primary care physicians and medical specialist physicians are able to send and receive information regarding laboratory tests; to order prescription medicines; and to communicate electronically with other physician offices, hospitals, physiotherapists and municipalities. Primary care physicians and medical specialists are using e-prescription services where their prescriptions are submitted electronically. Most of these requests (80%) are transferred electronically to a prescription repository that is accessible by all pharmacies for dispensing. All primary care physicians (general practitioners) in Denmark will be required to use electronic medical records for their patients by 1 April 2013.

Hospitals in Denmark are able to share electronically by means of EDI or web services: laboratory information, medications lists, and diagnosis and treatment information. All lab test results are accessible to health professionals working within hospitals through a national lab test portal. All hospitals and private labs exchange data using structured international EDI/XML standards. This includes 100% of discharge summaries, outpatient notes, casualty ward notes, x-ray reports, lab test orders, and lab test results. This information is shared among hospitals and between hospitals and primary care physicians and private medical specialist physicians.

A common electronic medications list has been implemented in three regions in Denmark and will be fully implemented in 2012. This medications list will be inclusive of both private and hospital dispensing. A common electronic journal for primary and secondary care is almost fully developed and is undergoing final pilot testing in 2012. The e-journal will enable physicians to see and update records for their patients including diagnosis and treatment information over time (coded diagnosis, episodes of care, treatments, and coded surgical interventions).

In *Estonia*, primary care and medical specialist physician offices and hospitals share a common functionality where all are able to send and receive lab tests and medical imaging results; to see and update an electronic medications list for their patients that includes any medications prescribed by other physicians; to see hospital in-patient and emergency room records for their patients electronically and to see and update an electronic health record for their patients including diagnosis and treatment information from multiple physicians and over time.

Finland results for primary care and medical specialist physicians refer to the public sector, where 100% of physicians are using electronic medical records. Most primary health care physicians in Finland work in the public sector and there is no data for the minority who work in the private sector. For medical specialist care, the proportion in the private sector that is using electronic records for their patient diagnosis and treatment information is about 60%.

In Finland, the sharing of records among health care providers, including primary care physician offices, medical specialist physician offices and hospitals, is at a regional level only. Most hospital districts (19 of 21) have joined a regional system for sharing patient data. All hospital districts have acute care hospitals as well as primary care and specialist physicians. Hospital districts have a local system for exchanging lab results and digital images, and most have implemented sharing of electronic patient records, written radiology statements, electronic referrals and electronic discharge letters.

Most primary care centres in Finland (68%) have joined at least one regional system for sharing data. Most share digital images (76%); radiology results (59%); lab tests and results (71%); electronic referrals (85%); hospital discharge letters (85%); and consultation letters from other health care providers (84%). Some (19%) use tele-video consultations with secondary care providers and 35% receive an electronic ECG from ambulances.

Sweden reports that primary and specialist care and hospitals are all fully using electronic records. Within Sweden, patient data is shared among different care units, including hospitals and primary care that are located within the same county council (health authority). Individual care givers that are contracted by the health authority typically share patient data within the county's system. There are, however, some exceptions.

Belgium reports the sharing of electronic patient records among primary care physician and medical specialist physician offices and hospitals. Data shared include laboratory results, access to patient longitudinal data about diagnosis and treatments, patient summary information, electronic prescribing and secured messaging. Primary care physicians in Belgium have the responsibility to update and publish patient summaries.

France has recently begun implementing a national electronic health record system and some components of this system are still in the testing phase. At present, about 100 000 patients have an electronic health record in this system. The system enables primary care physician offices, medical specialist offices and hospitals to share information about patient diagnosis, treatment, emergency-room care, prescription medicines, laboratory tests and medical images. Records are also shared with other health care providers, such as nurses and physiotherapists. The only exception is for pharmacists who hold records in a separate system, for now. Patient consent is required before information is shared. There are legal provisions in place for emergency situations where access to an EHR may be required and a patient is unable to give consent.

All primary care physicians use the same EHR system in *Iceland*. Electronic records are shared among providers within each of Iceland's seven health care districts, but not yet across districts. Among medical specialist physicians, however, there is little sharing of electronic records. Some laboratory test results and medical imaging results are shared across districts via a secured Internet with results available to physicians and hospitals. Physician discharge letters are shared electronically across providers (physicians and hospitals) and across geographic boundaries. There is a project underway to enable prescription medications information to be similarly shared. Planning for the connection of district EHR systems is also anticipated.

In *Germany*, physician offices and hospitals are required to capture data on diagnosis and treatment to support billing claims. Electronic documentation for medical purposes beyond billing is less common, but is increasing. According to a recent survey of the German Medical Association (BÄK), 93% of physicians use electronic systems for diagnosis, 75% for procedures, 69% for management of a medication plan, and 43% for communications. Some physicians (14%) use e-mail to communicate information to patients, 15% use e-mail to communicate with other physicians and 8% to communicate with hospitals. Hospitals in Germany focus on in-patient care, with ambulatory emergency treatment provided by physician offices. Electronic capture and sharing of radiology and laboratory results is common between hospitals and other physicians. Some hospitals (14%) use e-mail for communications. The exchange of structured data is limited in Germany.

In *Portugal*, most primary care physician offices and half of medical specialist offices are using electronic medical records and some are also able to send and receive laboratory test and medical imaging results electronically; to see and update an electronic medications list for their patients that includes medications prescribed by other physicians; to see hospital in-patient and emergency room records for their patients; and to contribute to their patient's shared electronic health record. There is no sharing of information thus far, however, between the private and public sectors. Most hospitals are capturing in-patient (70%) and patient emergency room (95%) records electronically. Public sector hospitals receive clinical referral information from all primary care units. Some hospitals in the Northern Region share a common imaging database as well as emergency services records for paediatrics. Some hospitals also have outposts in primary care centres that are connected with the hospital's central database.

In *Austria*, primary care physician and medical specialist physician offices are receiving laboratory test results, medical image results, and hospital discharge letters electronically. Hospitals also receive laboratory test and medical image results electronically and, within regions, there is some sharing of electronic patient records among hospitals.

The *Netherlands* reports physicians are required to record patient encounters for billing purposes. The sharing of electronic clinical information about patients between primary care physicians and after-hours health providers is very common. The electronic sharing of information between physicians and hospitals is also occurring, but paper forms are still often used. There are very few systems that enable the sharing of electronic patient information among primary care physician offices and other health care providers. Virtually all hospitals use electronic patient records. In some regions, hospitals share and exchange data with regional care givers, such as primary care physicians, laboratories and pharmacists. In other regions, sharing is more limited. There are some hospitals that do not share information electronically, even among hospital wards.

Slovenia reports a high proportion of physician offices and hospitals using electronic records. Sharing of electronic laboratory orders and results occurs in hospitals, certain larger primary and specialist care organisations and between some independent laboratories and physician offices. Laboratory test results are not shared, however, among hospitals. Some dental care practices have electronic access to x-ray images. The health insurance card enables providers to access all medications prescribed to patients that were reimbursed by national insurance. A teleradiology pilot project is underway to share images among major hospitals and even with some home-based radiology specialists.

Results for the *United States* are for all office-based physicians in both primary and specialty care that have at least a partially electronic system for capturing patient information. Results for hospitals are for those who have replaced paper forms with electronic records in at least one unit as reported by the 2011 American Hospital Association Annual Survey, Information Technology Supplement. In the United States, a growing number of hospitals are attesting that they meet the requirements of federal regulations related to the implementation of certified electronic patient record technologies and the proportion is expected to rise. While there is no specific data on hospital emergency rooms, there is anecdotal evidence that hospital emergency departments tend to be the first hospital services to convert to electronic records from paper forms. The most common form of electronic patient data sharing among office-based physicians and hospitals are e-prescribing, laboratory and diagnostic findings, and care summaries at points where patients transition from one provider to another. Exchange types and rates of usage vary by state, by region, by organisation, by network of health care organisations, and by health care trading area.

In *Korea*, results reported for primary care physician offices, with 63.5% using electronic records to capture patient diagnosis and treatment information, are from a 2005 survey and are for clinics. No clinics are exchanging patient information electronically. All public health care centres (providing primary care), however, are using electronic medical records and are sharing information on prescription medications electronically. Medical specialist physicians in Korea work within tertiary/general hospitals and other hospitals. A 2001 survey indicated that 66% of tertiary/general hospitals and 52% of hospitals were using electronic medical records.

Some hospital groups in Korea are using proprietary standards to share clinical information within their own network. As part of the Seoul National University Bundang Hospital Information Interchange Pilot Project, 35 clinics in Seongnam City and Yongin City are sharing patient information, diagnosis, laboratory test results, prescription medications and medical imaging results using HL7 CDA transfer standards and semantic standards (coded data).

Spain reports that most primary care centres and physician offices are using electronic medical records. Sharing of electronic records in primary care occurs within health centres or primary care networks. Primary care offices may also request specialist consultations within hospitals for patients electronically. It is common for primary care offices and medical specialists to order tests and to receive laboratory test results, medical images and/or medical image results electronically. The use of electronic patient records varies widely among regions and hospitals in Spain and estimates for specialists and hospitals are approximate and are based on public health care networks. Within hospitals, sharing of records typically does not extend beyond the hospital or the hospital's network. In a group of regions, however, there is a project underway to enable hospitals to share a minimum set of clinical reports including lab results, medical images and other reports with other hospitals throughout the country.

Switzerland reports that the use of ICT is common for reimbursement processes but not yet for medical documentation within primary care physician and medical specialist physician offices. There are several regional projects to share patient information electronically among health care providers. Health Info Net (HIN) offers secure data exchange among physician offices and can be used for a variety of information including reports, and radiology and laboratory results. This secure connection is offered to 80% of physician offices. By 2011, 50% of hospitals in Switzerland had an electronic clinical information system implemented and 40% were in the process of implementing this system. The use of ICT to send and receive data among hospitals is rapidly increasing. There are, however, major differences among hospitals in data sharing capabilities because of differences in regional needs.

Israel reports a high degree of use of electronic records among physician offices and hospitals; however, at present, records are shared among providers within each of Israel's four HMOs only. As part of the national EHR plan, a project to develop data sharing across HMOs and between physicians and hospitals was initiated in 2012 and is to be completed in two years.

Results for *Canada* for primary care and medical specialist care are from a national physician survey and are therefore for physicians and not physician offices (National Physician Survey, 2010). Results identify the percentage of physicians that use electronic records to enter or retrieve patient clinical notes. The survey found that the most commonly reported shared information was laboratory tests and diagnostic images (41.5% of primary care physicians and 33.4% of medical specialists). A smaller share of physicians had access to an external pharmacy or pharmacist electronically (9.9% of primary care physicians and 6.6% of specialists) or to other external systems (24.6% of primary care physicians and 26.4% of medical specialists). Hospitals in Canada are encouraged to adopt electronic patient records and to exchange information via electronic health record systems as they are deployed. There are no statistics for this sector.

In *Japan*, there is no clear distinction between primary care and medical specialist physicians and the statistics presented refer to both. A small proportion of pioneering hospitals and clinics have introduced electronic medical record systems. According to a survey of health care facilities in Japan in 2008, a small proportion of acute care hospitals (14.2%) and clinics (15.2%) were using electronic medical records and only 1.5% of both groups were sharing patient data electronically with other health care providers.

Physicians in *Japan* are encouraged to develop official networks to provide better disease-specific care pathways for patients through the use of financial incentives. The sharing of electronic medical records, however, is not a prerequisite and only a small number of hospitals and clinics have introduced EMRs. It is likely that the financial incentives currently provided to establish networks are not sufficient to motivate providers to introduce electronic medical records.

In *Mexico*, the largest federal health care institutions (IMSS and ISSSTE), offering both primary and tertiary care, are using electronic health records for patients and do enable physicians to share patient information electronically within the same institution. Physicians are also able to order services electronically. Other public and private health care providers in Mexico have varying levels of deployment and exchange of electronic records. Private medical specialist physician offices in Mexico are not connected to the electronic health record systems of the federal institutions. Few are able to exchange electronic information among service providers in their network.

The sharing of electronic records across primary care physician offices in *Singapore* is limited; however, national plans are in place to extend clinical communications capability in future. Results for hospitals are for public sector institutions. Public sector institutions in Singapore, and the medical specialist physicians working within them, are often sharing documents with other public sector institutions through an exchange solution (EMRX). Electronic records shared include radiology and laboratory results, prescribed medications, and diagnostic results.

While hospitals in *Slovakia* are not currently sharing patient data electronically, work is underway for the future use of an archive for medical images and for electronic communications. In *Indonesia*, there are electronic patient records in use by primary care and medical specialists offices and in hospitals but the implementation of electronic medical records varies widely as does the sharing of patient information electronically. The most common tool is an electronic record of patient diagnosis and treatment.

ORGANISATION FOR ECONOMIC CO-OPERATION AND DEVELOPMENT

The OECD is a unique forum where governments work together to address the economic, social and environmental challenges of globalisation. The OECD is also at the forefront of efforts to understand and to help governments respond to new developments and concerns, such as corporate governance, the information economy and the challenges of an ageing population. The Organisation provides a setting where governments can compare policy experiencerewardeds, seek answers to common problems, identify good practice and work to co-ordinate domestic and international policies.

The OECD member countries are: Australia, Austria, Belgium, Canada, Chile, the Czech Republic, Denmark, Estonia, Finland, France, Germany, Greece, Hungary, Iceland, Ireland, Israel, Italy, Japan, Korea, Luxembourg, Mexico, the Netherlands, New Zealand, Norway, Poland, Portugal, the Slovak Republic, Slovenia, Spain, Sweden, Switzerland, Turkey, the United Kingdom and the United States. The European Union takes part in the work of the OECD.

OECD Publishing disseminates widely the results of the Organisation's statistics gathering and research on economic, social and environmental issues, as well as the conventions, guidelines and standards agreed by its members.